DATE DUE

HEMINGWAY ON HUNTING

Books by Ernest Hemingway

Three Stories & Ten Poems

In Our Time

The Torrents of Spring

The Sun Also Rises

Men Without Women

A Farewell to Arms

Death in the Afternoon

Winner Take Nothing

Green Hills of Africa

To Have and Have Not

The Fifth Column and the First Forty-Nine Stories

For Whom the Bell Tolls

Across the River and into the Trees

The Old Man and the Sea

A Moveable Feast

By-Line: Ernest Hemingway

Islands in the Stream

The Nick Adams Stories

The Dangerous Summer

The Garden of Eden

The Hemingway Reader

The Complete Short Stories of Ernest Hemingway

Ernest Hemingway, Selected Letters, 1917–1961

True at First Light

Hemingway on Fishing

Hemingway on Hunting

HEMINGWAY ON HUNTING

ERNEST HEMINGWAY

Edited and with an Introduction by
SEAN HEMINGWAY

Foreword by Patrick Hemingway

THE LYONS PRESS
Guilford, Connecticut
An imprint of The Globe Pequot Press

This edition is for Colette Czapski Hemingway
a.k.a. 'Pistol P'

Contents

I

From up in Michigan to the Serengeti

Contents

II

Dispatches from the Field

III

A Hunter's Return to the Good Country

A Brief Hunter's Chronology

1899   July 21. Born in Oak Park, Illinois.

1899   September. Clarence and Grace Hemingway take their infant
        son to Walloon Lake near Petoskey, Michigan—his first trip into
        the American wild. EH will spend July and August of every
        summer of his youth at the family's Windemere Cottage.

1909   After leaving the presidency of the United States, Theodore
        Roosevelt makes an almost yearlong trip to Africa on a safari.

1909   July 21. EH receives his first gun, a 20-gauge, single-barrel shot-
        gun, from his grandfather Anson Hemingway.

1910   Roosevelt comes to Oak Park on a whistle-stop tour after his
        African safari of the previous year. EH, with his grandfather
        Anson, cheers him on.

1913   Summer. EH and Harold Sampson shoot a porcupine in the
        woods near Walloon Lake.

1915   July 30. EH illegally shoots a blue heron and runs away from the
        game warden. Eventually he faces the judge and pays the oblig-
        atory $15 fine.

1919   Summer. After returning from the Italian front of World War I, EH summers at Walloon Lake and hunts in the autumn around Petoskey, Michigan.

1922   Shoots quail in the prairies of Thrace while covering the Greco-Turkish war.

1928   March. Begins *A Farewell to Arms* (1929), which includes EH's recollections of bird shooting in the woods of the Abruzzi, Italy.

1928   August–September. Travels to see Yellowstone National Park and the Grand Teton Mountains—his first taste of the West.

1930   Fall. Hunts quail in Piggott, Arkansas.

1930   Fall–Winter. First visit to Charles Nordquist's L-Bar-T ranch in Wyoming. Shoots two grizzly bears using a dead horse as bait. Around this time, Uncle Gus Pfeiffer puts up $25,000 of stock to underwrite the African safari.

1931   December. A fire in the Pfeiffers' barn destroys EH's typewriter, boots and several of his guns.

1932   July–October. EH hunts sage hens, elk, rabbits and bear at the Nordquist ranch. Charles Thompson joins EH for a mountain goat hunt (unsuccessful). In September, EH kills a seven-point bull elk up on Timber Creek. EH keeps lucky bullet from the kill for many years.

1933   December 20. Hemingway party, with their guide Philip Percival, depart Nairobi for a two-month safari.

1934   March 1. EH and his friend, Charles Thompson, compete in the XVIth International Concours de Tir aux Pigeons shotgun shooting competition in Paris. EH later attends another at Monaco.

1934   May 11. Begins *Green Hills of Africa* (1935).

1936   February. Finishes drafts of "The Snows of Kilimanjaro" and "The Short Happy Life of Francis Macomber."

1936   July–October. Patrick accompanies his father on a grizzly bear hunt that summer, and EH makes a three-day antelope hunt.

1939   Fall. Visits Sun Valley, Idaho for the first time.

1940   September. Hunts duck, pheasant, snipe and grouse with sons, Jack, Patrick and Gregory, and Martha Gellhorn in Sun Valley. Organizes rabbit hunt.

1941   September. Gregory joins his father on an antelope hunt on horseback in Idaho, described in the story "The Shot."

1941   November–November 1944. With the Pilar outfitted with machine guns, EH and crew patrol Cuban waters for German submarines.

1948   September–April 1949. EH hunts widgeon, mallards and pintails in the Veneto for the first time. Also enjoys excellent duck shooting on Torcello and at the Villa Aprile in Cortina.

1949   March. Begins *Across the River and Into the Trees* (1950).

1952   May 4. Begins "The Last Good Country."

1953   May 15. Signs contract with *Look* magazine for a photojournalism piece on his 1953–54 safari.

1953   September–January 1954. Hemingways, with their guide, Philip Percival, are on safari in Kenya.

1954   December 30. EH is appointed an Honorary Game Warden of Kenya.

1955   October 28. Wins Nobel Prize. Works on his African novel *True at First Light* (1999).

1958   October–December. Hunts pheasant and duck in Ketchum, Idaho, while renting the Heiss House.

1961   July 2. Dies in Ketchum.

Foreword

This book is meant to be a companion piece to *Hemingway on Fishing*, which Nick Lyons edited and to which he wrote an excellent and comprehensive introduction. My brother Jack wrote a short foreword for this book just six months before his death in December 2000, where he mentioned that hunting and fishing were always very much a family affair with Ernest Hemingway. I am sure Papa would be pleased with the job his grandson Seán has done in editing *Hemingway on Hunting*. For Seán this has been very much a voyage of discovery, since he was born too late to know his grandfather as a hunter except through the conversations of his own father, Gregory, and his two paternal uncles, Jack and Pat.

If kids don't have access to parents who live to fish and hunt and who are willing to take the time to share the fun with their young families, it will be much harder for boys and girls to become competent as adults in either of these pastimes. One of the best and most enthusiastic hunters I have ever known, and I have known a great many, was the city-bred son of a painter of religious murals for the archdiocese of Cologne, who never took his son, to the best of my knowledge, outside the limits of that city. I hope these two Hemingway books will inspire as many families as possible to hunt and fish and to stay together.

At the end of World War II, it was really my mother, Pauline, Ernest Hemingway's second wife and Seán Hemingway's grandmother, who launched my brother Gregory and me into the then not so crowded world of fly fishing for trout on public water in the American West. She managed to get hold of one of the very first Ford four-door sedans to come off the assembly line for civilians in 1945, but the prospect of her driving his two young sons all the way from Key West to fish in Wyoming, Yellowstone Park, Washington State, and then down the Pacific coast to her sister Jinny's home in Hollywood, frightened Papa. He suggested that she let Jack, who had been liberated near the end of the war from a German prison camp and was not out of the army, do the driving, for until Pauline had been divorced in 1940, she had not had a driver's license. Papa had no way of knowing that she had become a perfectly safe driver in the four years since their divorce.

It was a great job for Jack. He did not yet want to go back to college or to work in civilian life. He could teach his two younger brothers what he had learned about fly fishing before the war and get to check out the old fishing grounds he knew, and visit new ones as well. We had bought our first dry flies three weeks before at Dan Bailey's trout shop in Livingston, Montana, in preparation for driving up to Gardiner, and on to the Madison, the Gibbon, and the Firehole, where we would try them out.

Papa first taught Greg and me to bait-fish for trout with grasshoppers in the valley of the Clarke's Fork of the Yellowstone. It was always cold enough in the early morning to get a bunch of them before they warmed up along the grassy bank of what, in the 1930's, was as great a native cutthroat trout stream as those near Sheridan, Wyoming, which furnished food and sport to General Crook's 1876 command before and after their June fight on the Rosebud: "The hundreds and thousands of fine fish taken from that set of creeks and officers and soldiers, who had nothing but the rudest appliances, speaks of the wonderful resources of the country in game at that time . . . Mr. Wasson and I made an arrangement to peruse each day either one of Shakespeare's plays or an essay by Macaulay and to discuss them together."

Jack showed us how to use the dry fly on undercut band browns in the Gibbon: Dan Bailey's well-tied, stiff-hackled, all-purpose No. 12 Adams, vintage 1945. God knows what binomially nomenclatured real bug those browns preferred to eat, but fish were more literary than Latinists in their tastes half a century ago and any Adams (John, John Quincy, or Henry) would turn them on.

It was on the last stretch of this summer trip that Jack had his opportunity to fish for steelhead. I still have the picture vividly in mind. We were parked near the mouth of the Kalama River, where it empties into the north bank of the Columbia. Along came Jack, whistling to himself as he walked back downstream, holding up a silver-sided monster of a fish that was bigger than any of the trout we had seen mounted on the wall of Dan Bailey's.

When it comes to hunting, I know now how grateful I am that I was included in a fall hunt for grizzly bear in 1936 on the upper end of the Crandall Creek drainage, high above the Clarke's Fork Valley, although I was only eight and had failed to learn to read in the first grade. There were two families, the Shevlins and the Hemingways, and all the help, horses, gear and supplies necessary to sustain a two-week hunting pack trip. Mrs. Shevlin, who was from a high-born Russian émigré family, was more interested in ballet than in bullets. After the very first day's encounter with a mature grizzly sow and two almost fully grown cubs and the resulting firefight that had the sow and one cub, in the words of the hymn, bloodstained, distended, cold and dead, she asked Papa if he would mind covering her with his Springfield whenever she went to the bathroom.

My godfather, Chub Weaver, from Red Lodge, Montana, a person of many talents (horse breaking, bootlegging, and undertaking, to mention just a few) was the cook on the pack trip. Most days, I stayed in camp and he tutored me in déciphering the adventures of two young children of opposite gender in the Saint Joseph's parochial school reader in which I had made so little progress in the winter of 1935–36 in Key West.

On a few days, as a break from my studies, I got to go out riding with the grown-ups on my horse Pinky, a devilish old strawberry roan pony who knew every nasty trick in the book. His best trick was to swell up his belly when I saddled him, with Chub's help of course, and then later deflate, so that the saddle would suddenly slip to the right or left and dump me on the side of the trail. Pinky wasn't the worst of it, though. That was lunch. Someone had forgotten to pack the yeast, so Chub couldn't make bread. Instead, we had two grease-soaked pancakes with a thick slab of fatty grizzly bear meat in between, wrapped in the oilpaper that people used back then.

Papa did manage during the two weeks to shoot a mountain grouse (as I remember it, a blue one) with his Colt Woodsman .22 pistol. But as was only fair, he got to eat it all himself; or maybe he shared it with the ladies. He was always a perfect gentleman in that respect.

Despite real hardships, we all slept very well in our four-star Arctic Woods sleeping bags, laid atop beds made of interlaced fir branches. Although Mrs. Shevlin never went hunting again and eventually divorced Mr. Shevlin, and Papa also divorced my mother four years later, we all had a good time up there in Crandall Creek, and Chub had me reading by the time we broke camp.

In the 1930's, if you joined the NRA, you could still order from the Springfield Armory in Massachusetts a military version of the .30-06 bolt-action rifle, essentially the weapon that Theodore Roosevelt took with him to hunt in Africa when Ernest Hemingway was a young boy. Most sportsmen who could afford to do so sent their NRA Springfields on to a custom gunsmith for restocking and other modifications that transformed the utilitarian rifles into handsome sporting weapons. Papa sent his to Griffin & Howe, the gunsmithing subsidiary of the great New York sporting goods store, Abercrombie & Fitch. The finished product was as good, or better, than anything a British firm could have turned out as the time. It is interesting that this was not so in the 1930's for big-game fishing rods, where English Hardys were much better than anything made in America.

In the short story "Fathers and Sons," Papa credits my grandfather Clarence with superhuman eyesight, and so it must have seemed to the little boy who inherited my grandmother Grace's nearsightedness along with the rugged frame of his maternal grandfather, Ernest Hall, after whom he was named.

What struck Philip Percival—and he mentioned it later, when Carlos Baker interviews him in the 1960's—was how much Ernest Hemingway reminded him, when they first met, of the Roosevelt he had guided more than twenty years earlier on the Kapititi plains of Kenya. Both Hemingway and Roosevelt had taken up the challenge of reaching and maintaining themselves at a professional level of physical fitness through the sport of boxing, not just as an end in itself but as a necessary condition for mixing with men who lived by the performance of their bodies as well as their minds. Neither Roosevelt nor Hemingway ever hesitated to take up any man's physical challenge, though it did sometimes require them to take off their glasses.

Ernest Hemingway is not a professional contemporary outdoors writer, and if that is what the reader expects from him they may be very disappointed. Puccini loved to hunt ducks in the marshes near Venice. Italian duck hunters, most of whom are very rich industrialists or titled agricultural landowners, who are not particularly known for their adherence to conventional democratic conservation principles, are very proud of Puccini the duck hunter. All Italians revere Puccini as a composer of operas, an art form of which Italians are inordinately fond. Italian duck hunters are pleased that such a popular Italian also liked to hunt ducks.

Foreword

For the reader for whom English is a native language and for whom mathematics is a professional tool or even a profession in itself, I would recommend a story by Hemingway that is not in this book, "Homage to Switzerland." The only literary criticism of this piece that I think does it justice is the late Michael Reynolds's "'Homage to Switzerland': Einstein's Train Stops at Hemingway's Station." Since this paper, to the best of my knowledge, is unpublished and is not readily available even on the World Wide Web, I would suggest that readers compare *Relativity, The Special and the General Theory*, by Albert Einstein, with "Homage to Switzerland." In their respective fields, Einstein and Hemingway have become icons of the twentieth century. We should all be grateful to Albert Einstein for elucidating a peculiarity of the celestial mechanics of the planet Mercury not possible by the insights of Newtonian mechanics, and to Ernest Hemingway for taking us a little further than Shakespeare in the clear depiction of the unchanging human condition.

—Patrick Hemingway
Bozeman, Montana
August 2001

Acknowledgments

My sincere gratitude to Patrick Hemingway for considering me for this project, for working with me and suggesting a number of pieces to include in this volume, and for his thoughtful Foreword; to Gregory Hemingway for his encouragement, suggestions and critical reading of my text; to Jeffrey Meyers and Robert M. Myers for their helpful suggestions; to Megan Desnoyers of the Hemingway Archives at the John F. Kennedy Library for her tireless assistance with research pertaining to unpublished materials in the collection, to her assistant Lauren Constantino, and to Allan Goodrich, James Hill and Courtney Paquette at the A/V archives for invaluable help with the photographic material; to the Ernest Hemingway Foundation, Inc. for permission to publish excerpts from the letters; to Simon and Schuster for permission to reprint excerpts from published works, and to Lydia Zelaya for facilitating this permission; to Nick and Tony Lyons for their shared enthusiasm and efforts, and to Brando Skyhorse for his assistance; to the photographer John Bryson; to Patrice Czapski and Scott McManus for the use of their new home on Cape Cod as a place to write; and

Acknowledgments

to Carol Hemingway, Ida Hemingway, Valerie Hemingway, Angela Hemingway, Brian Gaisford and Joseph Czapski for their encouragement and suggestions. Finally, I reserve my warmest note of appreciation for my wife, Colette, for her assistance and never-ending support throughout this endeavor.

Introduction

1

In the summer of 1934, Hemingway wrote to a friend: ". . . outside of writing I have two well developed talents; for sea fishing where there is a current and migratory fish and shooting with a rifle on targets at unknown ranges where the vital spots are not marked but have to be understood to be hit. . . ." Hunting remained for Ernest Hemingway a favorite pastime when he was not writing and was a subject that he wrote about often throughout the course of his life. This book brings together for the first time the author's many fine short stories, selections from books, essays, and even excerpts from letters, that illuminate the art of hunting and the pleasures of being in the outdoors through recollections and carefully crafted tales of hunts in North America, Europe and Africa. It has been an especial pleasure for me to compile this rich collection of my grandfather's works on hunting because of my own love of the outdoors, a sentiment which my grandfather fostered in his three sons and which my father, Gregory, and my uncles, Patrick and Jack, engendered in me from childhood.

Hunting has been a defining characteristic of human behavior for over two million years. The magnificent cave paintings at Lascaux in France, among our earliest artistic representations, celebrate the hunt and its bounty. Beyond its fundamental function as a means of providing food and clothing, hunting is ritualized by many cultures and the sanctity of taking a life is acknowledged as a natural part of the cycle of life. It has been recorded that the Bushmen of the Kalahari, for example, always celebrate the success of an eland hunt with ritual dances. In ancient Greek mythology, the hunting and successful killing of stags and wild boars were distinguished as heroic acts of valor that marked the completion of a significant rite of passage. For the Greeks, the hunt was sacred to the goddess Artemis, and foremost among hunters was the hero Orion, who as a constellation shines brightly in the night sky, a harbinger of hunting season. Hunting constituted a social class in ancient Egypt, where the sport was reserved for rulers and their nobles; likewise, the kings of Assyria and later Persia were also partial to the chase, as is shown by hunting scenes depicted on the walls of their temples and palaces. In the first, second and third centuries, the Romans turned hunting wild animals into a spectacle, importing all manner of big game from Africa for mock hunts in the Coliseum and other amphitheaters throughout the empire. The distinction between hunting for food and hunting for sport, however, was made early on, and from the latter a code of behavior developed for the hunter. By the Middle Ages in Europe, codes of behavior demanded that a hunter track down and kill any animal he may have wounded.

Hunting game with firearms, which began in Europe as early as the 16th century, enabled the hunter to kill game at greater distances and in larger numbers. The extreme consequence of this innovation was that by the 19th century, overhunting of areas around the globe had led to the tragic extinction of a number of species, notably the passenger pigeon in America, and the virtual extermination of others, such as the American bison. The concept of game conservation soon developed, especially in Africa where conservationists recognized the need for stewardship in order to preserve wildlife and its natural habitat for future generations. Of course, the need for wildlife conservation is not simply a result of overhunting, as has been pointed out by many specialists, including Norman Carr, one of the first game wardens in Africa and an avid hunter and naturalist with whom I apprenticed in the Luangwa Valley, Zambia. Norman often said that even more important than managing wildlife—animals usually can look after themselves—it is important that there is sufficient habitat for the complete range of all the species to live in harmony with one another. As all of the world's landscapes become increasingly fragmented by human activity, the need for wildlife and habitat conservation remains acute.

Hunters are at the forefront of wildlife conservation in America, where hunting continues to have great appeal despite ever increasing urbanization and suburbanization. However, the act of killing is, I believe, a deeply personal matter about which every individual has strong views. Hemingway offered his own insight in his treatise on bullfighting, *Death in the Afternoon:* "Killing cleanly and in a way which gives you aesthetic pleasure and pride has always been one of the greatest enjoyments of a part of the human race. Because the other part, which does not enjoy killing, has always been more articulate and has furnished most of the good writers we have had a very few statements of the true enjoyment of killing. One of its greatest pleasures, aside from the purely aesthetic ones, such as wing shooting and the ones of pride, such as difficult game stalking, where it is the disproportionately increased importance of the fraction of a moment that it takes for the shot that furnishes the emotion, is the feeling of rebellion against death which comes from its administering. Once you accept the rule of death thou shalt not kill is an easily and naturally obeyed commandment. But when a man is still in rebellion against death he has a pleasure in taking to himself one of the Godlike attributes; that of giving it. This is one of the most profound feelings in those men who enjoy killing. These things are done in pride and pride, of course, is a Christian sin, and a pagan virtue." Hemingway, like the old man talking to Robert Jordan in *For Whom the Bell Tolls*, specifically refers to the killing of animals, not human beings, which, of course, is another matter entirely. The clarity and conviction evident in the above statement arises from an extraordinary combination of qualities: Hemingway's lifelong love and pursuit of hunting, and his carefully developed talent for writing as true as he could.

2

Born in 1899 in Oak Park, Illinois, the eldest son in a sporting family, Ernest Miller Hemingway grew up with the outdoors close at hand. His father, Clarence Edmonds Hemingway, loved to hunt and fish. From early on, he took the young boy along with him hunting near their summer cabin, Windemere, on Walloon Lake in Northern Michigan, and on outings in the fields flushing snipe north of Chicago. In 1902, when Hemingway was only two years old, his mother, Grace Hall Hemingway, reported that her son ". . . loves to play the sportsman. He straps on an old powder flask and shot pouch and half an old musket over his shoulder. He calls different shaped pieces of wood—respectively—'my blunderbus,' 'my shotgun,' 'my rifle,' 'my Winchester,' 'my pistol,' etc., and delights in shooting imaginary wolves, bears, lions, buffalo, etc." By the time he was three, Hemingway had learned to load, cock and shoot a gun by himself, and at four he was trekking as much as seven miles on hunting expeditions with his father, carrying his own gun over his shoulder. One wonders at such an early tutelage! In an anecdote in one of Grace's scrapbooks, she relates how the little hunter and provider shot a duck for their dinner, but with tongue in cheek added that Papa (Clarence) shot at the same time. Nonetheless, young Ernest continued to work at his marksmanship, later joining the rifle club in high school, where he recorded a consistent score of 112 out of 150, shooting a rifle prone at a twenty-yard range—all in spite of a defective left eye that was later to keep him from enlisting in the army.

Clarence Hemingway, a fine wing shot and a member of the Chicago Sharpshooters Association, taught his son how to shoot with a shotgun at an early age. In fact, all of the children, the girls included, worked up to shooting by themselves with their father's first and favorite shotgun, a 12-gauge, lever-action Winchester that shot a very close pattern. Once a week on Sundays during the summer months at Windemere Cottage, Clarence Hemingway would organize for his family shotgun target shooting with a hand trap and clay pigeons. Ernest received his first gun, a 20-gauge, single-barrel shotgun, from his grandfather, Anson Hemingway, on his tenth birthday, and Ernest celebrated his eleventh birthday at Windemere among friends and family with a barbecue followed by a shotgun shooting competition. There were also hunting trips in southern Illinois with his father on his uncle Frank Hines's farm, where the young boy shot pigeons and quail, and hunted raccoon and possum at night with dogs. Clarence taught him gun care and safety, how to dress a kill, and even how to make bullets from an old Civil War mold that his father, Anson, had given him.

Throughout his childhood Hemingway heard about the deeds of pioneers of the Old West and soldiers of the Civil War, especially from his grandfather Anson. The elder Hemingway had come West in a covered wagon when he himself was a boy and had later fought in the Civil War as a volunteer in the Illinois infantry regiment. Ernest's father told of his own hunting exploits as a young man, tracking and shooting bear in the Great Smoky Mountains of North Carolina. But for any young boy growing up in the first two decades of the twentieth century, it was Theodore Roosevelt—western rancher and huntsman, President of the United States, and later African hunter and South American explorer—who inspired the imagination and fueled the desire to explore and hunt in the great outdoors. Young Hemingway identified with much of Teddy Roosevelt's hunting prowess, enthusiasm and determination. In 1910, when Roosevelt came to Oak Park on a whistle-stop tour after his African safari of the previous year, Ernest, in his own little khaki safari outfit, was standing alongside his grandfather Anson, cheering on the great African hunter and rough rider of San Juan Hill. More than any other individual in his time, Roosevelt opened the African frontier to the imagination of America's youths. The fresh scent of a new frontier and the thrill of the hunt, both with their overwhelming sense of valor and excitement, would captivate Hemingway for the rest of his life.

Clarence Hemingway educated his boy about nature and taught him the fundamentals of scientific observation. He frequently read to Ernest from natural history books filled with colorful illustrations. At a young age, Ernest joined the Agassiz naturalist club, of which his father was a leading member. As part of his early instruction, young Hemingway would accompany his father to the Field Museum of Natural History in Chicago to see the zoological specimens, especially the incredibly lifelike displays of animals that were an innovation of the master taxidermist Carl Akeley. In particular, the great Hall of African Mammals, with its sealed glass cases enclosing gazelles, wildebeest, rhino, cheetah, leopard and kudu, would have impressed the boy, as frequent trips to the Roosevelt Hall of African Mammals at the American Museum of Natural History with my father did me in my childhood. Clarence was himself an amateur taxidermist and maintained a small collection of specimens of his own; some of his creations can still be seen at the Ernest Hemingway Foundation of Oak Park. He taught Ernest how to skin and prepare an animal.

Lessons learned in our youth often make a lasting impression. Early on, Clarence Hemingway taught his son the hunter's code—no killing solely for killing's sake. Although Clarence believed that wild animals and birds had been put on this earth to be hunted, he insisted that any animal killed must be eaten and that nothing should be wasted. When Ernest strayed from this principle and shot a porcupine with his friend Harold Sampson in the woods near Walloon Lake during the summer of 1913, his father insisted that the boys eat its leathery flesh. On another occasion, while hunting on the North Prairie near Oak Park, Ernest accidentally triggered his 20-gauge shotgun and barely missed his companion, Lewis Clarahan, a chilling reminder of the need for care when handling a firearm. Perhaps the most significant shooting incident of Ernest's youth, however, occurred in the summer of 1915. While out with his sister Sunny, exploring a remote area of Walloon Lake called the "Cracken," Ernest poached a great blue heron intending to add it to his father's collection of bird specimens. The son of the game warden, who lived on the lake, heard the shot and confiscated the bird. Later, the warden himself came by Windemere Cottage looking for Ernest, who fled and lay low for a while. The incident was resolved when Ernest turned himself in to a judge in Boyne City and paid the $15 fine. Hemingway never forgot this brush with the law, and he used the incident as the focus of his unfinished short story "The Last Good Country."

Northern Michigan and the Upper Peninsula, which even today retain their natural beauty, were remote and wild territories in Hemingway's youth. He knew the local Native Americans, the Ojibwa, who clung to their traditions, and old-timer fur trappers, whose way of life was rapidly vanishing. Some of his earliest fiction, such as the "Judgement of Manitou," a dark tale about two frontier trappers framed in the mysticism of Indian folklore, draws on these early impressions. Many of the Nick Adams stories were inspired by Hemingway's experiences hunting, fishing and exploring in Northern Michigan.

After returning, in 1919, from the Italian front of World War I, where he was wounded as a Red Cross volunteer, Hemingway spent much time up in Michigan, where for the first time he had the opportunity to hunt during the fall. When he moved to Paris as a foreign correspondent for *The Toronto Star* in the winter of 1921 with his new bride, Hadley Richardson Hemingway, he eagerly took to hunting in Europe and wrote his dad about his experiences. Even on assignment, he managed to work in some shooting. While covering the Greco-Turkish war in 1922, he shot quail in the open prairies of Thrace, bagging twenty-two birds in a single day. One of his very last journalistic pieces written for *The Toronto Star* was "Game Shooting in Europe," a matter-of-fact presentation of the fine big-game hunting and bird shooting that could be had in various parts of Europe. He describes the many Parisian hunters with their shotguns slung over their shoulders leaving Paris for a weekend in the country, something he himself did a number of times, notably to shoot pheasant outside the city with his friend Ben Gallagher.

Hemingway hunted in nearly every place he ever lived. When he returned to the United States early in 1928 to live in Key West, Florida, with his second wife, my grandmother Pauline Pfeiffer Hemingway, he managed to find good bird shooting on the remote Marquesas Keys, some twenty-five miles south of Key West, shooting plover, cranes and curlews. After their son Patrick was born that July in Kansas City, Ernest and Pauline took a trip to Yellowstone National Park and the Grand Teton Mountains, a first taste of what the West could offer. Upon their return to Florida, they decided to stay on for quail-hunting season with Pauline's family in Piggot, Arkansas, where there was "swell shooting" in the woods and cornfields, something he looked forward to in the coming years. Around this time, Hemingway was nearly finished with his second novel, *A Farewell to Arms*, a love story loosely based on his early experiences in northern Italy during World War I. Its charming recollections of bird shooting in the chestnut woods of the Abruzzi, for birds whose meat was especially tasty because they fed on a particular variety of grapes, reveal the refined gastronomical rewards of the well-educated hunter.

Introduction

In 1930 and again in 1932, soon after my father, Gregory Hemingway, was born, Ernest went West to hunt, fish and write while staying at Lawrence Nordquist's L-Bar-T Ranch. The conditions at the Nordquist ranch, located some twelve miles outside Cooke City, Montana, and just inside the Wyoming state line, were ideal for his writing—a quiet place surrounded by the great outdoors. The hunting was strenuous work, with a lot of riding on horseback in the high country, sometimes in heavy snow, and packing out all of the meat and trophies. Armed with his Springfield rifle, Hemingway had his first crack at grizzlies, just as Teddy Roosevelt had done in his western ranching days, as well as elk, deer, big horn sheep, coyotes and eagles. He considered grizzly bears to be the only dangerous animal in North America, and the best training for Africa, where he decided he must hunt next.

An African safari in those days was no small undertaking. After a stopover in Europe, Ernest, Pauline and their Key West friend Charles Thompson set sail from Marseilles on November 15, 1933, aboard the *General Metzinger*, bound for Mombasa with some twenty-one pieces of luggage in tow. The long sea voyage across the Mediterranean, through the Suez Canal, down the Red Sea, and into the Indian Ocean along the east coast of Africa involved weeks of less than desirable living conditions while traveling through the rising heat. From Mombasa they took the Kenya and Uganda Railway to Nairobi, and then went by motor car into the interior. Philip Percival, the 49-year-old legendary safari guide who was to be their professional hunter, came highly recommended, having taken Roosevelt on safari in 1909. Ernest later said that Percival was the finest man he knew; he was certainly the hunter that Hemingway admired most. Percival immediately saw in Hemingway a resemblance to Teddy Roosevelt, with his broad smile, strong shoulders and poor eyesight.

The beauty and expanse of Africa, which surpassed that of Montana and Wyoming, amazed Hemingway. Shooting primarily with his customized Springfield, as well as a .30-06 Mauser and

Pauline's 6.5 Mannlicher, Ernest had excellent hunting, bagging four of the 'Big Five,' cheetah, zebra, sixteen varieties of antelope, warthogs, jackals, spring hare, a serval cat and thirty hyenas. Much of this game, besides the hyenas, for which he had a particular dislike, was used to feed the dozens of staff and clients in the camp over the course of the two-month safari. Only a bout with dysentery at the beginning of the trip and Ernest's intense competitive nature when his friend Charles Thompson continually shot bigger and better trophies got the better of him at times. Philip Percival found Hemingway to be excellent company and paid him the professional compliment of allowing him to shoot alone with his gun bearer, M'Cola. Even as the safari ended, Hemingway began to think how and when he would be able to return to Africa. As he wrote in *Green Hills of Africa*: "All I wanted to do now was get back to Africa. We had not left it, yet, but when I would wake in the night I would lie, listening, homesick for it already."

My grandfather was a great teacher who loved to impart his knowledge of hunting to others. As his three sons grew older, he began to educate them in the ways of the sportsman, both by example and through explicit instruction. In 1939, Ernest began to go to Sun Valley, Idaho, especially for the fine bird shooting. The remote and well-watered country around Sun Valley was excellent for shooting duck and pheasant, as well as Hungarian partridge, snipe and "prairie chickens," the native sage grouse. Hemingway hunted all of these with his boys, as well as with celebrities, such as Gary Cooper and Jane Russell, who came to Sun Valley in the late 1930's and 40's. Cooper was a renowned rifle shot, and Hemingway prided himself on his wing shooting, favoring his over-and-under Browning 12-gauge shotgun. "General" Hemingway organized rabbit drives around the Freer Farm and, with up to twenty shooters and beaters, systematically swept across the big sage fields to kill in a single day thousands of rabbits that had been decimating the local farmer's crops. There were also hunts for antelope and mule deer. My father remembers well the difficult and long days on horseback during the antelope hunt of 1941 that Hemingway wrote about in the story "The Shot."

By the late 1930's, Hemingway had moved to Cuba, where he lived in a farmhouse called the Finca Vigia. From his house, he could walk into the country for hours with a gun and come upon snipe, guinea, doves and quail. He joined a shooting club, the Club de Cazadores del Cerro, about five miles from the Finca, where one could do every kind of shooting: rifle, trap, skeet and live pigeons. My dad remembers my grandfather teaching him to shoot a shotgun there. "Don't worry about shooting the pigeons, Gig, just concentrate on your form," Papa would tell him. "If you fire enough shots you'll start to get the leads down, that is, you'll learn how far to fire in front of a bird flying at an angle to you. The shot doesn't get there as soon as the gun goes off you know. It seems like it does, but it takes half a second or so to reach the bird, depending on how fast he's flying, how far away he is, the strength of the powder charge and a few other factors. But I'm only confusing you with all this explanation. Just concentrate on your form now. You're right handed, so put the stock of the gun firmly against your right shoulder, make sure it feels comfortable, and that the stock is up against your shoulder. If the gun isn't positioned correctly, a smaller percentage of your shoulder will receive its full recoil, and it will kick like hell. Then you'll start to flinch, jerking the trigger in anticipation of the pain of the recoil, and that will move your gun off target before the shot leaves the barrel. That's right, firm against the shoulder, keep your head down, weight on your left front foot, and close that left eye. I think you're ready for a 20-gauge shotgun this year—at eleven you're big enough for one. It will kick a little at first but if you hold it properly you won't even notice it after a while. Honest," he concluded, smiling. Only ten years old, my dad went on to tie for first place in the Cuban live pigeon shooting competition later that summer. Because my father was competing with a .410 shotgun and was by far the youngest competitor, this was a remarkable accomplishment and a very proud moment for him and my grand-father.

Even at sea, Hemingway's quarry sometimes took on a hunter's rather than a piscatorial air, one that was often steeped in bravado. He sometimes shot sharks with the Thompson's sub-machine gun that he kept on board his ship, the *Pilar*. With his crew, whom he dubbed "the Crook Factory," he hunted German submarines in the Gulf Stream during World War II. That summer of 1943 for target practice Patrick and Gregory shot flying fish from the bow of the ship with a .22 rifle as the fish skimmed the surface of the water. On another memorable outing on the *Pilar*, Hemingway attempted to spear a sperm whale with a harpoon propelled from a sawed-off shotgun specially jerry-rigged for the purpose.

In the summer of 1948, Hemingway traveled to Italy with his last wife, my godmother, Mary Welsh Hemingway. The vacation turned into a nine-month sojourn, with excellent duck shooting on the northern part of the Venetian lagoon at Baron Nanyuki Franchetti's hunting preserve, and on the marshes around Torcello—the most remote of the islands near Venice where they had taken up residence. Widgeon, mallards and pintails flocked to the lagoon, a hunter's paradise, especially in the fall and winter months. By moonlight or in the early-morning predawn darkness, Hemingway loved being poled out on a skiff to blinds fashioned from large sunken barrels in the marshes, where his guide would put out decoys along with two or three live callers. It was these experiences that he would use to describe duck hunting so beautifully in *Across the River and Into the Trees*.

An old Arab proverb states, "He that has drunk of Africa's fountains, will drink again." Hemingway had never forgotten his desire to return to Africa. With shacks spreading in the countryside around the Finca and crime on the rise, the Cuban landscape was changing and the bird shooting was no longer so good. In a letter of October, 1952, to Philip Percival, Hemingway expressed his wish to return to Africa with an eye to even moving there "for keeps."

Introduction

The time seemed right in 1953, when my uncle Patrick was now living in Tanganyika (modern Tanzania) and preparing to set up his own hunting-safari firm. A safari was arranged, and at age 69 Philip Percival agreed to come out of retirement and act as Hemingway's professional hunter again. Hoping that an enthusiastic article about hunting in Kenya by the famous author would help to improve tourism after the recent Mau Mau bloodshed, the Kenyan government opened to hunting, for the Hemingways' safari alone, an area on the Salengai River, the Southern Game Reserve in the Kajiado District, forty miles south of Nairobi. Accompanying Ernest and Mary were their Cuban friend Mayito Menocal, the *Look* photographer Earl Thiesen, Patrick Hemingway for brief stints, and a local game ranger, Dennis Zaphiro. Hemingway did not shoot well and had few clean kills of big game, although he managed to bag several fine trophies. He did have excellent wing shooting on great flocks of doves, sandgrouse and guineas. Both he and Mary were as enthralled with the natural beauty of the place and its abundant wildlife as with the hunting.

A belated Christmas gift to Mary—a game-viewing flight to Murchison Falls in Uganda—ended in disaster. The single-engine Cessna almost flew into a flock of ibis over the Nile River near the falls, and when the pilot attempted to avoid the birds he hit an old telegraph wire that nicked the propeller and damaged the tail assembly, resulting in a crash landing. A second plane crash before their return to Nairobi led to world-news coverage reporting Hemingway dead, even running his obituary. Fortunately no one had died, although Hemingway sustained serious internal injuries, as well as a severe concussion. His health would never be quite the same again.

In the winter of 1955–56, Hemingway talked about going back to Africa, as Patrick was still living in Tanganyika and my dad was also there hunting. It was not meant to be, however, and the trip never materialized, primarily for health reasons. In fact, Hemingway never hunted big game in Africa or even in America again, although his love of wing shooting remained passionate. In 1958 Ernest and Mary began returning to Idaho especially for bird shooting. That fall, they rented a house in Ketchum, the Heiss House, which was even equipped with a room for hanging game. Hemingway went bird shooting on Silver Creek and in the fields around Sun Valley with old friends Lloyd Arnold, Taylor Williams, Bud Purdy, Dr. George Saviers, and others. Even with the evident decline in his health and the onset of depression, wing shooting and clay pigeon shooting in the off-season remained favorite activities right up until the very end of his life.

3

For many people, especially those of his generation, Hemingway's persona was indelibly linked to his writing. However, he often said that his personal life should be kept apart and that his writing stood for itself. As you will see in this collection, it does that and more. This book celebrates a great hunter, a father and a grandfather, and his love of the sport. Hemingway once wrote: "A writer's job is to tell the truth. His standard of fidelity to the truth should be so high that his invention, out of his experience, should produce a truer account than anything factual can be. For facts can be observed badly; but when a good writer is creating something, he has time and scope to make of it an absolute truth." In his fiction and his nonfiction writing on hunting, Hemingway is trying to get the feeling of the hunt, not just a depiction of it. This includes not only the process of hunting, the actions leading up to the kill, but as many different dimensions as possible: the country, the weather, the element of chance, the hunter's thoughts, and, if conceivable, the perspective of the hunted.

The selections that make up this book are divided into three parts. The first is devoted to writings of fiction and nonfiction that

Hemingway completed during his lifetime. Excerpts from books are preceded by short stories, beginning with two Nick Adams tales. The first story, whose title echoes Ivan Turgenev's novel of rebellion, explores the bonds between fathers and sons, especially the importance of hunting as a shared activity with the memories and skills being passed from one generation to the next. In "The Three-Day Blow," you will find a marvelous portrayal of an impromptu hunt after shooting the breeze with friends at home—hunting appears second nature and just outside your door. The two African stories are among Hemingway's greatest works of fiction. In "The Short Happy Life of Francis Macomber," we see Macomber overcome fear and self-doubt through big-game hunting in Africa—a personal test of manly courage. Generations of scholars have debated whether his wife, realizing his newfound courage, shot and killed him intentionally.

Green Hills of Africa is a personal favorite, describing, as it does, my grandfather and grandmother's first safari, tales from which also captivated my dad and my uncle Pat when they were young. It was a departure for my grandfather at the time, being his first non-fiction novel. In the foreword, Hemingway wrote: "The writer has attempted to write an absolutely true book to see whether the shape of a country and the pattern of a month's action can, if truly presented, compete with a work of the imagination." I have made a selection of my favorite passages, trying also to include a variety of hunting experiences. I wholeheartedly encourage the reader, if entertained by this selection, to turn to the entire novel, where there are many other fine passages on hunting.

The second section is given to journalistic pieces on hunting or pieces related to hunting. Hemingway always said that these writings should be considered apart from his literature; they were not written to last. However, they provide a wealth of additional information on various hunting topics and are of interest precisely because they reflect the hunting of their time through personal insights by the author. Included are lesser known pieces, such as

"My Pal the Gorilla Gargantua" and "Safari," that have never before been published in a Hemingway anthology.

The final section consists of posthumously published writings on hunting in Michigan, Montana and Africa. These works, unfinished as they are, cannot be held to the same standard as the works completed in Hemingway's lifetime. Nonetheless, you will find that they include some remarkable writings on hunting and the great outdoors. A theme evident in these posthumous works is Hemingway's desire to return to the good country and, perhaps, the wish to relive the glory days of his youth. For it is not just the country that has changed; the hunter himself has grown older. Hemingway explored this idea by returning to his youthful character, Nick Adams, in the story "The Last Good Country," which contains some hauntingly beautiful descriptions of virgin forest in Michigan. Characteristically, he also physically sought out new experiences, returning to Africa, for example, where he knew there were still magnificent country and hunting to be had.

Ernest Hemingway was a writer who wrote about hunting, not a professional hunter who wrote. After the safari of 1933–34, Philip Percival went deep-sea fishing for the first time with Hemingway off the coast of East Africa. Percival kidded Ernest that he, Percival, could now write a story as an expert of big game fishing, alluding to Hemingway's own letters about their African safari that had been published in *Esquire*. The passage from *True at First Light* on the leopard hunt, which concludes this book, illustrates this human side of Hemingway the hunter through a less than perfect kill.

—Seán Hemingway
Brooklyn, New York
August 2001

I

From up in Michigan to the Serengeti

"You see I'm trying in all my stories to get the feeling of the actual life across—not to just depict life—or criticize it—but to actually make it alive. So that when you have read something by me you actually experience the thing. You can't do this without putting in the bad and the ugly as well as what is beautiful. Because if it is all beautiful you can't believe in it. Things aren't that way. It is only by showing both sides—3 dimensions and if possible 4 that you can write the way I want to."

—To his father, Clarence Hemingway, Paris,
March 20, 1925

"Everybody loses all the bloom—we're not peaches—that doesn't mean you get rotten—a gun is better worn and with bloom off— So is a saddle—People too by God."

—To F. Scott Fitzgerald, Hendaye, France,
September 13, 1929

"I like to shoot a rifle and I like to kill and Africa is where you do that."

—To Janet Flanner, Key West,
April 8, 1933

Fathers and Sons

There had been a sign to detour in the center of the main street of this town, but cars had obviously gone through, so, believing it was some repair which had been completed, Nicholas Adams drove on through the town along the empty, brick-paved street, stopped by traffic lights that flashed on and off on this traffic-less Sunday, and would be gone next year when the payments on the system were not met; on under the heavy trees of the small town that are a part of your heart if it is your town and you have walked under them, but that are only too heavy, that shut out the sun and that dampen the houses for a stranger; out past the last house and onto the highway that rose and fell straight away ahead with banks of red dirt sliced cleanly away and the second-growth timber on both sides. It was not his country but it was the middle of fall and all of this country was good to drive through and to see. The cotton was picked and in the clearings there were patches of corn, some cut with streaks of red sorghum, and, driving easily, his son asleep on the seat by his side, the day's run made, knowing the town he would reach for the night, Nick noticed which corn fields had soy beans or peas in them, how the thickets and the cut-over land lay, where the cabins and houses were in relation to the fields and the thickets; hunting the country in his mind as he went by; sizing up each clearing as to feed and cover and figuring where you would find a covey and which way they would fly.

In shooting quail you must not get between them and their habitual cover, once the dogs have found them, or when they flush they will come pouring at you, some rising steep, some skimming by your ears, whirring into a size you have never seen them in the air as they pass, the only way being to turn and take them over your shoulder as they go, before they set their wings and angle down into the thicket. Hunting this country for quail as his father had taught him, Nicholas Adams started thinking about his father. When he first thought about him it was always the eyes. The big frame, the quick movements, the wide shoulders, the hooked, hawk nose, the beard that covered the weak chin, you never thought about—it was always the eyes. They were protected in his head by the formation of the brows; set deep as though a special protection had been devised for some very valuable instrument. They saw much farther and much quicker than the human eye sees and they were the great gift his father had. His father saw as a big-horn ram or as an eagle sees, literally.

He would be standing with his father on one shore of the lake, his own eyes were very good then, and his father would say, "They've run up the flag." Nick could not see the flag or the flag pole. "There," his father would say, "it's your sister Dorothy. She's got the flag up and she's walking out onto the dock."

Nick would look across the lake and he could see the long wooded shore-line, the higher timber behind, the point that guarded the bay, the clear hills of the farm and the white of their cottage in the trees but he could not see any flag pole, or any dock, only the white of the beach and the curve of the shore.

"Can you see the sheep on the hillside toward the point?"

"Yes."

They were a whitish patch on the gray-green of the hill.

"I can count them," his father said.

Like all men with a faculty that surpasses human requirements, his father was very nervous. Then, too, he was sentimental, and, like most sentimental people, he was both cruel and abused. Also, he had much bad luck, and it was not all of it his own. He had died in a trap that he had helped only a little to set, and they had all betrayed him in their various ways before he died. All sentimental people are betrayed so many times. Nick could not write about him yet, although he would, later, but the quail country made him remember him as he was when Nick was a boy and he was very grateful to him for two things: fishing and shooting. His father was as sound on those two things as he was unsound on sex, for instance, and Nick was glad that it had been that way; for some one has to give you your first gun or the opportunity to get it and use it, and you have to live where there is game or fish if you are to learn about them, and now, at thirty-eight, he loved to fish and to shoot exactly as much as when he first had gone with his father. It was a passion that had never slackened and he was very grateful to his father for bringing him to know it.

While for the other, that his father was not sound about, all the equipment you will ever have is provided and each man learns all there is for him to know about it without advice; and it makes no difference where you live. He remembered very clearly the only two pieces of information his father had given him about that. Once when they were out shooting together Nick shot a red squirrel out of a hemlock tree. The squirrel fell, wounded, and when Nick picked him up bit the boy clean through the ball of the thumb.

"The dirty little bugger," Nick said and smacked the squirrel's head against the tree. "Look how he bit me."

His father looked and said, "Suck it out clean and put some iodine on when you get home."

"The little bugger," Nick said.

5

"Do you know what a bugger is?" his father asked him.

"We call anything a bugger," Nick said.

"A bugger is a man who has intercourse with animals."

"Why?" Nick said.

"I don't know," his father said. "But it is a heinous crime."

Nick's imagination was both stirred and horrified by this and he thought of various animals but none seemed attractive or practical and that was the sum total of direct sexual knowledge bequeathed him by his father except on one other subject. One morning he read in the paper that Enrico Caruso had been arrested for mashing.

"What is mashing?"

"It is one of the most heinous of crimes," his father answered. Nick's imagination pictured the great tenor doing something strange, bizarre, and heinous with a potato masher to a beautiful lady who looked like the pictures of Anna Held on the inside of cigar boxes. He resolved, with considerable horror, that when he was old enough he would try mashing at least once.

His father had summed up the whole matter by stating that masturbation produced blindness, insanity, and death, while a man who went with prostitutes would contract hideous venereal diseases and that the thing to do was to keep your hands off of people. On the other hand his father had the finest pair of eyes he had ever seen and Nick had loved him very much and for a long time. Now, knowing how it had all been, even remembering the earliest times before things had gone badly was not good remembering. If he wrote it he could get rid of it. He had gotten rid of many things by writing them. But it was still too early for that. There were still too many people. So he decided to think of something else. There was nothing to do about his father and he had thought it all through many times. The handsome job the undertaker had done on his father's face had not blurred in his mind and all the rest of it was quite clear, including the responsibilities. He had complimented the undertaker. The undertaker had been both proud and smugly pleased. But it was not the undertaker that had given him that last face. The undertaker had only made certain dashingly executed repairs of doubtful artistic merit. The face had been making itself and being made for a long time. It had modelled fast in the last three years. It was a good story but there were still too many people alive for him to write it.

Nick's own education in those earlier matters had been acquired in the hemlock woods behind the Indian camp. This was reached by a trail which ran from the cottage through the woods to the farm and then by a road which wound through the slashings to the camp. Now if he could still feel all of that trail with bare feet. First there was the pine-needle loam through the hemlock woods behind the cottage where the fallen logs crumbled into wood dust and long splintered pieces of wood hung like javelins in the tree that had been struck by lightning. You crossed the creek on a log and if you stepped off there was the black muck of the swamp. You climbed a fence out of the woods and the trail was hard in the sun across the field with cropped grass and sheep sorrel and mullen growing and to the left the quaky bog of the creek bottom where the killdeer plover fed. The spring house was in that creek. Below the barn there was fresh warm manure and the other older manure that was caked dry on top. Then there was another fence and the hard, hot trail from the barn to the house and the hot sandy road that ran down to the woods, crossing the creek, on a bridge this time, where the cat-tails grew that you soaked in kerosene to make jack-lights with for spearing fish at night.

Then the main road went off to the left, skirting the woods and climbing the hill, while you went into the woods on the wide clay and shale road, cool under the trees, and broadened for them to skid out the hemlock bark the Indians cut. The hemlock bark was piled in long rows of stacks, roofed over with more bark, like houses, and the peeled logs lay huge and yellow where the trees had been felled. They left the logs in the woods to rot, they did not even clear away or burn the tops. It was only the bark they wanted

7

for the tannery at Boyne City; hauling it across the lake on the ice in winter, and each year there was less forest and more open, hot, shadeless, weed-grown slashing.

But there was still much forest then, virgin forest where the trees grew high before there were any branches and you walked on the brown, clean, springy-needled ground with no undergrowth and it was cool on the hottest days and they three lay against the trunk of a hemlock wider than two beds are long, with the breeze high in the tops and the cool light that came in patches, and Billy said:

"You want Trudy again?"

"You want to?"

"Un Huh."

"Come on."

"No, here."

"But Billy—"

"I no mind Billy. He my brother."

Then afterwards they sat, the three of them, listening for a black squirrel that was in the top branches where they could not see him. They were waiting for him to bark again because when he barked he would jerk his tail and Nick would shoot where he saw any movement. His father gave him only three cartridges a day to hunt with and he had a single-barrel twenty-gauge shotgun with a very long barrel.

"Son of a bitch never move," Billy said.

"You shoot, Nickie. Scare him. We see him jump. Shoot him again," Trudy said. It was a long speech for her.

"I've only got two shells," Nick said.

"Son of a bitch," said Billy.

They sat against the tree and were quiet. Nick was feeling hollow and happy.

"Eddie says he going to come some night sleep in bed with you sister Dorothy."

8

"What?"

"He said."

Trudy nodded.

"That's all he want do," she said. Eddie was their older half-brother. He was seventeen.

"If Eddie Gilby ever comes at night and even speaks to Dorothy you know what I'd do to him? I'd kill him like this." Nick cocked the gun and hardly taking aim pulled the trigger, blowing a hole as big as your hand in the head or belly of that half-breed bastard Eddie Gilby. "Like that. I'd kill him like that."

"He better not come then," Trudy said. She put her hand in Nick's pocket.

"He better watch out plenty," said Billy.

"He's big bluff," Trudy was exploring with her hand in Nick's pocket. "But don't you kill him. You get plenty trouble."

"I'd kill him like that," Nick said. Eddie Gilby lay on the ground with all his chest shot away. Nick put his foot on him proudly.

"I'd scalp him," he said happily.

"No," said Trudy. "That's dirty."

"I'd scalp him and send it to his mother."

"His mother dead," Trudy said. "Don't you kill him, Nickie. Don't you kill him for me."

"After I scalped him I'd throw him to the dogs."

Billy was very depressed. "He better watch out," he said gloomily.

"They'd tear him to pieces," Nick said, pleased with the picture. Then, having scalped that half-breed renegade and standing, watching the dogs tear him, his face unchanging, he fell backward against the tree, held tight around the neck, Trudy holding, choking him, and crying, "No kill him! No kill him! No kill him! No. No. No. Nickie. Nickie. Nickie!"

"What's the matter with you?"

"No kill him."

"I got to kill him."

"He just a big bluff."

"All right," Nickie said. "I won't kill him unless he comes around the house. Let go of me."

"That's good," Trudy said. "You want to do anything now? I feel good now."

"If Billy goes away." Nick had killed Eddie Gilby, then pardoned him his life, and he was a man now.

"You go, Billy. You hang around all the time. Go on."

"Son a bitch," Billy said. "I get tired this. What we come? Hunt or what?"

"You can take the gun. There's one shell."

"All right. I get a big black one all right."

"I'll holler," Nick said.

Then, later, it was a long time after and Billy was still away.

"You think we make a baby?" Trudy folded her brown legs together happily and rubbed against him. Something inside Nick had gone a long way away.

"I don't think so," he said.

"Make plenty baby what the hell."

They heard Billy shoot.

"I wonder if he got one."

"Don't care," said Trudy.

Billy came through the trees. He had the gun over his shoulder and he held a black squirrel by the front paws.

"Look," he said. "Bigger than a cat. You all through?"

"Where'd you get him?"

"Over there. Saw him jump first."

"Got to go home," Nick said.

"No," said Trudy.

"I got to get there for supper."

"All right."

"Want to hunt tomorrow?"

"All right."

"You can have the squirrel."

"All right."

"Come out after supper?"

"No."

"How you feel?"

"Good."

"All right."

"Give me kiss on the face," said Trudy.

Now, as he rode along the highway in the car and it was getting dark, Nick was all through thinking about his father. The end of the day never made him think of him. The end of the day had always belonged to Nick alone and he never felt right unless he was alone at it. His father came back to him in the fall of the year, or in the early spring when there had been jacksnipe on the prairie, or when he saw shocks of corn, or when he saw a lake, or if he ever saw a horse and buggy, or when he saw, or heard, wild geese, or in a duck blind; remembering the time an eagle dropped through the whirling snow to strike a canvas-covered decoy, rising, his wings beating, the talons caught in the canvas. His father was with him, suddenly, in deserted orchards and in new-plowed fields, in thickets, on small hills, or when going through dead grass, whenever splitting wood or hauling water, by grist mills, cider mills and dams and always with open fires. The towns he lived in were not towns his father knew. After he was fifteen he had shared nothing with him.

His father had frost in his beard in cold weather and in hot weather he sweated very much. He liked to work in the sun on the farm because he did not have to and he loved manual work, which Nick did not. Nick loved his father but hated the smell of him and once when he had to wear a suit of his father's underwear that had gotten too small for his father it made him feel sick and he took it off and put it under two stones in the creek and said that he had lost it. He had told his father how it was when his father had made him put it on but his father had said it was freshly washed. It had been, too. When Nick had asked him to smell of it his father sniffed at it indignantly and said that it was clean and fresh. When Nick came home from fishing without it and said he lost it he was whipped for lying.

Afterwards he had sat inside the woodshed with the door open, his shotgun loaded and cocked, looking across at his father sitting on the screen porch reading the paper, and thought, "I can blow him to hell. I can kill him." Finally he felt his anger go out of him and he felt a little sick about it being the gun that his father had given him. Then he had gone to the Indian camp, walking there in the dark, to get rid of the smell. There was only one person in his family that he liked the smell of; one sister. All the others he avoided all contact with. That sense blunted when he started to smoke. It was a good thing. It was good for a bird dog but it did not help a man.

"What was it like, Papa, when you were a little boy and used to hunt with the Indians?"

"I don't know," Nick was startled. He had not even noticed the boy was awake. He looked at him sitting beside him on the seat. He had felt quite alone but this boy had been with him. He wondered for how long. "We used to go all day to hunt black squirrels," he said. "My father only gave me three shells a day because he said that would teach me to hunt and it wasn't good for a boy to go banging around. I went with a boy named Billy Gilby and his sister Trudy. We used to go out nearly every day all one summer."

"Those are funny names for Indians."

"Yes, aren't they," Nick said.

"But tell me what they were like."

"They were Ojibways," Nick said. "And they were very nice."

"But what were they like to be with?"

"It's hard to say," Nick Adams said. Could you say she did first what no one has ever done better and mention plump brown legs, flat belly, hard little breasts, well holding arms, quick searching tongue, the flat eyes, the good taste of mouth, then uncomfortably, tightly, sweetly, moistly, lovely, tightly, achingly, fully, finally, un-endingly, never-endingly, never-to-endingly, suddenly ended, the great bird flown like an owl in the twilight, only it was daylight in the woods and hemlock needles stuck against your belly. So that when you go in a place where Indians have lived you smell them gone and all the empty pain killer bottles and the flies that buzz do not kill the sweetgrass smell, the smoke smell and that other like a fresh cased marten skin. Nor any jokes about them nor old squaws take that away. Nor the sick sweet smell they get to have. Nor what they did finally. It wasn't how they ended. They all ended the same. Long time ago good. Now no good.

And about the other. When you have shot one bird flying you have shot all birds flying. They are all different and they fly in different ways but the sensation is the same and the last one is as good as the first. He could thank his father for that.

"You might not like them," Nick said to the boy. "But I think you would."

"And my grandfather lived with them too when he was a boy, didn't he?"

"Yes. When I asked him what they were like he said that he had many friends among them."

"Will I ever live with them?"

"I don't know," Nick said. "That's up to you."

"How old will I be when I get a shotgun and can hunt by myself?"

"Twelve years old if I see you are careful."

"I wish I was twelve now."

"You will be, soon enough."

"What was my grandfather like? I can't remember him except that he gave me an air rifle and an American flag when I came over from France that time. What was he like?"

"He's hard to describe. He was a great hunter and fisherman and he had wonderful eyes."

"Was he greater than you?"

"He was a much better shot and his father was a great wing shot too."

"I'll bet he wasn't better than you."

"Oh, yes he was. He shot very quickly and beautifully. I'd rather see him shoot than any man I ever knew. He was always very disappointed in the way I shot."

"Why do we never go to pray at the tomb of my grandfather?"

"We live in a different part of the country. It's a long way from here."

"In France that wouldn't make any difference. In France we'd go. I think I ought to go to pray at the tomb of my grandfather."

"Sometime we'll go."

"I hope we won't live somewhere so that I can never go to pray at your tomb when you are dead."

"We'll have to arrange it."

"Don't you think we might all be buried at a convenient place? We could all be buried in France. That would be fine."

"I don't want to be buried in France," Nick said.

"Well, then, we'll have to get some convenient place in America. Couldn't we all be buried out at the ranch?"

"That's an idea."

"Then I could stop and pray at the tomb of my grandfather on the way to the ranch."

"You're awfully practical."

"Well, I don't feel good never to have even visited the tomb of my grandfather."

"We'll have to go," Nick said. "I can see we'll have to go."

The Three-Day Blow

The rain stopped as Nick turned into the road that went up through the orchard. The fruit had been picked and the fall wind blew through the bare trees. Nick stopped and picked up a Wagner apple from beside the road, shiny in the brown grass from the rain. He put the apple in the pocket of his Mackinaw coat.

The road came out of the orchard on to the top of the hill. There was the cottage, the porch bare, smoke coming from the chimney. In back was the garage, the chicken coop and the second-growth timber like a hedge against the woods behind. The big trees swayed far over in the wind as he watched. It was the first of the autumn storms.

As Nick crossed the open field above the orchard the door of the cottage opened and Bill came out. He stood on the porch looking out.

"Well, Wemedge," he said.

"Hey, Bill," Nick said, coming up the steps.

They stood together, looking out across the country, down over the orchard, beyond the road, across the lower fields and the woods

15

of the point to the lake. The wind was blowing straight down the lake. They could see the surf along the Ten Mile point.

"She's blowing," Nick said.

"She'll blow like that for three days," Bill said.

"Is your dad in?" Nick said.

"No. He's out with the gun. Come on in."

Nick went inside the cottage. There was a big fire in the fireplace. The wind made it roar. Bill shut the door.

"Have a drink?" he said.

He went out to the kitchen and came back with two glasses and a pitcher of water. Nick reached the whisky bottle from the shelf above the fireplace.

"All right?" he said.

"Good," said Bill.

They sat in front of the fire and drank the Irish whisky and water.

"It's got a swell, smoky taste," Nick said, and looked at the fire through the glass.

"That's the peat," Bill said.

"You can't get peat into liquor," Nick said.

"That doesn't make any difference," Bill said.

"You ever seen any peat?" Nick asked.

"No," said Bill.

"Neither have I," Nick said.

His shoes, stretched out on the hearth, began to steam in front of the fire.

"Better take your shoes off," Bill said.

"I haven't got any socks on."

"Take them off and dry them and I'll get you some," Bill said. He went upstairs into the loft and Nick heard him walking about overhead. Upstairs was open under the roof and was where Bill and his father and he, Nick, sometimes slept. In back was a dressing room. They moved the cots back out of the rain and covered them with rubber blankets.

Bill came down with a pair of heavy wool socks.

"It's getting too late to go around without socks," he said.

"I hate to start them again," Nick said. He pulled the socks on and slumped back in the chair, putting his feet up on the screen in front of the fire.

"You'll dent in the screen," Bill said. Nick swung his feet over to the side of the fireplace.

"Got anything to read?" he asked.

"Only the paper."

"What did the Cards do?"

"Dropped a double header to the Giants."

"That ought to cinch it for them."

"It's a gift," Bill said. "As long as McGraw can buy every good ball player in the league there's nothing to it."

"He can't buy them all," Nick said.

"He buys all the ones he wants," Bill said. "Or he makes them discontented so they have to trade them to him."

"Like Heinie Zim," Nick agreed.

"That bonehead will do him a lot of good."

Bill stood up.

"He can hit," Nick offered. The heat from the fire was baking his legs.

"He's a sweet fielder, too," Bill said. "But he loses ball games."

"Maybe that's what McGraw wants him for," Nick suggested.

"Maybe," Bill agreed.

"There's always more to it than we know about," Nick said.

"Of course. But we've got pretty good dope for being so far away."

"Like how much better you can pick them if you don't see the horses."

"That's it."

Bill reached down the whisky bottle. His big hand went all the way around it. He poured the whisky into the glass Nick held out.

"How much water?"

"Just the same."

He sat down on the floor beside Nick's chair.

"It's good when the fall storms come, isn't it?" Nick said.

"It's swell."

"It's the best time of year," Nick said.

"Wouldn't it be hell to be in town?" Bill said.

"I'd like to see the World Series," Nick said.

"Well, they're always in New York or Philadelphia now," Bill said. "That doesn't do us any good."

"I wonder if the Cards will ever win a pennant?"

"Not in our lifetime," Bill said.

"Gee, they'd go crazy," Nick said.

"Do you remember when they got going that once before they had the train wreck?"

"Boy!" Nick said, remembering.

Bill reached over to the table under the window for the book that lay there, face down, where he had put it when he went to the door. He held his glass in one hand and the book in the other, leaning it back against Nick's chair.

"What are you reading?"

"*Richard Feverel.*"

"I couldn't get into it."

"It's all right," Bill said. "It ain't a bad book, Wemedge."

"What else have you got I haven't read?" Nick asked.

"Did you read the *Forest Lovers?*"

"Yup. That's the one where they go to bed every night with the naked sword between them."

"That's a good book, Wemedge."

"It's a swell book. What I couldn't ever understand was what good the sword would do. It would have to stay edge up all the time because if it went over flat you could roll right over it and it wouldn't make any trouble."

"It's a symbol," Bill said.

"Sure," said Nick, "but it isn't practical."

"Did you ever read *Fortitude*?"

"It's fine," Nick said. "That's a real book. That's where his old man is after him all the time. Have you got any more by Walpole?"

"*The Dark Forest*," Bill said. "It's about Russia."

"What does he know about Russia?" Nick asked.

"I don't know. You can't ever tell about those guys. Maybe he was there when he was a boy. He's got a lot of dope on it."

"I'd like to meet him," Nick said.

"I'd like to meet Chesterton," Bill said.

"I wish he was here now," Nick said. "We'd take him fishing to the 'Voix tomorrow."

"I wonder if he'd like to go fishing," Bill said.

"Sure," said Nick. "He must be about the best guy there is. Do you remember the *Flying Inn*?"

> " 'If an angel out of heaven
> Gives you something else to drink,
> Thank him for his kind intentions;
> Go and pour them down the sink.' "

"That's right," said Nick. "I guess he's a better guy than Walpole."

"Oh, he's a better guy, all right," Bill said.

"But Walpole's a better writer."

"I don't know," Nick said. "Chesterton's a classic."

"Walpole's a classic, too," Bill insisted.

"I wish we had them both here," Nick said. "We'd take them both fishing to the 'Voix tomorrow."

"Let's get drunk," Bill said.

"All right," Nick agreed.

"My old man won't care," Bill said.

"Are you sure?" said Nick.

"I know it," Bill said.

"I'm a little drunk now," Nick said.

"You aren't drunk," Bill said.

He got up from the floor and reached for the whisky bottle. Nick held out his glass. His eyes fixed on it while Bill poured.

Bill poured the glass half full of whisky.

"Put in your own water," he said. "There's just one more shot."

"Got any more?" Nick asked.

"There's plenty more but dad only likes me to drink what's open."

"Sure," said Nick.

"He says opening bottles is what makes drunkards," Bill explained.

"That's right," said Nick. He was impressed. He had never thought of that before. He had always thought it was solitary drinking that made drunkards.

"How is your dad?" he asked respectfully.

"He's all right," Bill said. "He gets a little wild sometimes."

"He's a swell guy," Nick said. He poured water into his glass out of the pitcher. It mixed slowly with the whisky. There was more whisky than water.

"You bet your life he is," Bill said.

"My old man's all right," Nick said.

"You're damn right he is," said Bill.

"He claims he's never taken a drink in his life," Nick said, as though announcing a scientific fact.

"Well, he's a doctor. My old man's a painter. That's different."

"He's missed a lot," Nick said sadly.

"You can't tell," Bill said. "Everything's got its compensations."

"He says he's missed a lot himself," Nick confessed.

"Well, dad's had a tough time," Bill said.

"It all evens up," Nick said.

They sat looking into the fire and thinking of this profound truth.

"I'll get a chunk from the back porch," Nick said. He had noticed while looking into the fire that the fire was dying down. Also he wished to show he could hold his liquor and be practical. Even if his father had never touched a drop Bill was not going to get him drunk before he himself was drunk.

"Bring one of the big beech chunks," Bill said. He was also being consciously practical.

Nick came in with the log through the kitchen and in passing knocked a pan off the kitchen table. He laid the log down and picked up the pan. It had contained dried apricots, soaking in water. He carefully picked up all the apricots off the floor, some of them had gone under the stove, and put them back in the pan. He dipped some more water onto them from the pail by the table. He felt quite proud of himself. He had been thoroughly practical.

He came in carrying the log and Bill got up from the chair and helped him put it on the fire.

"That's a swell log," Nick said.

"I'd been saving it for the bad weather," Bill said. "A log like that will burn all night."

"There'll be coals left to start the fire in the morning," Nick said.

"That's right," Bill agreed. They were conducting the conversation on a high plane.

"Let's have another drink," Nick said.

"I think there's another bottle open in the locker," Bill said.

He kneeled down in the corner in front of the locker and brought out a square-faced bottle.

"It's Scotch," he said.

"I'll get some more water," Nick said. He went out into the kitchen again. He filled the pitcher with the dipper dipping cold spring water from the pail. On his way back to the living room he passed a mirror in the dining room and looked in it. His face looked strange. He smiled at the face in the mirror and it grinned back at him. He winked at it and went on. It was not his face but it didn't make any difference.

Bill had poured out the drinks.

"That's an awfully big shot," Nick said.

"Not for us, Wemedge," Bill said.

"What'll we drink to?" Nick asked, holding up the glass.

"Let's drink to fishing," Bill said.

"All right," Nick said. "Gentlemen, I give you fishing."

"All fishing," Bill said. "Everywhere."

"Fishing," Nick said. "That's what we drink to."

"It's better than baseball," Bill said.

"There isn't any comparison," said Nick. "How did we ever get talking about baseball?"

"It was a mistake," Bill said. "Baseball is a game for louts."

They drank all that was in their glasses.

"Now let's drink to Chesterton."

"And Walpole," Nick interposed.

Nick poured out the liquor. Bill poured in the water. They looked at each other. They felt very fine.

"Gentlemen," Bill said, "I give you Chesterton and Walpole."

"Exactly, gentlemen," Nick said.

They drank. Bill filled up the glasses. They sat down in the big chairs in front of the fire.

"You were very wise, Wemedge," Bill said.

"What do you mean?" asked Nick.

"To bust off that Marge business," Bill said.

"I guess so," said Nick.

"It was the only thing to do. If you hadn't, by now you'd be back home working trying to get enough money to get married."

Nick said nothing.

"Once a man's married he's absolutely bitched," Bill went on. "He hasn't got anything more. Nothing. Not a damn thing. He's done for. You've seen the guys that get married."

Nick said nothing.

"You can tell them," Bill said. "They get this sort of fat married look. They're done for."

"Sure," said Nick.

"It was probably bad busting it off," Bill said. "But you always fall for somebody else and then it's all right. Fall for them but don't let them ruin you."

"Yes," said Nick.

"If you'd have married her you would have had to marry the whole family. Remember her mother and that guy she married."

Nick nodded.

"Imagine having them around the house all the time and going to Sunday dinners at their house, and having them over to dinner and her telling Marge all the time what to do and how to act."

Nick sat quiet.

"You came out of it damned well," Bill said. "Now she can marry somebody of her own sort and settle down and be happy. You can't mix oil and water and you can't mix that sort of thing any more than if I'd marry Ida that works for Strattons. She'd probably like it, too."

Nick said nothing. The liquor had all died out of him and left him alone. Bill wasn't there. He wasn't sitting in front of the fire or going fishing tomorrow with Bill and his dad or anything. He wasn't drunk. It was all gone. All he knew was that he had once had Marjorie and that he had lost her. She was gone and he had sent her away. That was all that mattered. He might never see her again. Probably he never would. It was all gone, finished.

"Let's have another drink," Nick said.

Bill poured it out. Nick splashed in a little water.

"If you'd gone on that way we wouldn't be here now," Bill said.

That was true. His original plan had been to go down home and get a job. Then he had planned to stay in Charlevoix all winter so he could be near Marge. Now he did not know what he was going to do.

"Probably we wouldn't even be going fishing tomorrow," Bill said. "You had the right dope, all right."

"I couldn't help it," Nick said.

"I know. That's the way it works out," Bill said.

"All of a sudden everything was over," Nick said. "I don't know why it was. I couldn't help it. Just like when the three-day blows come now and rip all the leaves off the trees."

"Well, it's over. That's the point," Bill said.

"It was my fault," Nick said.

"It doesn't make any difference whose fault it was," Bill said.

"No, I suppose not," Nick said.

The big thing was that Marjorie was gone and that probably he would never see her again. He had talked to her about how they would go to Italy together and the fun they would have. Places they would be together. It was all gone now.

"So long as it's over that's all that matters," Bill said. "I tell you, Wemedge, I was worried while it was going on. You played it right. I understand her mother is sore as hell. She told a lot of people you were engaged."

"We weren't engaged," Nick said.

"It was all around that you were."

"I can't help it," Nick said. "We weren't."

"Weren't you going to get married?" Bill asked.

"Yes. But we weren't engaged," Nick said.

"What's the difference?" Bill asked judicially.

"I don't know. There's a difference."

"I don't see it," said Bill.

"All right," said Nick. "Let's get drunk."

"All right," Bill said. "Let's get really drunk."

"Let's get drunk and then go swimming," Nick said.

He drank off his glass.

"I'm sorry as hell about her but what could I do?" he said. "You know what her mother was like!"

"She was terrible," Bill said.

"All of a sudden it was over," Nick said. "I oughtn't to talk about it."

"You aren't," Bill said. "I talked about it and now I'm through. We won't ever speak about it again. You don't want to think about it. You might get back into it again."

Nick had not thought about that. It had seemed so absolute. That was a thought. That made him feel better.

"Sure," he said. "There's always that danger."

He felt happy now. There was not anything that was irrevocable. He might go into town Saturday night. Today was Thursday.

"There's always a chance," he said.

"You'll have to watch yourself," Bill said.

"I'll watch myself," he said.

He felt happy. Nothing was finished. Nothing was ever lost. He would go into town on Saturday. He felt lighter, as he had felt before Bill started to talk about it. There was always a way out.

"Let's take the guns and go down to the point and look for your dad," Nick said.

"All right."

Bill took down the two shotguns from the rack on the wall. He opened a box of shells. Nick put on his Mackinaw coat and his shoes. His shoes were stiff from the drying. He was still quite drunk but his head was clear.

"How do you feel?" Nick asked.

"Swell. I've just got a good edge on." Bill was buttoning up his sweater.

"There's no use getting drunk."

"No. We ought to get outdoors."

They stepped out the door. The wind was blowing a gale.

"The birds will lie right down in the grass with this," Nick said.

They struck down toward the orchard.

"I saw a woodcock this morning," Bill said.

"Maybe we'll jump him," Nick said.

"You can't shoot in this wind," Bill said.

Outside now the Marge business was no longer so tragic. It was not even very important. The wind blew everything like that away.

"It's coming right off the big lake," Nick said.

Against the wind they heard the thud of a shotgun.

"That's dad," Bill said. "He's down in the swamp."

"Let's cut down that way," Nick said.

"Let's cut across the lower meadow and see if we jump anything," Bill said.

"All right," Nick said.

None of it was important now. The wind blew it out of his head. Still he could always go into town Saturday night. It was a good thing to have in reserve.

The Short Happy Life of Francis Macomber

It was now lunch time and they were all sitting under the double green fly of the dining tent pretending that nothing had happened.

"Will you have lime juice or lemon squash?" Macomber asked.

"I'll have a gimlet," Robert Wilson told him.

"I'll have a gimlet too. I need something," Macomber's wife said.

"I suppose it's the thing to do," Macomber agreed. "Tell him to make three gimlets."

The mess boy had started them already, lifting the bottles out of the canvas cooling bags that sweated wet in the wind that blew through the trees that shaded the tents.

"What had I ought to give them?" Macomber asked.

"A quid would be plenty," Wilson told him. "You don't want to spoil them."

"Will the headman distribute it?"

"Absolutely."

Francis Macomber had, half an hour before, been carried to his tent from the edge of the camp in triumph on the arms and shoulders of the cook, the personal boys, the skinner and the porters. The gun-bearers had taken no part in the demonstration. When the native boys put him down at the door of his tent, he had shaken all their hands, received their congratulations, and then gone into the tent and sat on the bed until his wife came in. She did not speak to him when she came in and he left the tent at once to wash his face and hands in the portable wash basin outside and go over to the dining tent to sit in a comfortable canvas chair in the breeze and the shade.

"You've got your lion," Robert Wilson said to him, "and a damned fine one too."

Mrs. Macomber looked at Wilson quickly. She was an extremely handsome and well-kept woman of the beauty and social position which had, five years before, commanded five thousand dollars as the price of endorsing, with photographs, a beauty product which she had never used. She had been married to Francis Macomber for eleven years.

"He is a good lion, isn't he?" Macomber said. His wife looked at him now. She looked at both these men as though she had never seen them before.

One, Wilson, the white hunter, she knew she had never truly seen before. He was about middle height with sandy hair, a stubby mustache, a very red face and extremely cold blue eyes with faint white wrinkles at the corners that grooved merrily when he smiled. He smiled at her now and she looked away from his face at the way his shoulders sloped in the loose tunic he wore with the four big cartridges held in loops where the left breast pocket should have been, at his big brown hands, his old slacks, his very dirty boots and back to his red face again. She noticed where the baked red of his face stopped in a white line that marked the circle left by his Stetson hat that hung now from one of the pegs of the tent pole.

"Well, here's to the lion," Robert Wilson said. He smiled at her again and, not smiling, she looked curiously at her husband.

Francis Macomber was very tall, very well built if you did not mind that length of bone, dark, his hair cropped like an oarsman, rather thin-lipped, and was considered handsome. He was dressed in the same sort of safari clothes that Wilson wore except that his were new, he was thirty-five years old, kept himself very fit, was good at court games, had a number of big-game fishing records, and had just shown himself, very publicly, to be a coward.

"Here's to the lion," he said. "I can't ever thank you for what you did."

Margaret, his wife, looked away from him and back to Wilson.

"Let's not talk about the lion," she said.

Wilson looked over at her without smiling and now she smiled at him.

"It's been a very strange day," she said. "Hadn't you ought to put your hat on even under the canvas at noon? You told me that, you know."

"Might put it on," said Wilson.

"You know you have a very red face, Mr. Wilson," she told him and smiled again.

"Drink," said Wilson.

"I don't think so," she said. "Francis drinks a great deal, but his face is never red."

"It's red today," Macomber tried a joke.

"No," said Margaret. "It's mine that's red today. But Mr. Wilson's is always red."

"Must be racial," said Wilson. "I say, you wouldn't like to drop my beauty as a topic, would you?"

"I've just started on it."

"Let's chuck it," said Wilson.

"Conversation is going to be so difficult," Margaret said.

"Don't be silly, Margot," her husband said.

"No difficulty," Wilson said. "Got a damn fine lion."

Margot looked at them both and they both saw that she was going to cry. Wilson had seen it coming for a long time and he dreaded it. Macomber was past dreading it.

"I wish it hadn't happened. Oh, I wish it hadn't happened," she said and started for her tent. She made no noise of crying but they could see that her shoulders were shaking under the rose-colored, sun-proofed shirt she wore.

"Women upset," said Wilson to the tall man. "Amounts to nothing. Strain on the nerves and one thing'n another."

"No," said Macomber. "I suppose that I rate that for the rest of my life now."

"Nonsense. Let's have a spot of the giant killer," said Wilson. "Forget the whole thing. Nothing to it anyway."

"We might try," said Macomber. "I won't forget what you did for me though."

"Nothing," said Wilson. "All nonsense."

So they sat there in the shade where the camp was pitched under some wide-topped acacia trees with a boulder-strewn cliff behind them, and a stretch of grass that ran to the bank of a boulder-filled stream in front with forest beyond it, and drank their just-cool lime drinks and avoided one another's eyes while the boys set the table for lunch. Wilson could tell that the boys all knew about it now and when he saw Macomber's personal boy looking curiously at his master while he was putting dishes on the table he snapped at him in Swahili. The boy turned away with his face blank.

"What were you telling him?" Macomber asked.

"Nothing. Told him to look alive or I'd see he got about fifteen of the best."

"What's that? Lashes?"

"It's quite illegal," Wilson said. "You're supposed to fine them."

"Do you still have them whipped?"

"Oh, yes. They could raise a row if they chose to complain. But they don't. They prefer it to the fines."

"How strange!" said Macomber.

"Not strange, really," Wilson said. "Which would you rather do? Take a good birching or lose your pay?"

Then he felt embarrassed at asking it and before Macomber could answer he went on, "We all take a beating every day, you know, one way or another."

This was no better. "Good God," he thought. "I am a diplomat, aren't I?"

"Yes, we take a beating," said Macomber, still not looking at him. "I'm awfully sorry about that lion business. It doesn't have to go any further, does it? I mean no one will hear about it, will they?"

"You mean will I tell it at the Mathaiga Club?" Wilson looked at him now coldly. He had not expected this. So he's a bloody four-letter man as well as a bloody coward, he thought. I rather liked him too until today. But how is one to know about an American?

"No," said Wilson. "I'm a professional hunter. We never talk about our clients. You can be quite easy on that. It's supposed to be bad form to ask us not to talk though."

He had decided now that to break would be much easier. He would eat, then, by himself and could read a book with his meals. They would eat by themselves. He would see them through the safari on a very formal basis—what was it the French called it? Distinguished consideration—and it would be a damn sight easier than having to go through this emotional trash. He'd insult him and make a good clean break. Then he could read a book with his meals and he'd still be drinking their whisky. That was the phrase for it when a safari went bad. You ran into another white hunter and you asked, "How is everything going?" and he answered, "Oh, I'm still drinking their whisky," and you knew everything had gone to pot.

"I'm sorry," Macomber said and looked at him with his American face that would stay adolescent until it became middle-aged, and Wilson noted his crew-cropped hair, fine eyes only faintly

31

shifty, good nose, thin lips and handsome jaw. "I'm sorry I didn't realize that. There are lots of things I don't know."

So what could he do, Wilson thought. He was all ready to break it off quickly and neatly and here the beggar was apologizing after he had just insulted him. He made one more attempt. "Don't worry about me talking," he said. "I have a living to make. You know in Africa no woman ever misses her lion and no white man ever bolts."

"I bolted like a rabbit," Macomber said.

Now what in hell were you going to do about a man who talked like that, Wilson wondered.

Wilson looked at Macomber with his flat, blue, machine-gunner's eyes and the other smiled back at him. He had a pleasant smile if you did not notice how his eyes showed when he was hurt.

"Maybe I can fix it up on buffalo," he said. "We're after them next, aren't we?"

"In the morning if you like," Wilson told him. Perhaps he had been wrong. This was certainly the way to take it. You most certainly could not tell a damned thing about an American. He was all for Macomber again. If you could forget the morning. But, of course, you couldn't. The morning had been about as bad as they come.

"Here comes the Memsahib," he said. She was walking over from her tent looking refreshed and cheerful and quite lovely. She had a very perfect oval face, so perfect that you expected her to be stupid. But she wasn't stupid, Wilson thought, no, not stupid.

"How is the beautiful red-faced Mr. Wilson? Are you feeling better, Francis, my pearl?"

"Oh, much," said Macomber.

"I've dropped the whole thing," she said, sitting down at the table. "What importance is there to whether Francis is any good at killing lions? That's not his trade. That's Mr. Wilson's trade. Mr. Wilson is really very impressive killing anything. You do kill anything, don't you?"

"Oh, anything," said Wilson. "Simply anything." They are, he thought, the hardest in the world; the hardest, the cruelest, the most predatory and the most attractive and their men have softened or gone to pieces nervously as they have hardened. Or is it that they pick men they can handle? They can't know that much at the age they marry, he thought. He was grateful that he had gone through his education on American women before now because this was a very attractive one.

"We're going after buff in the morning," he told her.

"I'm coming," she said.

"No, you're not."

"Oh, yes, I am. Mayn't I, Francis?"

"Why not stay in camp?"

"Not for anything," she said. "I wouldn't miss something like today for anything."

When she left, Wilson was thinking, when she went off to cry, she seemed a hell of a fine woman. She seemed to understand, to realize, to be hurt for him and for herself and to know how things really stood. She is away for twenty minutes and now she is back, simply enamelled in that American female cruelty. They are the damnedest women. Really the damnedest.

"We'll put on another show for you tomorrow," Francis Macomber said.

"You're not coming," Wilson said.

"You're very mistaken," she told him. "And I want *so* to see you perform again. You were lovely this morning. That is if blowing things' heads off is lovely."

"Here's the lunch," said Wilson. "You're very merry, aren't you?"

"Why not? I didn't come out here to be dull."

"Well, it hasn't been dull," Wilson said. He could see the boulders in the river and the high bank beyond with the trees and he remembered the morning.

"Oh, no," she said. "It's been charming. And tomorrow. You don't know how I look forward to tomorrow."

"That's eland he's offering you," Wilson said.

"They're the big cowy things that jump like hares, aren't they?"

"I suppose that describes them," Wilson said.

"It's very good meat," Macomber said.

"Did you shoot it, Francis?" she asked.

"Yes."

"They're not dangerous, are they?"

"Only if they fall on you," Wilson told her.

"I'm so glad."

"Why not let up on the bitchery just a little, Margot," Macomber said, cutting the eland steak and putting some mashed potato, gravy and carrot on the down-turned fork that tined through the piece of meat.

"I suppose I could," she said, "since you put it so prettily."

"Tonight we'll have champagne for the lion," Wilson said. "It's a bit too hot at noon."

"Oh, the lion," Margot said. "I'd forgotten the lion!"

So, Robert Wilson thought to himself, she *is* giving him a ride, isn't she? Or do you suppose that's her idea of putting up a good show? How should a woman act when she discovers her husband is a bloody coward? She's damn cruel but they're all cruel. They govern, of course, and to govern one has to be cruel sometimes. Still, I've seen enough of their damn terrorism.

"Have some more eland," he said to her politely.

That afternoon, late, Wilson and Macomber went out in the motor car with the native driver and the two gun-bearers. Mrs. Macomber stayed in the camp. It was too hot to go out, she said, and she was going with them in the early morning. As they drove off Wilson saw her standing under the big tree, looking pretty rather than beautiful in her faintly rosy khaki, her dark hair drawn back off her forehead and gathered in a knot low on her neck, her face as fresh, he thought, as though she were in England. She waved to them as the car went off through the swale of high grass and curved around through the trees into the small hills of orchard bush.

In the orchard bush they found a herd of impala, and leaving the car they stalked one old ram with long, wide-spread horns and Macomber killed it with a very creditable shot that knocked the buck down at a good two hundred yards and sent the herd off bounding wildly and leaping over one another's backs in long, leg-drawn-up leaps as unbelievable and as floating as those one makes sometimes in dreams.

"That was a good shot," Wilson said. "They're a small target."

"Is it a worth-while head?" Macomber asked.

"It's excellent," Wilson told him. "You shoot like that and you'll have no trouble."

"Do you think we'll find buffalo tomorrow?"

"There's a good chance of it. They feed out early in the morning and with luck we may catch them in the open."

"I'd like to clear away that lion business," Macomber said. "It's not very pleasant to have your wife see you do something like that."

I should think it would be even more unpleasant to do it, Wilson thought, wife or no wife, or to talk about it having done it. But he said, "I wouldn't think about that any more. Any one could be upset by his first lion. That's all over."

But that night after dinner and a whisky and soda by the fire before going to bed, as Francis Macomber lay on his cot with the mosquito bar over him and listened to the night noises it was not all over. It was neither all over nor was it beginning. It was there exactly as it happened with some parts of it indelibly emphasized and he was miserably ashamed at it. But more than shame he felt cold, hollow fear in him. The fear was still there like a cold slimy hollow in all the emptiness where once his confidence had been and it made him feel sick. It was still there with him now.

It had started the night before when he had wakened and heard the lion roaring somewhere up along the river. It was a deep sound and at the end there were sort of coughing grunts that made him seem just outside the tent, and when Francis Macomber woke in the night to hear it he was afraid. He could hear his wife breathing quietly, asleep. There was no one to tell he was afraid, nor to be afraid with him, and, lying alone, he did not know the Somali proverb that says a brave man is always frightened three times by a lion; when he first sees his track, when he first hears him roar and when he first confronts him. Then while they were eating breakfast by lantern light out in the dining tent, before the sun was up, the lion roared again and Francis thought he was just at the edge of camp.

"Sounds like an old-timer," Robert Wilson said, looking up from his kippers and coffee. "Listen to him cough."

"Is he very close?"

"A mile or so up the stream."

"Will we see him?"

"We'll have a look."

"Does his roaring carry that far? It sounds as though he were right in camp."

"Carries a hell of a long way," said Robert Wilson. "It's strange the way it carries. Hope he's a shootable cat. The boys said there was a very big one about here."

"If I get a shot, where should I hit him," Macomber asked, "to stop him?"

"In the shoulders," Wilson said. "In the neck if you can make it. Shoot for bone. Break him down."

"I hope I can place it properly," Macomber said.

"You shoot very well," Wilson told him. "Take your time. Make sure of him. The first one in is the one that counts."

"What range will it be?"

"Can't tell. Lion has something to say about that. Don't shoot unless it's close enough so you can make sure."

"At under a hundred yards?" Macomber asked.

Wilson looked at him quickly.

"Hundred's about right. Might have to take him a bit under. Shouldn't chance a shot at much over that. A hundred's a decent range. You can hit him wherever you want at that. Here comes the Memsahib."

"Good morning," she said. "Are we going after that lion?"

"As soon as you deal with your breakfast," Wilson said. "How are you feeling?"

"Marvellous," she said. "I'm very excited."

"I'll just go and see that everything is ready." Wilson went off. As he left the lion roared again.

"Noisy beggar," Wilson said. "We'll put a stop to that."

"What's the matter, Francis?" his wife asked him.

"Nothing," Macomber said.

"Yes, there is," she said. "What are you upset about?"

"Nothing," he said.

"Tell me," she looked at him. "Don't you feel well?"

"It's that damned roaring," he said. "It's been going on all night, you know."

"Why didn't you wake me," she said. "I'd love to have heard it."

"I've got to kill the damned thing," Macomber said, miserably.

"Well, that's what you're out here for, isn't it?"

"Yes. But I'm nervous. Hearing the thing roar gets on my nerves."

"Well then, as Wilson said, kill him and stop his roaring."

"Yes, darling," said Francis Macomber. "It sounds easy, doesn't it?"

"You're not afraid, are you?"

"Of course not. But I'm nervous from hearing him roar all night."

"You'll kill him marvellously," she said. "I know you will. I'm awfully anxious to see it."

"Finish your breakfast and we'll be starting."

"It's not light yet," she said. "This is a ridiculous hour."

Just then the lion roared in a deep-chested moaning, suddenly guttural, ascending vibration that seemed to shake the air and ended in a sigh and a heavy, deep-chested grunt.

"He sounds almost here," Macomber's wife said.

"My God," said Macomber. "I hate that damned noise."

"It's very impressive."

"Impressive. It's frightful."

Robert Wilson came up then carrying his short, ugly, shockingly big-bored .505 Gibbs and grinning.

"Come on," he said. "Your gun-bearer has your Springfield and the big gun. Everything's in the car. Have you solids?"

"Yes."

"I'm ready," Mrs. Macomber said.

"Must make him stop that racket," Wilson said. "You get in front. The Memsahib can sit back here with me."

They climbed into the motor car and, in the gray first daylight, moved off up the river through the trees. Macomber opened the breech of his rifle and saw he had metal-cased bullets, shut the bolt and put the rifle on safety. He saw his hand was trembling. He felt in his pocket for more cartridges and moved his fingers over the cartridges in the loops of his tunic front. He turned back to where Wilson sat in the rear seat of the doorless, box-bodied motor car beside his wife, them both grinning with excitement, and Wilson leaned forward and whispered,

"See the birds dropping. Means the old boy has left his kill."

On the far bank of the stream Macomber could see, above the trees, vultures circling and plummeting down.

"Chances are he'll come to drink along here," Wilson whispered. "Before he goes to lay up. Keep an eye out."

They were driving slowly along the high bank of the stream which here cut deeply to its boulder-filled bed, and they wound in and out through big trees as they drove. Macomber was watching the opposite bank when he felt Wilson take hold of his arm. The car stopped.

"There he is," he heard the whisper. "Ahead and to the right. Get out and take him. He's a marvellous lion."

Macomber saw the lion now. He was standing almost broadside, his great head up and turned toward them. The early morning breeze that blew toward them was just stirring his dark mane, and the lion looked huge, silhouetted on the rise of bank in the gray morning light, his shoulders heavy, his barrel of a body bulking smoothly.

"How far is he?" asked Macomber, raising his rifle.

"About seventy-five. Get out and take him."

"Why not shoot from where I am?"

"You don't shoot them from cars," he heard Wilson saying in his ear. "Get out. He's not going to stay there all day."

Macomber stepped out of the curved opening at the side of the front seat, onto the step and down onto the ground. The lion still stood looking majestically and coolly toward this object that his eyes only showed in silhouette, bulking like some super-rhino. There was no man smell carried toward him and he watched the object, moving his great head a little from side to side. Then watching the object, not afraid, but hesitating before going down the bank to drink with such a thing opposite him, he saw a man figure detach itself from it and he turned his heavy head and swung away toward the cover of the trees as he heard a cracking crash and felt the slam of a .30-06 220-grain solid bullet that bit his flank and ripped in sudden hot scalding nausea through his stomach. He trotted, heavy, big-footed, swinging wounded full-bellied, through the trees toward the tall grass and cover, and the crash came again to go past him ripping the air apart. Then it crashed again and he felt the blow as it hit his lower ribs and ripped on through, blood sudden hot and frothy in his mouth, and he galloped toward the high grass where he could crouch and not be seen and make them bring the crashing thing close enough so he could make a rush and get the man that held it.

Macomber had not thought how the lion felt as he got out of the car. He only knew his hands were shaking and as he walked away from the car it was almost impossible for him to make his legs move. They were stiff in the thighs, but he could feel the muscles fluttering. He raised the rifle, sighted on the junction of the lion's head and shoulders and pulled the trigger. Nothing happened though he pulled until he thought his finger would break. Then he knew he had the safety on and as he lowered the rifle to move the safety over he moved another frozen pace forward, and the lion seeing his silhouette flow clear of the silhouette of the car, turned and started off at a trot, and, as Macomber fired, he heard a whunk that meant that the bullet was home; but the lion kept on going. Macomber shot again and every one saw the bullet throw a spout of dirt beyond the trotting lion. He shot again, remembering to lower his aim, and they all heard the bullet hit, and the lion went into a gallop and was in the tall grass before he had the bolt pushed forward.

Macomber stood there feeling sick at his stomach, his hands that held the Springfield still cocked, shaking, and his wife and Robert Wilson were standing by him. Beside him too were the two gun-bearers chattering in Wakamba.

"I hit him," Macomber said. "I hit him twice."

"You gut-shot him and you hit him somewhere forward," Wilson said without enthusiasm. The gun-bearers looked very grave. They were silent now.

"You may have killed him," Wilson went on. "We'll have to wait a while before we go in to find out."

"What do you mean?"

"Let him get sick before we follow him up."

"Oh," said Macomber.

"He's a hell of a fine lion," Wilson said cheerfully. "He's gotten into a bad place though."

"Why is it bad?"

"Can't see him until you're on him."

"Oh," said Macomber.

"Come on," said Wilson. "The Memsahib can stay here in the car. We'll go to have a look at the blood spoor."

"Stay here, Margot," Macomber said to his wife. His mouth was very dry and it was hard for him to talk.

"Why?" she asked.

"Wilson says to."

"We're going to have a look," Wilson said. "You stay here. You can see even better from here."

"All right."

Wilson spoke in Swahili to the driver. He nodded and said, "Yes, Bwana."

Then they went down the steep bank and across the stream, climbing over and around the boulders and up the other bank, pulling up by some projecting roots, and along it until they found where the lion had been trotting when Macomber first shot. There was dark blood on the short grass that the gun-bearers pointed out with grass stems, and that ran away behind the river bank trees.

"What do we do?" asked Macomber.

"Not much choice," said Wilson. "We can't bring the car over. Bank's too steep. We'll let him stiffen up a bit and then you and I'll go in and have a look for him."

"Can't we set the grass on fire?" Macomber asked.

"Too green."

"Can't we send beaters?"

Wilson looked at him appraisingly. "Of course we can," he said. "But it's just a touch murderous. You see, we know the lion's wounded. You can drive an unwounded lion—he'll move on ahead of a noise—but a wounded lion's going to charge. You can't see him until you're right on him. He'll make himself perfectly flat in cover you wouldn't think would hide a hare. You can't very well send boys in there to that sort of a show. Somebody bound to get mauled."

"What about the gun-bearers?"

"Oh, they'll go with us. It's their *shauri*. You see, they signed on for it. They don't look too happy though, do they?"

"I don't want to go in there," said Macomber. It was out before he knew he'd said it.

41

"Neither do I," said Wilson very cheerily. "Really no choice though." Then, as an afterthought, he glanced at Macomber and saw suddenly how he was trembling and the pitiful look on his face.

"You don't have to go in, of course," he said. "That's what I'm hired for, you know. That's why I'm so expensive."

"You mean you'd go in by yourself? Why not leave him there?"

Robert Wilson, whose entire occupation had been with the lion and the problem he presented, and who had not been thinking about Macomber except to note that he was rather windy, suddenly felt as though he had opened the wrong door in a hotel and seen something shameful.

"What do you mean?"

"Why not just leave him?"

"You mean pretend to ourselves he hasn't been hit?"

"No. Just drop it."

"It isn't done."

"Why not?"

"For one thing, he's certain to be suffering. For another, some one else might run onto him."

"I see."

"But you don't have to have anything to do with it."

"I'd like to," Macomber said. "I'm just scared, you know."

"I'll go ahead when we go in," Wilson said, "with Kongoni tracking. You keep behind me and a little to one side. Chances are we'll hear him growl. If we see him we'll both shoot. Don't worry about anything. I'll keep you backed up. As a matter of fact, you know, perhaps you'd better not go. It might be much better. Why don't you go over and join the Memsahib while I just get it over with?"

"No, I want to go."

"All right," said Wilson. "But don't go in if you don't want to. This is my *shauri* now, you know."

"I want to go," said Macomber.

They sat under a tree and smoked.

"Want to go back and speak to the Memsahib while we're waiting?" Wilson asked.

"No."

"I'll just step back and tell her to be patient."

"Good," said Macomber. He sat there, sweating under his arms, his mouth dry, his stomach hollow feeling, wanting to find courage to tell Wilson to go on and finish off the lion without him. He could not know that Wilson was furious because he had not noticed the state he was in earlier and sent him back to his wife. While he sat there Wilson came up. "I have your big gun," he said. "Take it. We've given him time, I think. Come on."

Macomber took the big gun and Wilson said:

"Keep behind me and about five yards to the right and do exactly as I tell you." Then he spoke in Swahili to the two gun-bearers who looked the picture of gloom.

"Let's go," he said.

"Could I have a drink of water?" Macomber asked. Wilson spoke to the older gun-bearer, who wore a canteen on his belt, and the man unbuckled it, unscrewed the top and handed it to Macomber, who took it noticing how heavy it seemed and how hairy and shoddy the felt covering was in his hand. He raised it to drink and looked ahead at the high grass with the flat-topped trees behind it. A breeze was blowing toward them and the grass rippled gently in the wind. He looked at the gun-bearer and he could see the gun-bearer was suffering too with fear.

Thirty-five yards into the grass the big lion lay flattened out along the ground. His ears were back and his only movement was a slight twitching up and down of his long, black-tufted tail. He had turned at bay as soon as he had reached this cover and he was sick with the wound through his full belly, and weakening with the wound through his lungs that brought a thin foamy red to his mouth each time he breathed. His flanks were wet and hot and flies were on the little openings the solid bullets had made in his tawny hide, and his big yellow eyes, narrowed with hate, looked straight ahead, only blinking when the pain came as he breathed, and his claws dug in the soft baked earth. All of him, pain, sickness, hatred and all of his remaining strength, was tightening into an absolute concentration for a rush. He could hear the men talking and he waited, gathering all of himself into this preparation for a charge as soon as the men would come into the grass. As he heard their voices his tail stiffened to twitch up and down, and, as they came into the edge of the grass, he made a coughing grunt and charged.

Kongoni, the old gun-bearer, in the lead watching the blood spoor, Wilson watching the grass for any movement, his big gun ready, the second gun-bearer looking ahead and listening, Macomber close to Wilson, his rifle cocked, they had just moved into the grass when Macomber heard the blood-choked coughing grunt, and saw the swishing rush in the grass. The next thing he knew he was running; running wildly, in panic in the open, running toward the stream.

He heard the *ca-ra-wong!* of Wilson's big rifle, and again in a second crashing *carawong!* and turning saw the lion, horrible-looking now, with half his head seeming to be gone, crawling toward Wilson in the edge of the tall grass while the red-faced man worked the bolt on the short ugly rifle and aimed carefully as another blasting *carawong!* came from the muzzle, and the crawling, heavy, yellow bulk of the lion stiffened and the huge, mutilated head slid forward and Macomber, standing by himself in the clearing where he had run, holding a loaded rifle, while two black men and a white man looked back at him in contempt, knew the lion was dead. He came toward Wilson, his tallness all seeming a naked reproach, and Wilson looked at him and said:

"Want to take pictures?"

"No," he said.

That was all any one had said until they reached the motor car. Then Wilson had said:

"Hell of a fine lion. Boys will skin him out. We might as well stay here in the shade."

Macomber's wife had not looked at him nor he at her and he had sat by her in the back seat with Wilson sitting in the front seat. Once he had reached over and taken his wife's hand without looking at her and she had removed her hand from his. Looking across the stream to where the gun-bearers were skinning out the lion he could see that she had been able to see the whole thing. While they sat there his wife had reached forward and put her hand on Wilson's shoulder. He turned and she had leaned forward over the low seat and kissed him on the mouth.

"Oh, I say," said Wilson, going redder than his natural baked color.

"Mr. Robert Wilson," she said. "The beautiful red-faced Mr. Robert Wilson."

Then she sat down beside Macomber again and looked away across the stream to where the lion lay, with uplifted, white-muscled, tendon-marked naked forearms, and white bloating belly, as the black men fleshed away the skin. Finally the gun-bearers brought the skin over, wet and heavy, and climbed in behind with it, rolling it up before they got in, and the motor car started. No one had said anything more until they were back in camp.

That was the story of the lion. Macomber did not know how the lion had felt before he started his rush, nor during it when the unbelievable smash of the .505 with a muzzle velocity of two tons had hit him in the mouth, nor what kept him coming after that, when the second ripping crash had smashed his hind quarters and he had come crawling on toward the crashing, blasting thing that had destroyed him. Wilson knew something about it and only expressed it by saying, "Damned fine lion," but Macomber did not know how Wilson felt about things either. He did not know how his wife felt except that she was through with him.

His wife had been through with him before but it never lasted. He was very wealthy, and would be much wealthier, and he knew she would not leave him ever now. That was one of the few things that he really knew. He knew about that, about motor cycles—that

45

was earliest—about motor cars, about duck-shooting, about fishing, trout, salmon and big-sea, about sex in books, many books, too many books, about all court games, about dogs, not much about horses, about hanging on to his money, about most of the other things his world dealt in, and about his wife not leaving him. His wife had been a great beauty and she was still a great beauty in Africa, but she was not a great enough beauty any more at home to be able to leave him and better herself and she knew it and he knew it. She had missed the chance to leave him and he knew it. If he had been better with women she would probably have started to worry about him getting another new, beautiful wife; but she knew too much about him to worry about him either. Also, he had always had a great tolerance which seemed the nicest thing about him if it were not the most sinister.

All in all they were known as a comparatively happily married couple, one of those whose disruption is often rumored but never occurs, and as the society columnist put it, they were adding more than a spice of *adventure* to their much envied and ever-enduring *Romance* by a *Safari* in what was known as *Darkest Africa* until the Martin Johnsons lighted it on so many silver screens where they were pursuing *Old Simba* the lion, the buffalo, *Tembo* the elephant and as well collecting specimens for the Museum of Natural History. This same columnist had reported them *on the verge* at least three times in the past and they had been. But they always made it up. They had a sound basis of union. Margot was too beautiful for Macomber to divorce her and Macomber had too much money for Margot ever to leave him.

It was now about three o'clock in the morning and Francis Macomber, who had been asleep a little while after he had stopped thinking about the lion, wakened and then slept again, woke suddenly, frightened in a dream of the bloody-headed lion standing over him, and listening while his heart pounded, he realized that his wife was not in the other cot in the tent. He lay awake with that knowledge for two hours.

At the end of that time his wife came into the tent, lifted her mosquito bar and crawled cozily into bed.

"Where have you been?" Macomber asked in the darkness.

"Hello," she said. "Are you awake?"

"Where have you been?"

"I just went out to get a breath of air."

"You did, like hell."

"What do you want me to say, darling?"

"Where have you been?"

"Out to get a breath of air."

"That's a new name for it. You *are* a bitch."

"Well, you're a coward."

"All right," he said. "What of it?"

"Nothing as far as I'm concerned. But please let's not talk, darling, because I'm very sleepy."

"You think that I'll take anything."

"I know you will, sweet."

"Well, I won't."

"Please, darling, let's not talk. I'm so very sleepy."

"There wasn't going to be any of that. You promised there wouldn't be."

"Well, there is now," she said sweetly.

"You said if we made this trip that there would be none of that. You promised."

"Yes, darling. That's the way I meant it to be. But the trip was spoiled yesterday. We don't have to talk about it, do we?"

"You don't wait long when you have an advantage, do you?"

"Please let's not talk. I'm so sleepy, darling."

"I'm going to talk."

"Don't mind me then, because I'm going to sleep." And she did.

At breakfast they were all three at the table before daylight and Francis Macomber found that, of all the many men that he had hated, he hated Robert Wilson the most.

"Sleep well?" Wilson asked in his throaty voice, filling a pipe. "Did you?"

"Topping," the white hunter told him.

You bastard, thought Macomber, you insolent bastard.

So she woke him when she came in, Wilson thought, looking at them both with his flat, cold eyes. Well, why doesn't he keep his wife where she belongs? What does he think I am, a bloody plaster saint? Let him keep her where she belongs. It's his own fault.

"Do you think we'll find buffalo?" Margot asked, pushing away a dish of apricots.

"Chance of it," Wilson said and smiled at her. "Why don't you stay in camp?"

"Not for anything," she told him.

"Why not order her to stay in camp?" Wilson said to Macomber.

"You order her," said Macomber coldly.

"Let's not have any ordering, nor," turning to Macomber, "any silliness, Francis," Margot said quite pleasantly.

"Are you ready to start?" Macomber asked.

"Any time," Wilson told him. "Do you want the Memsahib to go?"

"Does it make any difference whether I do or not?"

The hell with it, thought Robert Wilson. The utter complete hell with it. So this is what it's going to be like. Well, this is what it's going to be like, then.

"Makes no difference," he said.

"You're sure you wouldn't like to stay in camp with her yourself and let me go out and hunt the buffalo?" Macomber asked.

"Can't do that," said Wilson. "Wouldn't talk rot if I were you."

"I'm not talking rot. I'm disgusted."

"Bad word, disgusted."

"Francis, will you please try to speak sensibly," his wife said.

"I speak too damned sensibly," Macomber said. "Did you ever eat such filthy food?"

"Something wrong with the food?" asked Wilson quietly.

"No more than with everything else."

"I'd pull yourself together, laddybuck," Wilson said very quietly. "There's a boy waits at table that understands a little English."

"The hell with him."

Wilson stood up and puffing on his pipe strolled away, speaking a few words in Swahili to one of the gun-bearers who was standing waiting for him. Macomber and his wife sat on at the table. He was staring at his coffee cup.

"If you make a scene I'll leave you, darling," Margot said quietly.

"No, you won't."

"You can try it and see."

"You won't leave me."

"No," she said. "I won't leave you and you'll behave your self."

"Behave myself? That's a way to talk. Behave myself."

"Yes. Behave yourself."

"Why don't *you* try behaving?"

"I've tried it so long. So very long."

"I hate that red-faced swine," Macomber said. "I loathe the sight of him."

"He's really *very* nice."

"Oh, *shut up*," Macomber almost shouted. Just then the car came up and stopped in front of the dining tent and the driver and the two gun-bearers got out. Wilson walked over and looked at the husband and wife sitting there at the table.

"Going shooting?" he asked.

"Yes," said Macomber, standing up. "Yes."

"Better bring a woolly. It will be cool in the car," Wilson said.

"I'll get my leather jacket," Margot said.

"The boy has it," Wilson told her. He climbed into the front with the driver and Francis Macomber and his wife sat, not speaking, in the back seat.

Hope the silly beggar doesn't take a notion to blow the back of my head off, Wilson thought to himself. Women *are* a nuisance on safari.

The car was grinding down to cross the river at a pebbly ford in the gray daylight and then climbed, angling up the steep bank, where Wilson had ordered a way shovelled out the day before so they could reach the parklike wooded rolling country on the far side.

It was a good morning, Wilson thought. There was a heavy dew and as the wheels went through the grass and low bushes he could smell the odor of the crushed fronds. It was an odor like verbena and he liked this early morning smell of the dew, the crushed bracken and the look of the tree trunks showing black through the early morning mist, as the car made its way through the untracked, parklike country. He had put the two in the back seat out of his mind now and was thinking about buffalo. The buffalo that he was after stayed in the daytime in a thick swamp where it was impossible to get a shot, but in the night they fed out into an open stretch of country and if he could come between them and their swamp with the car, Macomber would have a good chance at them in the open. He did not want to hunt buff with Macomber in thick cover. He did not want to hunt buff or anything else with Macomber at all, but he was a professional hunter and he had hunted with some rare ones in his time. If they got buff today there would only be rhino to come and the poor man would have gone through his dangerous game and things might pick up. He'd have nothing more to do with the woman and Macomber would get over that too. He must have gone through plenty of that before by the look of things. Poor beggar. He must have a way of getting over it. Well, it was the poor sod's own bloody fault.

He, Robert Wilson, carried a double size cot on safari to accommodate any windfalls he might receive. He had hunted for a certain clientele, the international, fast, sporting set, where the women did not feel they were getting their money's worth unless they had shared that cot with the white hunter. He despised them when he was away from them although he liked some of them well enough at the time, but he made his living by them; and their standards were his standards as long as they were hiring him.

They were his standards in all except the shooting. He had his own standards about the killing and they could live up to them or get some one else to hunt them. He knew, too, that they all respected him for this. This Macomber was an odd one though. Damned if he wasn't. Now the wife. Well, the wife. Yes, the wife. Hm, the wife. Well he'd dropped all that. He looked around at them. Macomber sat grim and furious. Margot smiled at him. She looked younger today, more innocent and fresher and not so professionally beautiful. What's in her heart God knows, Wilson thought. She hadn't talked much last night. At that it was a pleasure to see her.

The motor car climbed up a slight rise and went on through the trees and then out into a grassy prairie-like opening and kept in the shelter of the trees along the edge, the driver going slowly and Wilson looking carefully out across the prairie and all along its far side. He stopped the car and studied the opening with his field glasses. Then he motioned to the driver to go on and the car moved slowly along, the driver avoiding warthog holes and driving around the mud castles ants had built. Then, looking across the opening, Wilson suddenly turned and said,

"By God, there they are!"

And looking where he pointed, while the car jumped forward and Wilson spoke in rapid Swahili to the driver, Macomber saw three huge, black animals looking almost cylindrical in their long heaviness, like big black tank cars, moving at a gallop across the far edge of the open prairie. They moved at a stiff-necked, stiff bodied gallop and he could see the upswept wide black horns on their heads as they galloped heads out; the heads not moving.

"They're three old bulls," Wilson said. "We'll cut them off before they get to the swamp."

The car was going a wild forty-five miles an hour across the open and as Macomber watched, the buffalo got bigger and bigger until he could see the gray, hairless, scabby look of one huge bull and how his neck was a part of his shoulders and the shiny black of his horns as he galloped a little behind the others that were strung out in that steady plunging gait; and then, the car swaying as though it had just jumped a road, they drew up close and he could see the plunging hugeness of the bull, and the dust in his sparsely haired hide, the wide boss of horn and his outstretched, wide-nostrilled muzzle, and he was raising his rifle when Wilson shouted, "Not from the car, you fool!" and he had no fear, only hatred of Wilson, while the brakes clamped on and the car skidded, plowing sideways to an almost stop and Wilson was out on one side and he on the other, stumbling as his feet hit the still speeding-by of the earth, and then he was shooting at the bull as he moved away, hearing the bullets whunk into him, emptying his rifle at him as he moved steadily away, finally remembering to get his shots forward into the shoulder, and as he fumbled to re-load, he saw the bull was down. Down on his knees, his big head tossing, and seeing the other two still galloping he shot at the leader and hit him. He shot again and missed and he heard the *carawonging* roar as Wilson shot and saw the leading bull slide forward onto his nose.

"Get that other," Wilson said. "Now you're shooting!"

But the other bull was moving steadily at the same gallop and he missed, throwing a spout of dirt, and Wilson missed and the dust rose in a cloud and Wilson shouted, "Come on. He's too far!" and grabbed his arm and they were in the car again, Macomber and Wilson hanging on the sides and rocketing swayingly over the uneven ground, drawing up on the steady, plunging, heavy-necked, straight-moving gallop of the bull.

They were behind him and Macomber was filling his rifle, dropping shells onto the ground, jamming it, clearing the jam, then they were almost up with the bull when Wilson yelled "Stop," and the car skidded so that it almost swung over and Macomber fell forward onto his feet, slammed his bolt forward and fired as far forward as he could aim into the galloping, rounded black back, aimed and shot again, then again, then again, and the bullets, all of them hitting, had no effect on the buffalo that he could see. Then Wilson shot, the roar deafening him, and he could see the bull stagger. Macomber shot again, aiming carefully, and down he came, onto his knees.

"All right," Wilson said. "Nice work. That's the three."

Macomber felt a drunken elation.

"How many times did you shoot?" he asked.

"Just three," Wilson said. "You killed the first bull. The biggest one. I helped you finish the other two. Afraid they might have got into cover. You had them killed. I was just mopping up a little. You shot damn well."

"Let's go to the car," said Macomber. "I want a drink."

"Got to finish off that buff first," Wilson told him. The buffalo was on his knees and he jerked his head furiously and bellowed in pig-eyed, roaring rage as they came toward him.

"Watch he doesn't get up," Wilson said. Then, "Get a little broadside and take him in the neck just behind the ear."

Macomber aimed carefully at the center of the huge, jerking, rage-driven neck and shot. At the shot the head dropped forward.

"That does it," said Wilson. "Got the spine. They're a hell of a looking thing, aren't they?"

"Let's get the drink" said Macomber. In his life he had never felt so good.

In the car Macomber's wife sat very white-faced. "You were marvellous, darling," she said to Macomber. "What a ride."

"Was it rough?" Wilson asked.

"It was frightful. I've never been more frightened in my life."

"Let's all have a drink," Macomber said.

"By all means," said Wilson. "Give it to the Memsahib." She drank the neat whisky from the flask and shuddered a little when she swallowed. She handed the flask to Macomber who handed it to Wilson.

"It was frightfully exciting," she said. "It's given me a dreadful headache. I didn't know you were allowed to shoot them from cars though."

"No one shot from cars," said Wilson coldly.

"I mean chase them from cars."

"Wouldn't ordinarily," Wilson said. "Seemed sporting enough to me though while we were doing it. Taking more chance driving that way across the plain full of holes and one thing and another than hunting on foot. Buffalo could have charged us each time we shot if he liked. Gave him every chance. Wouldn't mention it to any one though. It's illegal if that's what you mean."

"It seemed very unfair to me," Margot said, "chasing those big helpless things in a motor car."

"Did it?" said Wilson.

"What would happen if they heard about it in Nairobi?"

"I'd lose my license for one thing. Other unpleasantnesses," Wilson said, taking a drink from the flask. "I'd be out of business."

"Really?"

"Yes, really."

"Well," said Macomber, and he smiled for the first time all day. "Now she has something on you."

"You have such a pretty way of putting things, Francis," Margot Macomber said. Wilson looked at them both. If a four-letter man marries a five-letter woman, he was thinking, what number of letters would their children be? What he said was, "We lost a gun-bearer. Did you notice it?"

"My God, no," Macomber said.

"Here he comes," Wilson said. "He's all right. He must have fallen off when we left the first bull."

Approaching them was the middle-aged gun-bearer, limping along in his knitted cap, khaki tunic, shorts and rubber sandals, gloomy-faced and disgusted looking. As he came up he called out to Wilson in Swahili and they all saw the change in the white hunter's face.

"What does he say?" asked Margot.

"He says the first bull got up and went into the bush," Wilson said with no expression in his voice.

"Oh," said Macomber blankly.

"Then it's going to be just like the lion," said Margot, full of anticipation.

"It's not going to be a damned bit like the lion," Wilson told her. "Did you want another drink, Macomber?"

"Thanks, yes," Macomber said. He expected the feeling he had had about the lion to come back but it did not. For the first time in his life he really felt wholly without fear. Instead of fear he had a feeling of definite elation.

"We'll go and have a look at the second bull," Wilson said. "I'll tell the driver to put the car in the shade."

"What are you going to do?" asked Margaret Macomber.

"Take a look at the buff," Wilson said.

"I'll come."

"Come along."

The three of them walked over to where the second buffalo bulked blackly in the open, head forward on the grass, the massive horns swung wide.

"He's a very good head," Wilson said. "That's close to a fifty-inch spread."

Macomber was looking at him with delight.

"He's hateful looking," said Margot. "Can't we go into the shade?"

"Of course," Wilson said. "Look," he said to Macomber, and pointed. "See that patch of bush?"

"Yes."

"That's where the first bull went in. The gun-bearer said when he fell off the bull was down. He was watching us helling along and the other two buff galloping. When he looked up there was the bull up and looking at him. Gun-bearer ran like hell and the bull went off slowly into that bush."

"Can we go in after him now?" asked Macomber eagerly.

Wilson looked at him appraisingly. Damned if this isn't a strange one, he thought. Yesterday he's scared sick and today he's a ruddy fire eater.

"No, we'll give him a while."

"Let's please go into the shade," Margot said. Her face was white and she looked ill.

They made their way to the car where it stood under a single, wide-spreading tree and all climbed in.

"Chances are he's dead in there," Wilson remarked. "After a while we'll have a look."

Macomber felt a wild unreasonable happiness that he had never known before.

"By God, that was a chase," he said. "I've never felt any such feeling. Wasn't it marvellous, Margot?"

"I hated it."

"Why?"

"I hated it," she said bitterly. "I loathed it."

"You know I don't think I'd ever be afraid of anything again," Macomber said to Wilson. "Something happened in me after we first saw the buff and started after him. Like a dam bursting. It was pure excitement."

"Cleans out your liver," said Wilson. "Damn funny things happen to people."

Macomber's face was shining. "You know something did happen to me," he said. "I feel absolutely different."

His wife said nothing and eyed him strangely. She was sitting far back in the seat and Macomber was sitting forward talking to Wilson who turned sideways talking over the back of the front seat.

"You know, I'd like to try another lion," Macomber said. "I'm really not afraid of them now. After all, what can they do to you?"

"That's it," said Wilson. "Worst one can do is kill you. How does it go? Shakespeare. Damned good. See if I can remember. Oh, damned good. Used to quote it to myself at one time. Let's see. 'By my troth, I care not; a man can die but once; we owe God a death and let it go which way it will, he that dies this year is quit for the next.' Damned fine, eh?"

He was very embarrassed, having brought out this thing he had lived by, but he had seen men come of age before and it always moved him. It was not a matter of their twenty-first birthday.

It had taken a strange chance of hunting, a sudden precipitation into action without opportunity for worrying beforehand, to bring this about with Macomber, but regardless of how it had happened it had most certainly happened. Look at the beggar now, Wilson thought. It's that some of them stay little boys so long, Wilson thought. Sometimes all their lives. Their figures stay boyish when they're fifty. The great American boy-men. Damned strange people. But he liked this Macomber now. Damned strange fellow. Probably meant the end of cuckoldry too. Well, that would be a damned good thing. Damned good thing. Beggar had probably been afraid all his life. Don't know what started it. But over now. Hadn't had time to be afraid with the buff. That and being angry too. Motor car too. Motor cars made it familiar. Be a damn fire eater now. He'd seen it in the war work the same way. More of a change than any loss of virginity. Fear gone like an operation. Something else grew in its place. Main thing a man had. Made him into a man. Women knew it too. No bloody fear.

From the far corner of the seat Margaret Macomber looked at the two of them. There was no change in Wilson. She saw Wilson as she had seen him the day before when she had first realized what his great talent was. But she saw the change in Francis Macomber now.

"Do you have that feeling of happiness about what's going to happen?" Macomber asked, still exploring his new wealth.

"You're not supposed to mention it," Wilson said, looking in the other's face. "Much more fashionable to say you're scared. Mind you, you'll be scared too, plenty of times."

"But you *have* a feeling of happiness about action to come?"

"Yes," said Wilson. "There's that. Doesn't do to talk too much about all this. Talk the whole thing away. No pleasure in anything if you mouth it up too much."

"You're both talking rot," said Margot. "Just because you've chased some helpless animals in a motor car you talk like heroes."

"Sorry," said Wilson. "I have been gassing too much." She's worried about it already, he thought.

"If you don't know what we're talking about why not keep out of it?" Macomber asked his wife.

"You've gotten awfully brave, awfully suddenly," his wife said contemptuously, but her contempt was not secure. She was very afraid of something.

Macomber laughed, a very natural hearty laugh. "You know I *have*," he said. "I really have."

"Isn't it sort of late?" Margot said bitterly. Because she had done the best she could for many years back and the way they were together now was no one person's fault.

"Not for me," said Macomber.

Margot said nothing but sat back in the corner of the seat.

"Do you think we've given him time enough?" Macomber asked Wilson cheerfully.

"We might have a look," Wilson said. "Have you any solids left?"

"The gun-bearer has some."

Wilson called in Swahili and the older gun-bearer, who was skinning out one of the heads, straightened up, pulled a box of solids out of his pocket and brought them over to Macomber, who filled his magazine and put the remaining shells in his pocket.

"You might as well shoot the Springfield," Wilson said. "You're used to it. We'll leave the Mannlicher in the car with the Memsahib. Your gun-bearer can carry your heavy gun. I've this damned cannon. Now let me tell you about them." He had saved this until the last because he did not want to worry Macomber. "When a buff comes he comes with his head high and thrust straight out. The boss of the horns covers any sort of a brain shot. The only shot is straight into the nose. The only other shot is into his chest or, if you're to one side, into the neck or the shoulders. After they've been hit once they take a hell of a lot of killing. Don't try anything fancy. Take the easiest shot there is. They've finished skinning out that head now. Should we get started?"

He called to the gun-bearers, who came up wiping their hands, and the older one got into the back.

"I'll only take Kongoni," Wilson said. "The other can watch to keep the birds away."

As the car moved slowly across the open space toward the island of brushy trees that ran in a tongue of foliage along a dry water course that cut the open swale, Macomber felt his heart pounding and his mouth was dry again, but it was excitement, not fear.

"Here's where he went in," Wilson said. Then to the gun-bearer in Swahili, "Take the blood spoor."

The car was parallel to the patch of bush. Macomber, Wilson and the gun-bearer got down. Macomber, looking back, saw his wife, with the rifle by her side, looking at him. He waved to her and she did not wave back.

The brush was very thick ahead and the ground was dry. The middle-aged gun-bearer was sweating heavily and Wilson had his hat down over his eyes and his red neck showed just ahead of Macomber. Suddenly the gun-bearer said something in Swahili to Wilson and ran forward.

"He's dead in there," Wilson said. "Good work," and he turned to grip Macomber's hand and as they shook hands, grinning at each other, the gun-bearer shouted wildly and they saw him coming out of the bush sideways, fast as a crab, and the bull coming, nose out, mouth tight closed, blood dripping, massive head straight out, coming in a charge, his little pig eyes bloodshot as he looked at them. Wilson, who was ahead, was kneeling shooting, and Macomber, as he fired, unhearing his shot in the roaring of Wilson's gun, saw fragments like slate burst from the huge boss of the horns, and the head jerked, he shot again at the wide nostrils and saw the horns jolt again and fragments fly, and he did not see Wilson now and, aiming carefully, shot again with the buffalo's huge bulk almost on him and his rifle almost level with the on-coming head, nose out, and he could see the little wicked eyes and the head started to lower and he felt a sudden white-hot, blinding flash explode inside his head and that was all he ever felt.

Wilson had ducked to one side to get in a shoulder shot. Macomber had stood solid and shot for the nose, shooting a touch high each time and hitting the heavy horns, splintering and chipping them like hitting a slate roof, and Mrs. Macomber, in the car, had shot at the buffalo with the 6.5 Mannlicher as it seemed about to gore Macomber and had hit her husband about two inches up and a little to one side of the base of his skull.

Francis Macomber lay now, face down, not two yards from where the buffalo lay on his side and his wife knelt over him with Wilson beside her.

"I wouldn't turn him over," Wilson said.

The woman was crying hysterically.

"I'd get back in the car," Wilson said. "Where's the rifle?"

She shook her head, her face contorted. The gun-bearer picked up the rifle.

"Leave it as it is," said Wilson. Then, "Go get Abdulla so that he may witness the manner of the accident."

He knelt down, took a handkerchief from his pocket, and spread it over Francis Macomber's crew-cropped head where it lay. The blood sank into the dry, loose earth.

Wilson stood up and saw the buffalo on his side, his legs out, his thinly-haired belly crawling with ticks. "Hell of a good bull," his brain registered automatically. "A good fifty inches, or better. Better." He called to the driver and told him to spread a blanket over the body and stay by it. Then he walked over to the motor car where the woman sat crying in the corner.

"That was a pretty thing to do," he said in a toneless voice. "He *would* have left you too."

"Stop it," she said.

"Of course it's an accident," he said. "I know that."

"Stop it," she said.

"Don't worry," he said. "There will be a certain amount of un-pleasantness but I will have some photographs taken that will be very useful at the inquest. There's the testimony of the gun-bearers and the driver too. You're perfectly all right."

"Stop it," she said.

"There's a hell of a lot to be done," he said. "And I'll have to send a truck off to the lake to wireless for a plane to take the three of us into Nairobi. Why didn't you poison him? That's what they do in England."

"Stop it. Stop it. Stop it," the woman cried.

Wilson looked at her with his flat blue eyes.

"I'm through now," he said. "I was a little angry. I'd begun to like your husband."

"Oh, please stop it," she said. "Please stop it."

"That's better," Wilson said. "Please is much better. Now I'll stop."

The Snows of Kilimanjaro

Kilimanjaro is a snow covered mountain 19,710 feet high, and is said to be the highest mountain in Africa. Its western summit is called the Masai "Ngàje Ngài," the House of God. Close to the western summit there is the dried and frozen carcass of a leopard. No one has explained what the leopard was seeking at that altitude.

"The marvellous thing is that it's painless," he said. "That's how you know when it starts."

"Is it really?"

"Absolutely. I'm awfully sorry about the odor though. That must bother you."

"Don't! Please don't."

"Look at them," he said. "Now is it sight or is it scent that brings them like that?"

The cot the man lay on was in the wide shade of a mimosa tree and as he looked out past the shade onto the glare of the plain there were three of the big birds squatted obscenely, while in the sky a dozen more sailed, making quick-moving shadows as they passed.

"They've been there since the day the truck broke down," he said. "Today's the first time any have lit on the ground. I watched the way they sailed very carefully at first in case I ever wanted to use them in a story. That's funny now."

"I wish you wouldn't," she said.

"I'm only talking," he said. "It's much easier if I talk. But I don't want to bother you."

"You know it doesn't bother me," she said. "It's that I've gotten so very nervous not being able to do anything. I think we might make it as easy as we can until the plane comes."

"Or until the plane doesn't come."

"Please tell me what I can do. There must be something I can do."

"You can take the leg off and that might stop it, though I doubt it. Or you can shoot me. You're a good shot now. I taught you to shoot, didn't I?"

"Please don't talk that way. Couldn't I read to you?"

"Read what?"

"Anything in the book bag that we haven't read."

"I can't listen to it," he said. "Talking is the easiest. We quarrel and that makes the time pass."

"I don't quarrel. I never want to quarrel. Let's not quarrel any more. No matter how nervous we get. Maybe they will be back with another truck today. Maybe the plane will come."

"I don't want to move," the man said. "There is no sense in moving now except to make it easier for you."

"That's cowardly."

"Can't you let a man die as comfortably as he can without calling him names? What's the use of slanging me?"

"You're not going to die."

"Don't be silly. I'm dying now. Ask those bastards." He looked over to where the huge, filthy birds sat, their naked heads sunk in the hunched feathers. A fourth planed down, to run quick-legged and then waddle slowly toward the others.

"They are around every camp. You never notice them. You can't die if you don't give up."

"Where did you read that? You're such a bloody fool."

"You might think about some one else."

"For Christ's sake," he said, "that's been my trade."

He lay then and was quiet for a while and looked across the heat shimmer of the plain to the edge of the bush. There were a few Tommies that showed minute and white against the yellow and, far off, he saw a herd of zebra, white against the green of the bush. This was a pleasant camp under big trees against a hill, with good water, and close by, a nearly dry water hole where sand grouse flighted in the mornings.

"Wouldn't you like me to read?" she asked. She was sitting on a canvas chair beside his cot. "There's a breeze coming up."

"No thanks."

"Maybe the truck will come."

"I don't give a damn about the truck."

"I do."

"You give a damn about so many things that I don't."

"Not so many, Harry."

"What about a drink?"

"It's supposed to be bad for you. It said in Black's to avoid all alcohol. You shouldn't drink."

"Molo!" he shouted.

"Yes Bwana."

"Bring whiskey-soda."

"Yes Bwana."

"You shouldn't," she said. "That's what I mean by giving up. It says it's bad for you. I know it's bad for you."

"No," he said. "It's good for me."

So now it was all over, he thought. So now he would never have a chance to finish it. So this was the way it ended in a bickering over a drink. Since the gangrene started in his right leg he had no pain and with the pain the horror had gone and all he felt now was a great tiredness and anger that this was the end of it. For this, that now was coming, he had very little curiosity. For years it had obsessed him; but now it meant nothing in itself. It was strange how easy being tired enough made it.

Now he would never write the things that he had saved to write until he knew enough to write them well. Well, he would not have to fail at trying to write them either. Maybe you could never write them, and that was why you put them off and delayed the starting. Well he would never know, now.

"I wish we'd never come," the woman said. She was looking at him holding the glass and biting her lip. "You never would have gotten anything like this in Paris. You always said you loved Paris. We could have stayed in Paris or gone anywhere. I'd have gone anywhere. I said I'd go anywhere you wanted. If you wanted to shoot we could have gone shooting in Hungary and been comfortable."

"Your bloody money," he said.

"That's not fair," she said. "It was always yours as much as mine. I left everything and I went wherever you wanted to go and I've done what you wanted to do. But I wish we'd never come here."

"You said you loved it."

"I did when you were all right. But now I hate it. I don't see why that had to happen to your leg. What have we done to have that happen to us?"

"I suppose what I did was to forget to put iodine on it when I first scratched it. Then I didn't pay any attention to it because I never infect. Then, later, when it got bad, it was probably using that weak carbolic solution when the other antiseptics ran out that paralyzed the minute blood vessels and started the gangrene." He looked at her, "What else?"

"I don't mean that."

"If we would have hired a good mechanic instead of a half baked kikuyu driver, he would have checked the oil and never burned out that bearing in the truck."

"I don't mean that."

"If you hadn't left your own people, your goddamned Old Westbury, Saratoga, Palm Beach people to take me on—"

"Why, I loved you. That's not fair. I love you now. I'll always love you. Don't you love me?"

"No," said the man. "I don't think so. I never have."

"Harry, what are you saying? You're out of your head."

"No. I haven't any head to go out of."

"Don't drink that," she said. "Darling, please don't drink that. We have to do everything we can."

"You do it," he said. "I'm tired."

Now in his mind he saw a railway station at Karagatch and he was standing with his pack and that was the headlight of the Simplon-Orient cutting the dark now and he was leaving Thrace then after the retreat. That was one of the things he had saved to write, with, in the morning at breakfast, looking out the window and seeing snow on the mountains in Bulgaria and Nansen's Secretary asking the old man if it were snow and the old man looking at it and saying, No, that's not snow. It's too early for snow. And the Secretary repeating to the other girls, No, you see. It's not snow and them all saying, It's not snow we were mistaken. But it was snow all right and he sent them on into it when he evolved exchange of populations. And it was snow they tramped along in until they died that winter.

It was snow too that fell all Christmas week that year up in the Gauertal, that year they lived in the woodcutter's house with the big square porcelain stove that filled half the room, and they slept on mattresses filled with beech leaves, the time the deserter came with his feet bloody in the snow. He said the police were right behind him and they gave him woolen socks and held the gendarmes talking until the tracks had drifted over.

In Schrunz, on Christmas day, the snow was so bright it hurt your eyes when you looked out from the weinstube and saw every one coming home from church. That was where they walked up the sleigh-smoothed urin-yellowed road along the river with the steep pine hills, skis heavy on the shoulder, and where they ran that great run down the glacier above the Madlener-haus, the snow as smooth to see as cake frosting and as light as powder and he remembered the noiseless rush the speed made as you dropped down like a bird.

They were snow-bound a week in the Madlener-haus that time in the blizzard playing cards in the smoke by the lantern light and the stakes were higher all the time as Herr Lent lost more. Finally he lost it all. Every-thing, the skichule money and all the season's profit and then his capital. He could see him with his long nose, picking up the cards and then opening, "Sans Voir." There was always gambling then. When there was no snow you gambled and when there was too much you gambled. He thought of all the time in his life he had spent gambling.

But he had never written a line of that, nor of that cold, bright Christ-mas day with the mountains showing across the plain that Barker had flown across the lines to bomb the Austrian officers' leave train, machine-gunning them as they scattered and ran. He remembered Barker after-wards coming into the mess and starting to tell about it. And how quiet it got and then somebody saying, "You bloody murderous bastard."

Those were the same Austrians they killed then that he skied with later. No not the same. Hans, that he skied with all that year, had been in the Kaiser-Jägers and when they went hunting hares together up the little valley above the saw-mill they had talked of the fighting on Pasubio and of the at-tack on Pertica and Asalone and he had never written a word of that. Nor of Monte Corno, nor the Siete Commun, nor of Arsiedo.

How many winters had he lived in the Voralberg and the Arlberg? It was four and then he remembered the man who had the fox to sell when they had walked into Bludenz, that time to buy presents, and the cherry-pit taste of good kirsch, the fast-slipping rush of running powder-snow on crust, singing "Hi! Ho! said Rolly!" as you ran down the last stretch to the steep drop, taking it straight, then running the orchard in three turns and out across the ditch and onto the icy road behind the inn. Knocking your bindings loose, kicking the skis free and leaning them up against the wooden wall of the inn, the lamp-light coming from the window, where inside, in the smoky, new-wine smelling warmth, they were playing the accordion.

"Where did we stay in Paris?" he asked the woman who was sitting by him in a canvas chair, now, in Africa.

"At the Crillon. You know that."

"Why do I know that?"

"That's where we always stayed."

"No. Not always."

"There and at the Pavillion Henri-Quatre in St. Gérmain. You said you loved it there."

"Love is a dunghill," said Harry. "And I'm the cock that gets on it to crow."

"If you have to go away," she said, "is it absolutely necessary to kill off everything you leave behind? I mean do you have to take away everything? Do you have to kill your horse, and your wife and burn your saddle and your armour?"

"Yes," he said. "Your damned money was my armour. My Swift and my Armour."

"Don't."

"All right. I'll stop that. I don't want to hurt you."

"It's a little bit late now."

"All right then. I'll go on hurting you. It's more amusing. The only thing I ever really liked to do with you I can't do now."

"No, that's not true. You liked to do many things and everything you wanted to do I did."

"Oh, for Christ sake stop bragging, will you?"

He looked at her and saw her crying.

"Listen," he said. "Do you think that it is fun to do this? I don't know why I'm doing it. It's trying to kill to keep yourself alive, I imagine. I was all right when we started talking. I didn't mean to start this, and now I'm crazy as a coot and being as cruel to you as I can be. Don't pay any attention, darling, to what I say. I love you, really. You know I love you. I've never loved any one else the way I love you."

He slipped into the familiar lie he made his bread and butter by. "You're sweet to me."

"You bitch," he said. "You rich bitch. That's poetry. I'm full of poetry now. Rot and poetry. Rotten poetry."

"Stop it. Harry, why do you have to turn into a devil now?"

"I don't like to leave anything," the man said. "I don't like to leave things behind."

* * *

It was evening now and he had been asleep. The sun was gone behind the hill and there was a shadow all across the plain and the small animals were feeding close to camp; quick dropping heads and switching tails, he watched them keeping well out away from the bush now. The birds no longer waited on the ground. They were all perched heavily in a tree. There were many more of them. His personal boy was sitting by the bed.

"Memsahib's gone to shoot," the boy said. "Does Bwana want?"

"Nothing."

She had gone to kill a piece of meat and, knowing how he liked to watch the game, she had gone well away so she would not disturb this little pocket of the plain that he could see. She was always thoughtful, he thought. On anything she knew about, or had read, or that she had ever heard.

It was not her fault that when he went to her he was already over. How could a woman know that you meant nothing that you said; that you spoke only from habit and to be comfortable? After he no longer meant what he said, his lies were more successful with women than when he had told them the truth.

It was not so much that he lied as that there was no truth to tell. He had had his life and it was over and then he went on living it again with different people and more money, with the best of the same places, and some new ones.

70

You kept from thinking and it was all marvellous. You were equipped with good insides so that you did not go to pieces that way, the way most of them had, and you made an attitude that you cared nothing for the work you used to do, now that you could no longer do it. But, in yourself, you said that you would write about these people; about the very rich; that you were really not of them but a spy in their country; that you would leave it and write of it and for once it would be written by some one who knew what he was writing of. But he would never do it, because each day of not writing, of comfort, of being that which he despised, dulled his ability and softened his will to work so that, finally, he did not work at all. The people he knew now were all much more comfortable when he did not work. Africa was where he had been happiest in the good time of his life, so he had come out here to start again. They had made this safari with the minimum of comfort. There was no hardship; but there was no luxury and he had thought that he could get back into training that way. That in some way he could work the fat off his soul the way a fighter went into the mountains to work and train in order to burn it out of his body.

She had liked it. She said she loved it. She loved anything that was exciting, that involved a change of scene, where there were new people and where things were pleasant. And he had felt the illusion of returning strength of will to work. Now if this was how it ended, and he knew it was, he must not turn like some snake biting itself because its back was broken. It wasn't this woman's fault. If it had not been she it would have been another. If he lived by a lie he should try to die by it. He heard a shot beyond the hill.

She shot very well this good, this rich bitch, this kindly caretaker and destroyer of his talent. Nonsense. He had destroyed his talent himself. Why should he blame this woman because she kept him well? He had destroyed his talent by not using it, by betrayals of himself and what he believed in, by drinking so much that he blunted the edge of his perceptions, by laziness, by sloth, and by snobbery, by pride and by prejudice, by hook and by crook. What

71

was this? A catalogue of old books? What was his talent anyway? It was a talent all right but instead of using it, he had traded on it. It was never what he had done, but always what he could do. And he had chosen to make his living with something else instead of a pen or a pencil. It was strange, too, wasn't it, that when he fell in love with another woman, that woman should always have more money than the last one? But when he no longer was in love, when he was only lying, as to this woman, now, who had the most money of all, who had all the money there was, who had had a husband and children, who had taken lovers and been dissatisfied with them, and who loved him dearly as a writer, as a man, as a companion and as a proud possession; it was strange that when he did not love her at all and was lying, that he should be able to give her more for her money than when he had really loved.

We must all but cut out for what we do, he thought. However you make your living is where your talent lies. He had sold vitality, in one form or another, all his life and when your affections are not too involved you give much better value for the money. He had found that out but he would never write that, now, either. No, he would not write that, although it was well worth writing.

Now she came in sight, walking across the open toward the camp. She was wearing jodphurs and carrying her rifle. The two boys had a Tommie slung and they were coming along behind her. She was still a good-looking woman, he thought, and she had a pleasant body. She had a great talent and appreciation for the bed, she was not pretty, but he liked her face, she read enormously, liked to ride and shoot and, certainly, she drank too much. Her husband had died when she was still a comparatively young woman and for a while she had devoted herself to her two just-grown children, who did not need her and were embarrassed at having her about, to her stable of horses, to books, and to bottles. She liked to read in the evening before dinner and she drank Scotch and soda while she read. By dinner she was fairly drunk and after a bottle of wine at dinner she was usually drunk enough to sleep.

That was before the lovers. After she had the lovers she did not drink so much because she did not have to be drunk to sleep. But the lovers bored her. She had been married to a man who had never bored her and these people bored her very much.

Then one of her two children was killed in a plane crash and after that was over she did not want the lovers, and drink being no anæsthetic she had to make another life. Suddenly, she had been acutely frightened of being alone. But she wanted some one that she respected with her.

It had begun very simply. She liked what he wrote and she had always envied the life he led. She thought he did exactly what he wanted to. The steps by which she had acquired him and the way in which she had finally fallen in love with him were all part of a regular progression in which she had built herself a new life and he had traded away what remained of his old life.

He had traded it for security, for comfort too, there was no denying that, and for what else? He did not know. She would have bought him anything he wanted. He knew that. She was a damned nice woman too. He would as soon be in bed with her as any one; rather with her, because she was richer, because she was very pleasant and appreciative and because she never made scenes. And now this life that she had built again was coming to a term because he had not used iodine two weeks ago when a thorn had scratched his knee as they moved forward trying to photograph a herd of waterbuck standing, their heads up, peering while their nostrils searched the air, their ears spread wide to hear the first noise that would send them rushing into the bush. They had bolted, too, before he got the picture.

Here she came now.

He turned his head on the cot to look toward her. "Hello," he said.

"I shot a Tommy ram," she told him. "He'll make you good broth and I'll have them mash some potatoes with the Klim. How do you feel?"

"Much better."

"Isn't that lovely? You know I thought perhaps you would. You were sleeping when I left."

"I had a good sleep. Did you walk far?"

"No. Just around behind the hill. I made quite a good shot on the Tommy."

"You shoot marvellously, you know."

"I love it. I've loved Africa. Really. If *you're* all right it's the most fun that I've ever had. You don't know the fun it's been to shoot with you. I've loved the country."

"I love it too."

"Darling, you don't know how marvellous it is to see you feeling better. I couldn't stand it when you felt that way. You won't talk to me like that again, will you? Promise me?"

"No," he said. "I don't remember what I said."

"You don't have to destroy me. Do you? I'm only a middle-aged woman who loves you and wants to do what you want to do. I've been destroyed two or three times already. You wouldn't want to destroy me again, would you?"

"I'd like to destroy you a few times in bed," he said.

"Yes. That's the good destruction. That's the way we're made to be destroyed. The plane will be here tomorrow."

"How do you know?"

"I'm sure. It's bound to come. The boys have the wood all ready and the grass to make the smudge. I went down and looked at it again today. There's plenty of room to land and we have the smudges ready at both ends."

"What makes you think it will come tomorrow?"

"I'm sure it will. It's overdue now. Then, in town, they will fix up your leg and then we will have some good destruction. Not that dreadful talking kind."

"Should we have a drink? The sun is down."

"Do you think you should?"

"I'm having one."

"We'll have one together. *Molo, letti dui whiskey-soda!*" she called.

"You'd better put on your mosquito boots," he told her.

"I'll wait till I bathe . . ."

While it grew dark they drank and just before it was dark and there was no longer enough light to shoot, a hyena crossed the open on his way around the hill.

"That bastard crosses there every night," the man said. "Every night for two weeks."

"He's the one makes the noise at night. I don't mind it. They're a filthy animal though."

Drinking together, with no pain now except the discomfort of lying in the one position, the boys lighting a fire, its shadow jumping on the tents, he could feel the return of acquiescence in this life of pleasant surrender. She *was* very good to him. He had been cruel and unjust in the afternoon. She was a fine woman, marvellous really. And just then it occurred to him that he was going to die.

It came with a rush; not as a rush of water nor of wind; but of a sudden evil-smelling emptiness and the odd thing was that the hyena slipped lightly along the edge of it.

"What is it, Harry?" she asked him.

"Nothing," he said. "You had better move over to the other side. To windward."

"Did Molo change the dressing?"

"Yes. I'm just using the boric now."

"How do you feel?"

"A little wobbly."

"I'm going in to bathe," she said. "I'll be right out. I'll eat with you and then we'll put the cot in."

So, he said to himself, we did well to stop the quarrelling. He had never quarrelled much with this woman, while with the women that he loved he had quarrelled so much they had finally, always, with the corrosion of the quarreling, killed what they had together. He had loved too much, demanded too much, and he wore it all out.

*   *   *

He thought about alone in Constantinople that time, having quarrelled in Paris before he had gone out. He had whored the whole time and then, when that was over, and he had failed to kill his loneliness, but only made it worse, he had written her, the first one, the one who left him, a letter telling her how he had never been able to kill it. . . . How when he thought he saw her outside the Regence *one time it made him go all faint and sick inside, and that he would follow a woman who looked like her in some way, along the Boulevard, afraid to see it was not she, afraid to lose the feeling it gave him. How every one he had slept with had only made him miss her more. How what she had done could never matter since he knew he could not cure himself of loving her. He wrote this letter at the Club, cold sober, and mailed it to New York asking her to write him at the office in Paris. That seemed safe. And that night missing her so much it made him feel hollow sick inside, he wandered up past Taxim's, picked a girl up and took her out to supper. He had gone to a place to dance with her afterward, she danced badly, and left her for a hot Armenian slut, that swung her belly against him so it almost scalded. He took her away from a British gunner subaltern after a row. The gunner asked him outside and they fought in the street on the cobbles in the dark. He'd hit him twice, hard, on the side of the jaw and when he didn't go down he knew he was in for a fight. The gunner hit him in the body, then beside his eye. He swung with his left again and landed and the gunner fell on him and grabbed his coat and tore the sleeve off and he clubbed him twice behind the ear and then smashed him with his right as he pushed him away. When the gunner went down his head hit first and he ran with the girl because they heard the M.P.'s coming. They got into a taxi and drove out to Rimmily Hissa along the Bosphorus, and around, and back in the cool night and went to bed and she felt as over-ripe as she looked but smooth, rose-petal, syrupy, smooth-bellied, big-breasted and needed no pillow under her buttocks, and he left her before she was awake looking blousy enough in the first daylight and turned up at the Pera Palace with a black eye, carrying his coat because one sleeve was missing.*

That same night he left for Anatolia and he remembered, later on that trip, riding all day through fields of the poppies that they raised for opium and how strange it made you feel, finally, and all the distances seemed wrong, to where they had made the attack with the newly arrived Constantine officers, that did not know a god-damned thing, and the artillery had fired into the troops and the British observer had cried like a child.

That was the day he'd first seen dead men wearing white ballet skirts and upturned shoes with pompons on them. The Turks had come steadily and lumpily and he had seen the skirted men running and the officers shooting into them and running then themselves and he and the British observer had run too until his lungs ached and his mouth was full of the taste of pennies and they stopped behind some rocks and there were the Turks coming as lumpily as ever. Later he had seen the things that he could never think of and later still he had seen much worse. So when he got back to Paris that time he could not talk about it or stand to have it mentioned. And there in the café as he passed was that American poet with a pile of saucers in front of him and a stupid look on his potato face talking about the Dada movement with a Roumanian who said his name was Tristan Tzara, who always wore a monocle and had a headache, and, back at the apartment with his wife that now he loved again, the quarrel all over, the madness all over, glad to be home, the office sent his mail up to the flat. So then the letter in answer to the one he'd written came in on a platter one morning and when he saw the handwriting he went cold all over and tried to slip the letter underneath another. But his wife said, "Who is that letter from, dear?" and that was the end of the beginning of that.

He remembered the good times with them all, and the quarrels. They always picked the finest places to have the quarrels. And why had they always quarrelled when he was feeling best? He had never written any of that because, at first, he never wanted to hurt any one and then it seemed as though there was enough to write without it. But he had always thought that he would write it finally. There was so much to write. He had seen the world change; not just the events; although he had seen many of them and had watched the people, but he had seen the subtler change and he could remember how the people were at different times. He had been in it and he had watched it and it was his duty to write of it; but now he never would.

*   *   *

"How do you feel?" she said. She had come out from the tent now after her bath.

"All right."

"Could you eat now?" He saw Molo behind her with the folding table and the other boy with the dishes.

"I want to write," he said.

"You ought to take some broth to keep your strength up."

"I'm going to die tonight," he said. "I don't need my strength up."

"Don't be melodramatic, Harry, please," she said.

"Why don't you use your nose? I'm rotted half way up my thigh now. What the hell should I fool with broth for? Molo bring whiskey-soda."

"Please take the broth," she said gently.

"All right."

The broth was too hot. He had to hold it in the cup until it cooled enough to take it and then he just got it down without gagging.

"You're a fine woman," he said. "Don't pay any attention to me."

She looked at him with her well-known, well-loved face from *Spur* and *Town and Country,* only a little the worse for drink, only a little the worse for bed, but *Town and Country* never showed those good breasts and those useful thighs and those lightly small-of-back caressing hands, and as he looked and saw her well known pleasant smile, he felt death come again. This time there was no rush. It was a puff, as of a wind that makes a candle flicker and the flame go tall.

"They can bring my net out later and hang it from the tree and build the fire up. I'm not going in the tent tonight. It's not worth moving. It's a clear night. There won't be any rain."

So this was how you died, in whispers that you did not hear. Well, there would be no more quarrelling. He could promise that. The one experience that he had never had he was not going to spoil now. He probably would. You spoiled everything. But perhaps he wouldn't.

"You can't take dictation, can you?"

"I never learned," she told him.

"That's all right."

There wasn't time, of course, although it seemed as though it telescoped so that you might put it all into one paragraph if you could get it right.

There was a log house, chinked white with mortar, on a hill above the lake. There was a bell on a pole by the door to call the people in to meals. Behind the house were fields and behind the fields was the timber. A line of lombardy poplars ran from the house to the dock. Other poplars ran along the point. A road went up to the hills along the edge of the timber and along that road he picked blackberries. Then that log house was burned down and all the guns that had been on deer foot racks above the open fire place were burned and afterwards their barrels, with the lead melted in the magazines, and the stocks burned away, lay out on the heap of ashes that were used to make lye for the big iron soap kettles, and you asked Grandfather if you could have them to play with, and he said, no. You see they were his guns still and he never bought any others. Nor did he hunt any more. The house was rebuilt in the same place out of lumber now and painted white and from its porch you saw the poplars and the lake beyond; but there were never any more guns. The barrels of the guns that had hung on the deer feet on the wall of the log house lay out there on the heap of ashes and no one ever touched them.

In the Black Forest, after the war, we rented a trout stream and there were two ways to walk to it. One was down the valley from Triberg and around the valley road in the shade of the trees that bordered the white road, and then up a side road that went up through the hills past many small farms, with the big Schwarzwald houses, until that road crossed the stream. That was where our fishing began.

79

The other way was to climb steeply up to the edge of the woods and then go across the top of the hills through the pine woods, and then out to the edge of a meadow and down across this meadow to the bridge. There were birches along the stream and it was not big, but narrow, clear and fast, with pools where it had cut under the roots of the birches. At the Hotel in Triberg the proprietor had a fine season. It was very pleasant and we were all great friends. The next year came the inflation and the money he had made the year before was not enough to buy supplies to open the hotel and he hanged himself.

You could dictate that, but you could not dictate the Place Contrescarpe where the flower sellers dyed their flowers in the street and the dye ran over the paving where the autobus started and the old men and the women, always drunk on wine and bad marc; and the children with their noses running in the cold; the smell of dirty sweat and poverty and drunkenness at the Café des Amateurs and the whores at the Bal Musette they lived above. The Concierge who entertained the trooper of the Garde Republicaine in her loge, his horse-hair-plumed helmet on a chair. The locataire across the hall whose husband was a bicycle racer and her joy that morning at the Cremerie when she had opened L'Auto and seen where he placed third in Paris-Tours, his first big race. She had blushed and laughed and then gone upstairs crying with the yellow sporting paper in her hand. The husband of the woman who ran the Bal Musette drove a taxi and when he, Harry, had to take an early plane the husband knocked upon the door to wake him and they each drank a glass of white wine at the zinc of the bar before they started. He knew his neighbors in that quarter then because they were all poor.

Around that Place *there were two kinds; the drunkards and the sportifs. The drunkards killed their poverty that way; the sportifs took it out in exercise. They were the descendants of the Communards and it was no struggle for them to know their politics. They knew who had shot their fathers, their relatives, their brothers, and their friends when the Versailles troops came in and took the town after the Commune and executed any one they could catch with calloused hands, or who wore a cap, or carried any other sign he was a working man. And in that poverty, and in that quarter across the street from a Boucherie Chevaline and a wine co-operative he had written the start of all he was to do. There never was another part of Paris that he loved like that, the sprawling trees, the old white plastered houses painted brown below, the long green of the autobus in that round square, the purple flower dye upon the paving, the sudden drop down the hill of the rue Cardinal Lemoine to the River, and the other way the narrow crowded world of the rue Mouffetard. The street that ran up toward the Pantheon and the other that he always took with the bicycle, the only asphalted street in all that quarter, smooth under the tires, with the high narrow houses and the cheap tall hotel where Paul Verlaine had died. There were only two rooms in the apartments where they lived and he had a room on the top floor of that hotel that cost him sixty francs a month where he did his writing, and from it he could see the roofs and chimney pots and all the hills of Paris.*

From the apartment you could only see the wood and coal man's place. He sold wine too, bad wine. The golden horse's head outside the Boucherie Chevaline where the carcasses hung yellow gold and red in the open window, and the green painted co-operative where they bought their wine; good wine and cheap. The rest was plaster walls and the windows of the neighbors. The neighbors who, at night, when some one lay drunk in the street, moaning and groaning in that typical French ivresse *that you were propaganded to believe did not exist, would open their windows and then the murmur of talk.*

"Where is the policeman? When you don't want him the bugger is always there. He's sleeping with some concierge. Get the Agent." *Till some one threw a bucket of water from a window and the moaning stopped. "What's that? Water. Ah, that's intelligent." And the windows shutting. Marie, his femme de menage, protesting against the eight-hour day saying, "If a husband works until six he gets only a little drunk on the way home and does not waste too much. If he works only until five he is drunk every night and one has no money. It is the wife of the working man who suffers from this shortening of hours."*

"Wouldn't you like some more broth?" the woman asked him now.

"No, thank you very much. It was awfully good."

"Try just a little."

"I would like a whiskey-soda."

"It's not good for you."

"No. It's bad for me. Cole Porter wrote the words and the music. This knowledge that you're going mad for me."

"You know I like you to drink."

"Oh yes. Only it's bad for me."

When she goes, he thought. I'll have all I want. Not all I want but all there is. Ayee he was tired. Too tired. He was going to sleep a little while. He lay still and death was not there. It must have gone around another street. It went in pairs, on bicycles, and moved absolutely silently on the pavements.

No, he had never written about Paris. Not the Paris that he cared about. But what about the rest that he had never written?

What about the ranch and the silvered gray of the sage brush, the quick, clear water in the irrigation ditches, and the heavy green of the alfalfa. The trail went up into the hills and the cattle in the summer were shy as deer. The bawling and the steady noise and slow moving mass raising a dust as you brought them down in the fall. And behind the mountains, the clear sharpness of the peak in the evening light and, riding down along the trail in the moonlight, bright across the valley. Now he remembered coming down through the timber in the dark holding the horse's tail when you could not see and all the stories that he meant to write.

About the half-wit chore boy who was left at the ranch that time and told not to let any one get any hay, and that old bastard from the Forks who had beaten the boy when he had worked for him stopping to get some feed. The boy refusing and the old man saying he would beat him again. The boy got the rifle from the kitchen and shot him when he tried to come into the barn and when they came back to the ranch he'd been dead a week, frozen in the corral, and the dogs had eaten part of him. But what was left you packed on a sled wrapped in a blanket and roped on and you got the boy to help you haul it, and the two of you took it out over the road on skis, and sixty miles down to town to turn the boy over. He having no idea that he would be arrested. Thinking he had done his duty and that you were his friend and he would be rewarded. He'd helped to haul the old man in so everybody could know how bad the old man had been and how he'd tried to steal some feed that didn't belong to him, and when the sheriff put the handcuffs on the boy he couldn't believe it. Then he'd started to cry. That was one story he had saved to write. He knew at least twenty good stories from out there and he had never written one. Why?

"You tell them why," he said.

"Why what, dear?"

"Why nothing."

She didn't drink so much, now, since she had him. But if he lived he would never write about her, he knew that now. Nor about any of them. The rich were dull and they drank too much, or they played too much backgammon. They were dull and they were repetitious. He remembered poor Julian and his romantic awe of them and how he had started a story once that began, "The very rich are different from you and me." And how some one had said to Julian, Yes, they have more money. But that was not humorous to Julian. He thought they were a special glamourous race and when he found they weren't it wrecked him just as much as any other thing that wrecked him.

He had been contemptuous of those who wrecked. You did not have to like it because you understood it. He could beat anything, he thought, because no thing could hurt him if he did not care.

All right. Now he would not care for death. One thing he had always dreaded was the pain. He could stand pain as well as any man, until it went on too long, and wore him out, but here he had something that had hurt frightfully and just when he had felt it breaking him, the pain had stopped.

He remembered long ago when Williamson, the bombing officer, had been hit by a stick bomb some one in a German patrol had thrown as he was coming in through the wire that night and, screaming, had begged every one to kill him. He was a fat man, very brave, and a good officer, although addicted to fantastic shows. But that night he was caught in the wire, with a flare lighting him up and his bowels spilled out into the wire, so when they brought him in, alive, they had to cut him loose. Shoot me, Harry. For Christ sake shoot me. They had had an argument one time about our Lord never sending you anything you could not bear and some one's theory had been that that meant that at a certain time the pain passed you out automatically. But he had always remembered Williamson, that night. Nothing passed out Williamson until he gave him all his morphine tablets that he had always saved to use himself and then they did not work right away.

Still this now, that he had, was very easy; and if it was no worse as it went on there was nothing to worry about. Except that he would rather be in better company.

He thought a little about the company that he would like to have.

No, he thought, when everything you do, you do too long, and do too late, you can't expect to find the people still there. The people are all gone. The party's over and you are with your hostess now.

I'm getting as bored with dying as with everything else, he thought.

"It's a bore," he said out loud.

"What is, my dear?"

"Anything you do too bloody long."

He looked at her face between him and the fire. She was leaning back in the chair and the firelight shone on her pleasantly lined face and he could see that she was sleepy. He heard the hyena make a noise just outside the range of the fire.

"I've been writing," he said. "But I got tired."

"Do you think you will be able to sleep?"

"Pretty sure. Why don't you turn in?"

"I like to sit here with you."

"Do you feel anything strange?" he asked her.

"No. Just a little sleepy."

"I do," he said.

He had just felt death come by again.

"You know the only thing I've never lost is curiosity," he said to her.

"You've never lost anything. You're the most complete man I've ever known."

"Christ," he said. "How little a woman knows. What is that? Your intuition?"

Because, just then, death had come and rested its head on the foot of the cot and he could smell its breath.

"Never believe any of that about a scythe and a skull," he told her. "It can be two bicycle policemen as easily, or be a bird. Or it can have a wide snout like a hyena."

It had moved up on him now, but it had no shape any more. It simply occupied space.

"Tell it to go away."

It did not go away but moved a little closer.

"You've got a hell of a breath," he told it. "You stinking bastard."

It moved up closer to him still and now he could not speak to it, and when it saw he could not speak it came a little closer, and now he tried to send it away without speaking, but it moved in on him so its weight was all upon his chest, and while it crouched there and he could not move, or speak, he heard the woman say, "Bwana is asleep now. Take the cot up very gently and carry it into the tent."

He could not speak to tell her to make it go away and it crouched now, heavier, so he could not breathe. And then, while they lifted the cot, suddenly it was all right and the weight went from his chest.

It was morning and had been morning for some time and he heard the plane. It showed very tiny and then made a wide circle and the boys ran out and lit the fires, using kerosene, and piled on grass so there were two big smudges at each end of the level place and the morning breeze blew them toward the camp and the plane circled twice more, low this time, and then glided down and levelled off and landed smoothly and, coming walking toward him, was old Compton in slacks, a tweed jacket and a brown felt hat.

"What's the matter, old cock?" Compton said.

"Bad leg," he told him. "Will you have some breakfast?"

"Thanks. I'll just have some tea. It's the Puss Moth you know. I won't be able to take the Memsahib. There's only room for one. Your lorry is on the way."

Helen had taken Compton aside and was speaking to him. Compton came back more cheery than ever.

"We'll get you right in," he said. "I'll be back for the Mem. Now I'm afraid I'll have to stop at Arusha to refuel. We'd better get going."

"What about the tea?"

"I don't really care about it you know."

The boys had picked up the cot and carried it around the green tents and down along the rock and out onto the plain and along past the smudges that were burning brightly now, the grass all consumed, and the wind fanning the fire, to the little plane. It was difficult getting him in, but once in he lay back in the leather seat, and the leg was stuck straight out to one side of the seat where Compton sat. Compton started the motor and got in. He waved to Helen and to the boys and, as the clatter moved into the old familiar roar, they swung around with Compie watching for wart-hog holes and roared, bumping, along the stretch between the fires and with the last bump rose and he saw them all standing below, waving, and the camp beside the hill, flattening now, and the plain spreading, clumps of trees, and the bush flattening, while the game trails ran now smoothly to the dry waterholes, and there was a new water that he had never known of. The zebra, small rounded backs now, and the wildebeeste, big-headed dots seeming to climb as they moved in long fingers across the plain, now scattering as the shadow came toward them, they were tiny now, and the movement had no gallop, and the plain as far as you could see, gray-yellow now and ahead old Compie's tweed back and the brown felt hat. Then they were over the first hills and the wildebeeste were trailing up them, and then they were over mountains with sudden depths of green-rising forest and the solid bamboo slopes, and then the heavy forest again, sculptured into peaks and hollows until they crossed, and hills sloped down and then another plain, hot now, and purple brown, bumpy with heat and Compie looking back to see how he was riding. Then there were other mountains dark ahead.

And then instead of going on to Arusha they turned left, he evidently figured that they had the gas, and looking down he saw a pink sifting cloud, moving over the ground, and in the air, like the first snow in a blizzard, that comes from nowhere, and he knew the locusts were coming up from the South. Then they began to climb and they were going to the East it seemed, and then it darkened and they were in a storm, the rain so thick it seemed like flying through a waterfall, and then they were out and Compie turned his head and grinned and pointed and there, ahead, all he could see, as wide as all the world, great, high, and unbelievably white in the sun, was the square top of Kilimanjaro. And then he knew that there was where he was going.

Just then the hyena stopped whimpering in the night and started to make a strange, human, almost crying sound. The woman heard it and stirred uneasily. She did not wake. In her dream she was at the house on Long Island and it was the night before her daughter's début. Somehow her father was there and he had been very rude. Then the noise the hyena made was so loud she woke and for a moment she did not know where she was and she was very afraid. Then she took the flashlight and shone it on the other cot that they had carried in after Harry had gone to sleep. She could see his bulk under the mosquito bar but somehow he had gotten his leg out and it hung down alongside the cot. The dressings had all come down and she could not look at it.

"Molo," she called, "Molo! Molo!"

Then she said, "Harry, Harry!" Then her voice rising, "Harry! Please, Oh Harry!"

There was no answer and she could not hear him breathing.

Outside the tent the hyena made the same strange noise that had awakened her. But she did not hear him for the beating of her heart.

"Memories of Hunting in the Abruzzi"

(from *A Farewell to Arms*)

"I would like you to go to Abruzzi," the priest said. The others were shouting. "There is good hunting. You would like the people and though it is cold it is clear and dry. You could stay with my family. My father is a famous hunter."

"Come on," said the captain. "We go whorehouse before it shuts."

"Good-night," I said to the priest.

"Good-night," he said.

* * *

That night at the mess I sat next to the priest and he was disappointed and suddenly hurt that I had not gone to the Abruzzi. He had written to his father that I was coming and they had made preparations. I myself felt as badly as he did and could not understand why I had not gone. It was what I had wanted to do and I tried to explain how one thing had led to another and finally he saw it and understood that I had really wanted to go and it was almost all right. I had drunk much wine and afterward coffee and Strega and I explained, winefully, how we did not do the things we wanted to do; we never did such things.

We two were talking while the others argued. I had wanted to go to Abruzzi. I had gone to no place where the roads were frozen and hard as iron, where it was clear cold and dry and the snow was dry and powdery and hare-tracks in the snow and the peasants took off their hats and called you Lord and there was good hunting. I had gone to no such place but to the smoke of cafés and nights when the room whirled and you needed to look at the wall to make it stop, nights in bed, drunk, when you knew that that was all there was, and the strange excitement of waking and not knowing who it was with you, and the world all unreal in the dark and so exciting that you must resume again unknowing and not caring in the night, sure that this was all and all and all and not caring. Suddenly to care very much and to sleep to wake with it sometimes morning and all that had been there gone and everything sharp and hard and clear and sometimes a dispute about the cost. Sometimes still pleasant and fond and warm and breakfast and lunch. Sometimes all niceness gone and glad to get out on the street but always another day starting and then another night. I tried to tell about the night and the difference between the night and the day and how the night was better unless the day was very clean and cold and I could not tell it; as I cannot tell it now. But if you have had it you know. He had not had it but he understood that I had really wanted to go to the Abruzzi but had not gone and we were still friends, with many tastes alike, but with the difference between us. He had always known what I did not know and what, when I learned it, I was always able to forget. But I did not know that then, although I learned it later. In the meantime we were all at the mess, the meal was finished, and the argument went on. We two stopped talking and the captain shouted, "Priest not happy. Priest not happy without girls."

"I am happy," said the priest.

"Priest not happy. Priest wants Austrians to win the war," the captain said. The others listened. The priest shook his head.

"No," he said.

"Priest wants us never to attack. Don't you want us never to attack?"

"No. If there is a war I suppose we must attack."

"Must attack. Shall attack!"

The priest nodded.

"Leave him alone," the major said. "He's all right."

"He can't do anything about it anyway," the captain said. We all got up and left the table.

*   *   *

"Did you always love God?"

"Ever since I was a little boy."

"Well," I said. I did not know what to say. "You are a fine boy," I said.

"I am a boy," he said. "But you call me father."

"That's politeness."

He smiled.

"I must go, really," he said. "You do not want me for anything?" he asked hopefully.

"No. Just to talk."

"I will take your greetings to the mess."

"Thank you for the many fine presents."

"Nothing."

"Come and see me again."

"Yes. Good-by," he patted my hand.

"So long," I said in dialect.

"Ciaou," he repeated.

It was dark in the room and the orderly, who had sat by the foot of the bed, got up and went out with him. I liked him very much and I hoped he would get back to the Abruzzi some time. He had a rotten life in the mess and he was fine about it but I thought how he would be in his own country. At Capracotta, he had told me, there were trout in the stream below the town. It was forbidden to play the flute at night. When the young men serenaded only the flute was forbidden. Why, I had asked. Because it was bad for the girls to hear the flute at night. The peasants all called you "Don" and when you met them they took off their hats. His father hunted every day and stopped to eat at the houses of peasants. They were always honored. For a foreigner to hunt he must present a certificate that he had never been arrested. There were bears on the Gran Sasso D'Italia but it was a long way. Aquila was a fine town. It was cool in the summer at night and the spring in Abruzzi was the most beautiful in Italy. But what was lovely was the fall to go hunting through the chestnut woods. The birds were all good because they fed on grapes and you never took a lunch because the peasants were always honored if you would eat with them at their houses. After a while I went to sleep.

"The Way to Hunt"

(from *Green Hills of Africa*)

Now it is pleasant to hunt something that you want very much over a long period of time, being outwitted, out-manœuvred, and failing at the end of each day, but having the hunt and knowing every time you are out that, sooner or later, your luck will change and that you will get the chance that you are seeking. But it is not pleasant to have a time limit by which you must get your kudu or perhaps never get it, nor even see one. It is not the way hunting should be. It is too much like those boys who used to be sent to Paris with two years in which to make good as writers or painters after which, if they had not made good, they could go home and into their fathers' business. The way to hunt is for as long as you live against as long as there is such and such an animal; just as the way to paint is as long as there is you and colors and canvas, and to write as long as you can live and there is pencil and paper or ink or any machine to do it with, or anything you care to write about, and you feel a fool, and you are a fool, to do it any other way.

93

"The Need to Hunt"

(from *Green Hills of Africa*)

"And what do you want?"

"To write as well as I can and learn as I go along. At the same time I have my life which I enjoy and which is a damned good life."

"Hunting kudu?"

"Yes. Hunting kudu and many other things."

"What other things?"

"Plenty of other things."

"And you know what you want?"

"Yes."

"You really like to do this, what you do now, this silliness of kudu?"

"Just as much as I like to be in the Prado."

"One is not better than the other?"

"One is as necessary as the other. There are other things, too."

95

"Naturally. There must be. But this sort of thing means something to you, really?"

"Truly."

"And you know what you want?"

"Absolutely, and I get it all the time."

"But it takes money."

"I could always make money and besides I have been very lucky."

"The Hyena"

(from *Green Hills of Africa*)

Highly humorous was the hyena obscenely loping, full belly dragging, at daylight on the plain, who, shot from the stern, skittered on
into speed to tumble end over end. Mirth provoking was the hyena
that stopped out of range by an alkali lake to look back and, hit in
the chest, went over on his back, his four feet and his full belly in
the air. Nothing could be more jolly than the hyena coming suddenly wedge-headed and stinking out of high grass by a *donga*, hit
at ten yards, who raced his tail in three narrowing, scampering circles until he died.

 It was funny to M'Cola to see a hyena shot at close range.
There was that comic slap of the bullet and the hyena's agitated
surprise to find death inside of him. It was funnier to see a hyena
shot at a great distance, in the heat shimmer of the plain, to see
him go over backwards, to see him start that frantic circle, to see
that electric speed that meant that he was racing the little nick-
elled death inside him. But the great joke of all, the thing M'Cola

97

waved his hands across his face about, and turned away and shook his head and laughed, ashamed even of the hyena; the pinnacle of hyenic humor, was the hyena, the classic hyena, that hit too far back while running, would circle madly, snapping and tearing at himself until he pulled his own intestines out, and then stood there, jerking them out and eating them with relish.

"*Fisi*," M'Cola would say and shake his head in delighted sorrow at there being such an awful beast. Fisi, the hyena, hermaphroditic, self-eating devourer of the dead, trailer of calving cows, ham-stringer, potential biter-off of your face at night while you slept, sad yowler, camp-follower, stinking, foul, with jaws that crack the bones the lion leaves, belly dragging, loping away on the brown plain, looking back, mongrel dog-smart in the face; whack from the little Mannlicher and then the horrid circle starting. "*Fisi*," M'Cola laughed, ashamed of him, shaking his bald black head. "*Fisi*. Eats himself. *Fisi*."

"P. O. M.'s Lion"

(from *Green Hills of Africa*)

The evening we killed the first lion it was dark when we came in sight of camp. The killing of the lion had been confused and unsatisfactory. It was agreed beforehand that P. O. M. should have the first shot but since it was the first lion any of us had ever shot at, and it was very late in the day, really too late to take the lion on, once he was hit we were to make a dogfight of it and any one was free to get him. This was a good plan as it was nearly sundown and if the lion got into cover, wounded, it would be too dark to do anything about it without a mess. I remember seeing the lion looking yellow and heavy-headed and enormous against a scrubby-looking tree in a patch of orchard bush and P. O. M. kneeling to shoot and wanting to tell her to sit down and make sure of him. Then there was the short-barrelled explosion of the Mannlicher and the lion was going to the left on a run, a strange, heavy-shouldered, foot-swinging, cat run. I hit him with the Springfield and he went down and spun over and I shot again, too quickly, and threw a cloud of dirt over him. But there he was, stretched out, on his belly, and, with the sun just over the top of the trees, and the grass very green, we walked up on him like a posse, or a gang of Black and Tans, guns ready and cocked, not knowing whether he was stunned or dead. When we were close M'Cola threw a stone at him. It hit him in the flank and from the way it hit you could tell he was a dead animal. I was sure P. O. M. had hit him but there was only one bullet hole, well back, just below the spine and ranging forward to come to the surface under the skin of the chest. You could feel the bullet under the skin and M'Cola made a slit and cut it out. It was a 220-grain solid bullet from the Springfield and it had raked him, going through lungs and heart.

I was so surprised by the way he had rolled over dead from the shot after we had been prepared for a charge, for heroics, and for drama, that I felt more let down than pleased. It was our first lion and we were very ignorant and this was not what we had paid to see. Charo and M'Cola both shook P. O. M.'s hand and then Charo came over and shook hands with me.

"Good shot, B'wana," he said in Swahili. "*Piga m'uzuri.*"

"Did you shoot, Karl?" I asked.

"No. I was just going to when you shot."

"You didn't shoot him, Pop?"

"No. You'd have heard it." He opened the breech and took out the two big .450 No. 2's.

"I'm sure I missed him," P. O. M. said.

"I was sure you hit him. I still think you hit him," I said.

"Mama hit," M'Cola said.

"Where?" Charo asked.

"Hit," said M'Cola. "Hit."

"You rolled him over," Pop said to me. "God, he went over like a rabbit."

"I couldn't believe it."

"Mama *piga*," M'Cola said. "*Piga Simba.*"

As we saw the camp fire in the dark ahead of us, coming in that night, M'Cola suddenly commenced to shout a stream of high-pitched, rapid, singing words in Wakamba ending in the word *"Simba."* Some one at the camp shouted back one word.

"Mama!" M'Cola shouted. Then another long stream. Then "Mama! Mama!"

Through the dark came all the porters, the cook, the skinner, the boys, and the headman.

"Mama!" M'Cola shouted. "Mama *piga Simba.*"

The boys came dancing, crowding, and beating time and chanting something from down in their chests that started like a cough and sounded like *"Hey la Mama! Hay la Mama! Hey la Mama!"*

The rolling-eyed skinner picked P. O. M. up, the big cook and the boys held her, and the others pressing forward to lift, and if not to lift to touch and hold, they danced and sang through the dark, around the fire and to our tent.

"Hey la Mama! huh! huh! huh! Hay la Mama! huh! huh! huh!" they sang the lion dance with that deep, lion asthmatic cough in it. Then at the tent they put her down and every one, very shyly, shook hands, the boys saying *"m'uzuri, Memsahib,"* and M'Cola and the porters all saying *"m'uzuri,* Mama" with much feeling in the accenting of the word "Mama."

Afterwards in the chairs in front of the fire, sitting with the drinks, Pop said, "You shot it. M'Cola would kill any one who said you didn't."

"You know, I feel as though I did shoot it," P. O. M. said. "I don't believe I'd be able to stand it if I really had shot it. I'd be too proud. Isn't triumph marvellous?"

"Good old Mama," Karl said.

"I believe you did shoot him," I said.

"Oh, let's not go into that," P. O. M. said. "I feel so wonderful about just being supposed to have killed him. You know people never used to carry me on their shoulders much at home."

"No one knows how to behave in America," Pop said. "Most uncivilized."

"We'll carry you in Key West," Karl said. "Poor old Mama."

"Let's not talk about it," P. O. M. said. "I like it too much. Shouldn't I maybe distribute largess?"

"They didn't do it for that," Pop said. "But it is all right to give something to celebrate."

"Oh, I want to give them all a great deal of money," P. O. M. said. "Isn't triumph simply marvellous?"

"Good old Mama," I said. "You killed him."

"No I didn't. Don't lie to me. Just let me enjoy my triumph."

"The Rhino"

(from *Green Hills of Africa*)

We went to bed early and in the night it rained a little, not a real
rain but a shower from the mountains, and in the morning we were
up before daylight and had climbed up to the top of the steep
grassy ridge that looked down onto the camp, onto the ravine of
the river bed, and across to the steep opposite bank of the stream,
and from where we could see all the hilly slopes and the edge of
the forest. It was not yet light when some geese flew overhead and
the light was still too gray to be able to see the edge of the forest
clearly in the glasses. We had scouts out on three different hill tops
and we were waiting for it to be light enough for us to see them if
they signalled.

Then Pop said, "Look at that son of a bitch," and shouted at
M'Cola to bring the rifles. M'Cola went jumping down the hill, and
across the stream, directly opposite us, a rhino was running with a
quick trot along the top of the bank. As we watched he speeded up
and came, fast trotting, angling down across the face of the bank.

He was a muddy red, his horn showed clearly, and there was nothing ponderous in his quick, purposeful movement. I was very excited at seeing him.

"He'll cross the stream," Pop said. "He's shootable."

M'Cola put the Springfield in my hand and I opened it to make sure I had solids. The rhino was out of sight now but I could see the shaking of the high grass.

"How far would you call it?"

"All of three hundred."

"I'll bust the son of a bitch."

I was watching, freezing myself deliberately inside, stopping the excitement as you close a valve, going into that impersonal state you shoot from.

He showed, trotting into the shallow, boulder filled stream. Thinking of one thing, that the shot was perfectly possible, but that I must lead him enough, must get ahead, I got on him, then well ahead of him, and squeezed off. I heard the *whonk* of the bullet and, from his trot, he seemed to explode forward. With a whooshing snort he smashed ahead, splashing water and snorting. I shot again and raised a little column of water behind him, and shot again as he went into the grass; behind him again.

"Piga," M'Cola said. "Piga!"

Droopy agreed.

"Did you hit him?" Pop said.

"Absolutely," I said. "I think I've got him."

Droopy was running and I re-loaded and ran off after him. Half the camp was strung out across the hills waving and yelling. The rhino had come in right below where they were and gone on up the valley toward where the forest came close down into the head of the valley.

Pop and P. O. M. came up. Pop with his big gun and M'Cola carrying mine.

"Droopy will get the tracks," Pop said. "M'Cola swears you hit him."

"Piga!" M'Cola said.

"He snorted like a steam engine," P. O. M. said. "Didn't he look wonderful going along there?"

"He was late getting home with the milk," Pop said. "Are you *sure* you hit him? It was a godawful long shot."

"I *know* I hit him. I'm *pretty* sure I've killed him."

"Don't tell any one if you did," Pop said. "They'll never believe you. Look! Droopy's got blood."

Below, in the high grass Droop was holding up a grass blade toward us. Then, stooped, he went on trailing fast by the blood spoor.

"Piga," M'Cola said. "M'uzuri!"

"We'll keep up above where we can see if he makes a break," Pop said. "Look at Droopy."

Droop had removed his fez and held it in his hand.

"That's all the precautions he needs," Pop said. "We bring up a couple of heavy guns and Droopy goes in after him with one article less of clothing."

Below us Droopy and his partner who was trailing with him had stopped. Droopy held up his hand.

"They hear him," Pop said. "Come on."

We started toward them. Droopy came toward us and spoke to Pop.

"He's in there," Pop whispered. "They can hear the tick birds. One of the boys says he heard the faro, too. We'll go in against the wind. You go ahead with Droopy. Let the Memsahib stay behind me. Take the big gun. All right."

The rhino was in high grass, somewhere in there behind some bushes. As we went forward we heard a deep, moaning sort of groan. Droopy looked around at me and grinned. The noise came again, ending this time like a blood-choked sigh. Droopy was laughing. "Faro," he whispered and put his hand palm open on the side of his head in the gesture that means to go to sleep. Then in a jerky-flighted, sharp-beaked little flock we saw the tick birds rise and fly away. We knew where he was and, as we went slowly forward, parting the high grass, we saw him. He was on his side, dead.

"Better shoot him once to make sure," Pop said. M'Cola handed me the Springfield he had been carrying. I noticed it was cocked, looked at M'Cola, furious with him, kneeled down and shot the rhino in the sticking place. He never moved. Droopy shook my hand and so did M'Cola.

"He had that damned Springfield cocked," I said to Pop. The cocked gun, behind my back, made me black angry.

That meant nothing to M'Cola. He was very happy, stroking the rhino's horn, measuring it with his fingers spread, looking for the bullet hole.

"It's on the side he's lying on," I said.

"You should have seen him when he was protecting Mama," Pop said. "That's why he had the gun cocked."

"Can he shoot?"

"No," Pop said. "But he would."

"Shoot me in the pants," I said. "Romantic bastard." When the whole outfit came up, we rolled the rhino into a sort of kneeling position and cut away the grass to take some pictures. The bullet hole was fairly high in the back, a little behind the lungs.

"That was a hell of a shot," Pop said. "A hell of a shot. Don't ever tell any one you made that one."

"You'll have to give me a certificate."

"That would just make us both liars. They're a strange beast, aren't they?"

There he was, long-hulked, heavy-sided, prehistoric looking, the hide like vulcanized rubber and faintly transparent looking, scarred with a badly healed horn wound that the birds had pecked at, his tail thick, round, and pointed, flat many-legged ticks crawling on him, his ears fringed with hair, tiny pig eyes, moss growing on the base of his horn that grew out forward from his nose. M'Cola looked at him and shook his head. I agreed with him. This was the hell of an animal.

"The Buffalo"

(from *Green Hills of Africa*)

We stood now in the shade of trees with great smooth trunks, circled at their base with the line of roots that showed in rounded ridges up the trunks like arteries; the trunks the yellow green of a French forest on a day in winter after rain. But these trees had a great spread of branches and were in leaf and below them, in the stream bed in the sun, reeds like papyrus grass grew thick as wheat and twelve feet tall. There was a game trail through the grass along the stream and Droopy was bent down looking at it. M'Cola went over and looked and they both followed it a little way, stooped close over it, then came back to us.

"Nyati," M'Cola whispered. "Buffalo." Droopy whispered to Pop and then Pop said, softly in his throaty, whiskey whisper, "They're buff gone down the river. Droop says there are some big bulls. They haven't come back."

"Let's follow them," I said. "I'd rather get another buff than rhino."

"It's as good a chance as any for rhino, too," Pop said.

"By God, isn't it a great looking country?" I said.

"Splendid," Pop said. "Who would have imagined it?"

"The trees are like André's pictures," P. O. M. said. "It's simply beautiful. Look at that green. It's Masson. Why can't a good painter see this country?"

"How are your boots?"

"Fine."

As we trailed the buffalo we went very slowly and quietly. There was no wind and we knew that when the breeze came up it would be from the east and blow up the canyon toward us. We followed the game trail down the river-bed and as we went the grass was much higher. Twice we had to get down to crawl and the reeds were so thick you could not see two feet into them. Droop found a fresh rhino track, too, in the mud. I began to think about what would happen if a rhino came barging along this tunnel and who would do what. It was exciting but I did not like it. It was too much like being in a trap and there was P. O. M. to think about. Then as the stream made a bend and we came out of the high grass to the bank I smelled game very distinctly. I do not smoke, and hunting at home I have several times smelled elk in the rutting season before I have seen them and I can smell clearly where an old bull has lain in the forest. The bull elk has a strong musky smell. It is a strong but pleasant odor and I know it well, but this smell I did not know.

"I can smell them," I whispered to Pop. He believed me.

"What is it?"

"I don't know but it's plenty strong. Can't you?"

"No."

"Ask Droop."

Droopy nodded and grinned.

"They take snuff," Pop said. "I don't know whether they can scent or not."

We went on into another bed of reeds that were high over our heads, putting each foot down silently before lifting the other, walking as quietly as in a dream or a slow motion picture. I could smell whatever it was clearly now, all of the time, sometimes stronger than at others. I did not like it at all. We were close to the bank now, and, ahead the game trail went straight out into a long slough of higher reeds than any we had come through.

"I can smell them close as hell," I whispered to Pop. "No kidding. Really."

"I believe you," Pop said. "Should we get up here onto the bank and skirt this bit? We'll be above it."

"Good." Then, when we were up, I said, "That tall stuff had me spooked. I wouldn't like to hunt in that."

"How'd you like to hunt elephant in that?" Pop whispered.

"I wouldn't do it."

"Do you really hunt elephant in grass like that?" P. O. M. asked.

"Yes," Pop said. "Get up on somebody's shoulders to shoot."

Better men than I am do it, I thought. I wouldn't do it.

We went along the grassy right bank, on a sort of shelf, now in the open, skirting a slough of high dry reeds. Beyond on the opposite bank were the heavy trees and above them the steep bank of the canyon. You could not see the stream. Above us, on the right, were the hills, wooded in patches of orchard bush. Ahead, at the end of the slough of reeds the banks narrowed and the branches of the big trees almost covered the stream. Suddenly Droopy grabbed me and we both crouched down. He put the big gun in my hand and took the Springfield. He pointed and around a curve in the bank I saw the head of a rhino with a long, wonderful-looking horn. The head was swaying and I could see the ears forward and twitching, and see the little pig eyes. I slipped the safety catch and motioned Droopy down. Then I heard M'Cola saying, "Toto! Toto!" and he grabbed my arm. Droopy was whispering, "Manamouki! Manamouki! Manamouki!" very fast and he and M'Cola were frantic that I should not shoot. It was a cow rhino with a calf and as I lowered the gun, she gave a snort, crashed in the reeds, and was gone. I never saw the calf. We could see the reeds swaying where the two of them were moving and then it was all quiet.

"Damn shame," Pop whispered. "She had a beautiful horn."

"I was all set to bust her," I said. "I couldn't tell she was a cow."

"M'Cola saw the calf."

M'Cola was whispering to Pop and nodding his head emphatically.

"He says there's another rhino in there," Pop said. "That he heard him snort."

"Let's get higher, where we can see them if they break, and throw something in," I said.

"Good idea," Pop agreed. "Maybe the bull's there."

We went a little higher up the bank where we could look out over the lake of high reeds and, with Pop holding his big gun ready and I with the safety off mine, M'Cola threw a club into the reeds where he had heard the snort. There was a wooshing snort and no movement, not a stir in the reeds. Then there was a crashing further away and we could see the reeds swaying with the rush of something through them toward the opposite bank, but could not see what was making the movement. Then I saw the black back, the wide-swept, point-lifted horns and then the quick-moving, climbing rush of a buffalo up the other bank. He went up, his neck up and out, his head horn-heavy, his withers rounded like a fighting bull, in fast strong-legged climb. I was holding on the point where his neck joined his shoulder when Pop stopped me.

"He's not a big one," he said softly. "I wouldn't take him unless you want him for meat."

He looked big to me and now he stood, his head up, broadside, his head swung toward us.

"I've got three more on the license and we're leaving their country," I said.

"It's awfully good meat," Pop whispered. "Go ahead then. Bust him. But be ready for the rhino after you shoot."

I sat down, the big gun feeling heavy and unfamiliar, held on the buff's shoulder, squeezed off and flinched without firing. Instead of the sweet clean pull of the Springfield with the smooth, unhesitant release at the end, this trigger came to what, in a squeeze, seemed metal stuck against metal. It was like when you shoot in a nightmare. I couldn't squeeze it and I corrected from my flinch, held my breath, and pulled the trigger. It pulled off with a jerk and the big gun made a rocking explosion out of which I came, seeing the buffalo still on his feet, and going out of sight to the left in a climbing run, to let off the second barrel and throw a burst of rock dust and dirt over his hind quarters. He was out of shot before I could reload the double-barrelled .470 and we had all heard the snorting and the crashing of another rhino that had gone out of the lower end of the reeds and on under the heavy trees on our side without showing more than a glimpse of his bulk in the reeds.

"It was the bull," Pop said. "He's gone down the stream."

"N'Dio. Doumi! Doumi!" Droopy insisted it was a bull.

"I hit the damned buff," I said. "God knows where. To hell with those heavy guns. The trigger pull put me off."

"You'd have killed him with the Springfield," Pop said.

"I'd know where I hit him anyway. I thought with the four-seventy I'd kill him or miss him," I said. "Instead, now we've got him wounded."

"He'll keep," Pop said. "We want to give him plenty of time."

"I'm afraid I gut-shot him."

"You can't tell. Going off fast like that he might be dead in a hundred yards."

"The hell with that four-seventy," I said. "I can't shoot it. The trigger's like the last turn of the key opening a sardine can."

"Come on," Pop said. "We've got God knows how many rhino scattered about here."

"What about the buff?"

"Plenty of time for him later. We must let him stiffen up. Let him get sick."

"Suppose we'd been down in there with all that stuff coming out."

"Yes," said Pop.

All this in whispers. I looked at P. O. M. She was like some one enjoying a good musical show.

"Did you see where it hit him?"

"I couldn't tell," she whispered. "Do you suppose there are any more in there?"

"Thousands," I said. "What do we do, Pop?"

"That bull may be just around the bend," Pop said. "Come on."

We went along the bank, our nerves cocked, and as we came to the narrow end of the reeds there was another rush of something heavy through the tall stalks. I had the gun up waiting for whatever it was to show. But there was only the waving of the reeds. M'Cola signalled with his hand not to shoot.

"The goddamned calf," Pop said. "Must have been two of them. Where's the bloody bull?"

"How the hell do you see them?"

"Tell by the size."

Then we were standing looking down into the stream bed, into the shadows under the branches of the big trees, and off ahead down the stream when M'Cola pointed up the hill on our right.

"Faro," he whispered and reached me the glasses.

There on the hillside, head-on, wide, black, looking straight toward us, ears twitching and head lifted, swaying as the nose searched for the wind, was another rhino. He looked huge in the glasses. Pop was studying him with his binoculars.

"He's no better than what you have," he said softly.

"I can bust him right in the sticking place," I whispered.

"You only have one more," Pop whispered. "You want a good one."

I offered the glasses to P. O. M.

"I can see him without," she said. "He's huge."

"He may charge," Pop said. "Then you'll have to take him."

Then, as we watched, another rhino came into sight from behind a wide feathery-topped tree. He was quite a bit smaller.

"By God, it's a calf," Pop said. "That one's a cow. Good thing you didn't shoot her. She bloody well *may* charge too."

"Is it the same cow?" I whispered.

"No. That other one had a hell of a horn."

We all had the nervous exhilaration, like a laughing drunk, that a sudden over-abundance, idiotic abundance of game makes. It is a feeling that can come from any sort of game or fish that is ordinarily rare and that, suddenly, you find in a ridiculously unbelievable abundance.

"Look at her. She knows there's something wrong. But she can't see us or smell us."

"She heard the shots."

"She knows we're here. But she can't make it out."

The rhino looked so huge, so ridiculous, and so fine to see, and I sighted on her chest.

"It's a nice shot."

"Perfect," Pop said.

"What are we going to do?" P. O. M. said. She was practical.

"We'll work around her," Pop said.

"If we keep low I don't believe our scent will carry up there once we're past."

"You can't tell," Pop said. "We don't want her to charge."

She did not charge, but dropped her head, finally, and worked up the hill followed by the nearly full-grown calf.

"Now," said Pop, "we'll let Droop go ahead and see if he can find the bull's tracks. We might as well sit down."

We sat in the shade and Droopy went up one side of the stream and the local guide the other. They came back and said the bull had gone on down.

"Did any one ever see what sort of horn he had?" I asked.

"Droop said he was good."

M'Cola had gone up the hill a little way. Now he crouched and beckoned.

"Nyati," he said with his hand up to his face.

"Where?" Pop asked him. He pointed, crouched down, and as we crawled up to him he handed me the glasses. They were a long way away on the jutting ridge of one of the steep hillsides on the far side of the canyon, well down the stream. We could see six, then eight, buffalo, black, heavy necked, the horns shining, standing on the point of a ridge. Some were grazing and others stood, their heads up, watching.

"That one's a bull," Pop said, looking through the glasses.

"Which one?"

"Second from the right."

"They all look like bulls to me."

"They're a long way away. That one's a good bull. Now we've got to cross the stream and work down toward them and try to get above them."

"Will they stay there?"

"No. Probably they'll work down into this stream bed as soon as it's hot."

"Let's go."

We crossed the stream on a log and then another log and on the other side, half way up the hillside, there was a deeply worn game trail that graded along the bank under the heavily leafed branches of the trees. We went along quite fast, but walking carefully, and below us, now, the stream bed was covered solidly with foliage. It was still early in the morning but the breeze was rising and the leaves stirred over our heads. We crossed one ravine that came down to the stream, going into the thick bush to be out of sight and stooping as we crossed behind trees in the small open place, then, using the shoulder of the ravine as protection, we climbed so that we might get high up the hillside above the buffalo and work down to them. We stopped in the shelter of the ridge, me sweating heavily and fixing a handkerchief inside the sweatband of my Stetson, and sent Droop ahead to look. He came back to say they were gone. From above we could see nothing of them, so we cut across the ravine and the hillside thinking we might intercept them on their way down into the river bed. The next hillside had been burned and at the bottom of the hill there was a burned area of bush. In the ash dust were the tracks of the buffalo as they came down and into the thick jungle of the stream bed. Here it was too overgrown and there were too many vines to follow them. There were no tracks going down the stream so we knew they were down in that part of the stream bed we had looked down on from the game trail. Pop said there was nothing to do about them in there. It was so thick that if we jumped them we could not get a shot. You could not tell one from another, he said. All you would see would be a rush of black. An old bull would be gray but a good herd bull might be as black as a cow. It wasn't any good to jump them like that.

It was ten o'clock now and very hot in the open, the sun pegged and the breeze lifted the ashes of the burned-over ground as we walked. Everything would be in the thick cover now. We decided to find a shady place and lie down and read in the cool; to have lunch and kill the hot part of the day.

* * *

When they woke up we had lunch of cold sliced tenderloin, bread, and mustard, and a can of plums, and drank the third, and last, bottle of beer. Then we read again and all went to sleep. I woke thirsty and was unscrewing the top from a water bottle when I heard a rhino snort and crash in the brush of the river bed. Pop was awake and heard it too and we took our guns, without speaking, and started toward where the noise had come from. M'Cola found the tracks. The rhino had come up the stream, evidently he had winded us when he was only about thirty yards away, and had gone on up. We could not follow the tracks the way the wind was blowing so we circled away from the stream and back to the edge of the burned place to get above him and then hunted very carefully against the wind along the stream through very thick bush, but we did not find him. Finally Droopy found where he had gone up the other side and on into the hills. From the tracks it did not seem a particularly large one.

We were a long way from camp, at least four hours as we had come, and much of it up-hill going back, certainly there would be that long climb out of the canyon; we had a wounded buffalo to deal with, and when we came out on the edge of the burned country again, we agreed that we should get P. O. M. and get started. It was still hot, but the sun was on its way down and for a good way we would be on the heavily shaded game trail on the high bank above the stream. When we found P. O. M. she pretended to be indignant at our going off and leaving her alone but she was only teasing us.

We started off, Droop and his spearsman in the lead, walking along the shadow of the trail that was broken by the sun through the leaves. Instead of the cool early morning smell of the forest there was a nasty stink like the mess cats make.

"What makes the stink?" I whispered to Pop.

"Baboons," he said.

A whole tribe of them had gone on just ahead of us and their droppings were everywhere. We came up to the place where the rhinos and the buff had come out of the reeds and I located where I thought the buff had been when I shot. M'Cola and Droopy were casting about like hounds and I thought they were at least fifty yards too high up the bank when Droop held up a leaf.

"He's got blood," Pop said. We went up to them. There was a great quantity of blood, black now on the grass, and the trail was easy to follow. Droop and M'Cola trailed one on each side, leaving the trail between them, pointing to each blood spot formally with a long stem of grass. I always thought it would be better for one to trail slowly and the other cast ahead but this was the way they trailed, stooped heads, pointing each dried splash with their grass stems and occasionally, when they picked up the tracks after losing them, stooping to pluck a grass blade or a leaf that had the black stain on it. I followed them with the Springfield, then came Pop, with P. O. M. behind him. Droop carried my big gun and Pop had his. M'Cola had P. O. M.'s Mannlicher slung over his shoulder. None of us spoke and every one seemed to regard it as a pretty se-

116

rious business. In some high grass we found blood, at a pretty good height on the grass leaves on both sides of the trail where the buff had gone through the grass. That meant he was shot clean through. You could not tell the original color of the blood now, but I had a moment of hoping he might be shot through the lungs. But further on we came on some droppings in the rocks with blood in them and then for a while he had dropped dung wherever he climbed and all of it was blood-spotted. It looked, now, like a gut shot or one through the paunch. I was more ashamed of it all the time.

"If he comes don't worry about Droopy or the others," Pop whispered. "They'll get out of his way. Stop him."

"Right up the nose," I said.

"Don't try anything fancy," Pop said. The trail climbed steadily, then twice looped back on itself and for a time seemed to wander, without plan, among some rocks. Once it led down to the stream, crossed a rivulet of it and then came back up on the same bank, grading up through the trees.

"I think we'll find him dead," I whispered to Pop. That aimless turn had made me see him, slow and hard hit, getting ready to go down.

"I hope so," Pop said.

But the trail went on, where there was little grass now, and trailing was much slower and more difficult. There were no tracks now that I could see, only the probable line he would take, verified by a shiny dark splatter of dried blood on a stone. Several times we lost it entirely and, the three of us making casts, one would find it, point and whisper "Damu," and we would go on again. Finally it led down from a rocky hillside with the last of the sun on it, down into the stream bed where there was a long, wide patch of the highest dead reeds that we had seen. These were higher and thicker even than the slough the buff had come out of in the morning and there were several game trails that went into them.

"Not good enough to take the little Memsahib in there," Pop said.

117

"Let her stay here with M'Cola," I said.

"It's not good enough for the little Memsahib," Pop repeated. "I don't know why we let her come."

"She can wait here. Droop wants to go on."

"Right you are. We'll have a look."

"You wait here with M'Cola," I whispered over my shoulder.

We followed Droopy into the thick, tall grass that was five feet above our heads, walking carefully on the game trail, stooping forward, trying to make no noise breathing. I was thinking of the buff the way I had seen them when we had gotten the three that time, how the old bull had come out of the bush, groggy as he was, and I could see the horns, the boss coming far down, the muzzle out, the little eyes, the roll of fat and muscle on his thin-haired, gray, scaly-hided neck, the heavy power and the rage in him, and I admired him and respected him, but he was slow, and all the while we shot I felt that it was fixed and that we had him. This was different, this was no rapid fire, no pouring it on him as he comes groggy into the open, if he comes now I must be quiet inside and put it down his nose as he comes with the head out. He will have to put the head down to hook, like any bull, and that will uncover the old place the boys wet their knuckles on and I will get one in there and then must go sideways into the grass and he would be Pop's from then on unless I could keep the rifle when I jumped. I was sure I could get that one in and jump if I could wait and watch his head come down. I knew I could do that and that the shot would kill him but how long would it take? That was the whole thing. How long would it take? Now, going forward, sure he was in here, I felt the elation, the best elation of all, of certain action to come, action in which you had something to do, in which you can kill and come out of it, doing something you are ignorant about and so not scared, no one to worry about and no responsibility except to perform something you feel sure you can perform, and I was walking softly ahead watching Droopy's back and remembering to keep the sweat out of my glasses when

I heard a noise behind us and turned my head. It was P. O. M. with M'Cola coming on our tracks.

"For God's sake," Pop said. He was furious.

We got her back out of the grass and up onto the bank and made her realize that she must stay there. She had not understood that she was to stay behind. She had heard me whisper something but thought it was for her to come behind M'Cola.

"That spooked me," I said to Pop.

"She's like a little terrier," he said. "But it's not good enough."

We were looking out over that grass.

"Droop wants to go still," I said. "I'll go as far as he will. When he says no that lets us out. After all, I gut-shot the son of a bitch."

"Mustn't do anything silly, though."

"I can kill the son of a bitch if I get a shot at him. If he comes he's got to give me a shot."

The fright P. O. M. had given us about herself had made me noisy.

"Come on," said Pop. We followed Droopy back in and it got worse and worse and I do not know about Pop but about half way I changed to the big gun and kept the safety off and my hand over the trigger guard and I was plenty nervous by the time Droopy stopped and shook his head and whispered "Hapana." It had gotten so you could not see a foot ahead and it was all turns and twists. It was really bad and the sun was only on the hillside now. We both felt good because we had made Droopy do the calling off and I was relieved as well. What we had followed him into had made my fancy shooting plans seem very silly and I knew all we had in there was Pop to blast him over with the four-fifty number two after I'd maybe miss him with that lousy four-seventy. I had no confidence in anything but its noise any more.

We were back trailing when we heard the porters on the hillside shout and we ran crashing through the grass to try to get to a high enough place to see to shoot. They waved their arms and shouted that the buffalo had come out of the reeds and gone past them and then M'Cola and Droopy were pointing and Pop had me by the sleeve trying to pull me to where I could see them and then, in the sunlight, high up on the hillside against the rocks I saw two buffalo. They shone very black in the sun and one was much bigger than the other and I remember thinking this was our bull and that he had picked up a cow and she had made the pace and kept him going. Droop had handed me the Springfield and I slipped my arm through the sling and sighting, the buff now all seen through the aperture, I froze myself inside and held the bead on the top of his shoulder and as I started to squeeze he started running and I swung ahead of him and loosed off. I saw him lower his head and jump like a bucking horse as he comes out of the chutes and as I threw the shell, slammed the bolt forward and shot again, behind him as he went out of sight, I knew I had him. Droopy and I started to run and as we were running I heard a low bellow. I stopped and yelled at Pop, "Hear him? I've got him, I tell you!"

"You hit him," said Pop. "Yes."

"Goddamn it, I killed him. Didn't you hear him bellow?"

"No."

"Listen!" We stood listening and there it came, clear, a long, moaning, unmistakable bellow.

"By God," Pop said. It was a very sad noise.

M'Cola grabbed my hand and Droopy slapped my back and all laughing we started on a running scramble, sweating, rushing, up the ridge through the trees and over rocks. I had to stop for breath, my heart pounding, and wiped the sweat off my face and cleaned my glasses.

"Kufa!" M'Cola said, making the word for dead almost explosive in its force. "N'Dio! Kufa!"

"Kufa!" Droopy said grinning.

"Kufa!" M'Cola repeated and we shook hands again before we went on climbing. Then, ahead of us, we saw him, on his back, throat stretched out to the full, his weight on his horns, wedged against a tree. M'Cola put his finger in the bullet hole in the center of the shoulder and shook his head happily.

Pop and P. O. M. came up, followed by the porters.

"By God, he's a better bull than we thought," I said.

"He's not the same bull. This is a real bull. That must have been our bull with him."

"I thought he was with a cow. It was so far away I couldn't tell."

"It must have been four hundred yards. By God, you *can* shoot that little pipsqueak."

"When I saw him put his head down between his legs and buck I knew we had him. The light was wonderful on him."

"I knew you had hit him, and I knew he wasn't the same bull. So I thought we had two wounded buffalo to deal with. I didn't hear the first bellow."

"It was wonderful when we heard him bellow," P. O. M. said. "It's such a sad sound. It's like hearing a horn in the woods."

"It sounded awfully jolly to me," Pop said. "By God, we deserve a drink on this. That was a shot. Why didn't you ever tell us you could shoot?"

"Go to hell."

"You know he's a damned good tracker, too, and what kind of a bird shot?" he asked P. O. M.

"Isn't he a beautiful bull?" P. O. M. asked.

"He's a fine one. He's not old but it's a fine head."

We tried to take pictures but there was only the little box camera and the shutter stuck and there was a bitter argument about the shutter while the light failed, and I was nervous now, irritable, righteous, pompous about the shutter and inclined to be abused because we could get no picture. You cannot live on a plane of the sort of elation I had felt in the reeds and having killed, even when it is only a buffalo, you feel a little quiet inside. Killing is not a feeling that you share and I took a drink of water and told P. O. M. I was sorry I was such a bastard about the camera. She said it was all right and we were all right again looking at the buff with M'Cola making the cuts for the headskin and we standing close together and feeling fond of each other and understanding everything, camera and all. I took a drink of the whiskey and it had no taste and I felt no kick from it.

"Let me have another," I said. The second one was all right.

We were going on ahead to camp with the chased-by-a-rhino spearsman as guide and Droop was going to skin out the head and they were going to butcher and cache the meat in trees so the hyenas would not get it. They were afraid to travel in the dark and I told Droopy he could keep my big gun. He said he knew how to shoot so I took out the shells and put on the safety and handing it to him told him to shoot. He put it to his shoulder, shut the wrong eye, and pulled hard on the trigger, and again, and again. Then I showed him about the safety and had him put it on and off and snap the gun a couple of times. M'Cola became very superior during Droopy's struggle to fire with the safety on and Droopy seemed to get much smaller. I left him the gun and two cartridges and they were all busy butchering in the dusk when we followed the spearsman and the tracks of the smaller buff, which had no blood on them, up to the top of the hill and on our way toward home. We climbed around the tops of valleys, went across gulches, up and down ravines and finally came onto the main ridge, it dark and cold in the evening, the moon not yet up, we plodded along, all tired. Once M'Cola, in the dark, loaded with Pop's heavy gun and an assortment of water bottles, binoculars, and a musette bag of books, sung out a stream of what sounded like curses at the guide who was striding ahead.

"What's he say?" I asked Pop.

"He's telling him not to show off his speed. That there is an old man in the party."

"Who does he mean, you or himself?"

"Both of us."

We saw the moon come up, smoky red over the brown hills, and we came down through the chinky lights of the village, the mud houses all closed tight, and the smells of goats and sheep, and then across the stream and up the bare slope to where the fire was burning in front of our tents. It was a cold night with much wind.

"Pursuit and Failure"

(from *Green Hills of Africa*)

Standing in front of the canvas circle of the latrine I looked, as each morning, at that fuzzy blur of stars that the romanticists of astronomers called the Southern Cross. Each morning at this moment I observed the Southern Cross in solemn ceremony.

Pop was at the car. M'Cola handed me the Springfield and I got in the front. The tragedian and his tracker were in the back. M'Cola climbed in with them.

"Good luck," Pop said. Some one was coming from toward the tents. It was P. O. M. in her blue robe and mosquito boots. "*Oh*, good luck," she said. "*Please*, good luck."

I waved and we started, the headlights showing the way to the road.

There was nothing on the salt when we came up to it after leaving the car about three miles away and making a very careful stalk. Nothing came all morning. We sat with our heads down in the blind, each covering a different direction through openings in

125

the thatched withes, and always I expected the miracle of a bull kudu coming majestic and beautiful through the open scrub to the gray, dusty opening in the trees where the salt lick was worn, grooved, and trampled. There were many trails to it through the trees and on any one a bull might come silently. But nothing came. When the sun was up and we were warmed after the misty cold of the morning I settled my rump deeper in the dust and lay back against the wall of the hole, resting against the small of my back and my shoulders and still able to see out through the slit in the blind. Putting the Springfield across my knees I noticed that there was rust on the barrel. Slowly I pulled it along and looked at the muzzle. It was freshly brown with rust.

"The bastard never cleaned it last night after that rain," I thought and, very angry, I lifted the lug and slipped the bolt out. M'Cola was watching me with his head down. The other two were looking out through the blind. I held the rifle in one hand for him to look through the breech and then put the bolt back in and shoved it forward softly, lowering it with my finger on the trigger so that it was ready to cock rather than keeping it on the safety.

M'Cola had seen the rusty bore. His face had not changed and I had said nothing but I was full of contempt and there had been indictment, evidence, and condemnation without a word being spoken. So we sat there, he with his head bent so only the bald top showed, me leaning back and looking out through the slit, and we were no longer partners, no longer good friends; and nothing came to the salt.

At ten o'clock the breeze, which had come up in the east, began to shift around and we knew it was no use. Our scent was being scattered in all directions around the blind as sure to frighten any animals as though we were revolving a searchlight in the dark. We got up out of the blind and went over to look in the dust of the lick for tracks. The rain had moistened it but it was not soaked and we saw several kudu tracks, probably made early in the night and one big bull track, long, narrow, heart-shaped; clearly, deeply cut.

We took the track and followed it on the damp reddish earth for two hours in thick bush that was like second-growth timber at home. Finally we had to leave it in stuff we could not move through. All this time I was angry about the uncleaned rifle and yet happy and eager with anticipation that we might jump the bull and get a snap at him in the brush. But we did not see him and now, in the big heat of noon, we made three long circles around some hills and finally came out into a meadow full of little, humpy Masai cattle and, leaving all shade behind, trailed back across the open country under the noon sun to the car.

Kamau, sitting in the car, had seen a kudu bull pass a hundred yards away. He was headed toward the salt lick at about nine o'clock when the wind began to be tricky, had evidently caught our scent and gone back into the hills. Tired, sweating, and feeling more sunk than angry now, I got in beside Kamau and we headed the car toward camp. There was only one evening left now, and no reason to expect we would have any better luck than we were having. As we came to camp, and the shade of the heavy trees cool as a pool, I took the bolt out of the Springfield and handed the rifle, boltless, to M'Cola without speaking or looking at him. The bolt I tossed inside the opening of our tent onto my cot.

Pop and P. O. M. were sitting under the dining tent.

"No luck?" Pop asked gently.

"Not a damn bit. Bull went by the car headed toward the salt. Must have spooked off. We hunted all over hell."

"Didn't you see anything?" P. O. M. asked. "Once we thought we heard you shoot."

"That was Garrick shooting his mouth off. Did the scouts get anything?"

"Not a thing. We've been watching both hills."

"Hear from Karl?"

"Not a word."

"I'd like to have seen one," I said. I was tired out and slipping into bitterness fast. "God damn them. What the hell did he have to blow that lick to hell for the first morning and gut-shoot a lousy bull and chase him all over the son-of-a-bitching country spooking it to holy bloody hell?"

"Bastards," said P. O. M., staying with me in my unreasonableness. "Sonsabitches."

"The Kudu"

(from *Green Hills of Africa*)

It was late afternoon now and the sky was heavy with clouds. I was wet to the waist and my socks were mud soaked. Also I was sweating from pushing on the car and from chopping.

"When do we start?" I asked.

"Tomorrow," Garrick answered without bothering to question the Roman.

"No," I said. "Tonight."

"Tomorrow," Garrick said. "Late now. One hour light." He showed me one hour on my watch.

I dictionaried. "Hunt tonight. Last hour best hour."

Garrick implied that the kudu were too far away. That it was impossible to hunt and return, all this with gestures, "Hunt tomorrow."

"You bastard," I said in English. All this time the Roman and the old man had been standing saying nothing. I shivered. It was cold with the sun under the clouds in spite of the heaviness of the air after rain.

"Old man," I said.

"Yes, Master," said the old man. Dictionary-ing carefully, I said, "Hunt kudu tonight. Last hour best hour. Kudu close?"

"Maybe."

"Hunt now?"

They talked together.

"Hunt tomorrow," Garrick put in.

"Shut up, you actor," I said. "Old man. Little hunt now?"

"Yes," said old man and Roman nodded. "Little while."

"Good," I said and went to find a shirt and undershirt and a pair of socks.

"Hunt now," I told M'Cola.

"Good," he said. "M'uzuri."

With the clean feeling of dry shirt, fresh socks and a change of boots I sat on the petrol case and drank a whiskey and water while I waited for the Roman to come back. I felt certain I was going to have a shot at kudu and I wanted to take the edge off so I would not be nervous. Also I wanted not to catch a cold. Also I wanted the whiskey for itself, because I loved the taste of it and because, being as happy as I could be, it made me feel even better.

I saw the Roman coming and I pulled the zippers up on my boots, checked the cartridges in the magazine of the Springfield, took off the foresight protector and blew through the rear aperture. Then I drank what was left in the tin cup that was on the ground by the box and stood up, checking that I had a pair of handkerchiefs in my shirt pockets.

M'Cola came carrying his knife and Pop's big glasses.

"You stay here," I said to Garrick. He did not mind. He thought we were silly to go out so late and he was glad to prove us wrong. The Wanderobo wanted to go.

"That's plenty," I said and waved the old man back and we started out of the corral with the Roman ahead, carrying a spear, then me, then M'Cola with glasses and the Mannlicher, full of solids, and last the Wanderobo-Masai with another spear.

It was after five when we struck off across the maize field and down to the stream, crossing where it narrowed in high grass a hundred yards above the dam and then, walking slowly and carefully, went up the grassy bank on the far side getting soaked to the waist as we stooped going through the wet grass and bracken. We had not been gone ten minutes and were moving carefully up the stream bank, when, without warning, the Roman grabbed my arm and pulled me bodily down to the ground as he crouched; me pulling back the bolt to cock the rifle as I dropped. Holding his breath he pointed and across the stream on the far bank at the edge of the trees was a large, gray animal, white stripes showing on his flanks and huge horns curling back from his head as he stood, broadside to us, head up, seeming to be listening. I raised the rifle but there was a bush in the way of the shot. I could not shoot over the bush without standing.

"Piga," whispered M'Cola. I shook my finger and commenced to crawl forward to be clear of the bush, sick afraid the bull would jump while I was trying to make the shot certain, but remembering Pop's "Take your time." When I saw I was clear I got on one knee, saw the bull through the aperture, marvelling at how big he looked and then, remembering not to have it matter, that it was the same as any other shot, I saw the bead centered exactly where it should be just below the top of the shoulder and squeezed off. At the roar he jumped and was going into the brush, but I knew I had hit him. I shot at a show of gray between the trees as he went in and M'Cola was shouting, "Piga! Piga!" meaning, "He's hit! He's hit!" and the Roman was slapping me on the shoulder, then he had his toga up around his neck and was running naked, and the four of us were running now, full speed, like hounds, splashing across the stream, tearing up the bank, the Roman ahead, crashing naked through the brush, then stooping and holding up a leaf with bright blood, slamming me on the back, M'Cola saying, "Damu! Damu!" blood, blood, then the deep cut tracks off to the right, me reloading, we all trailing in a dead run, it almost dark in the timber, the Roman, confused a

131

moment by the trail, making a cast off to the right, then picking up blood once more, then pulling me down again with a jerk on my arm and none of us breathing as we saw him standing in a clearing a hundred yards ahead, looking to me hard-hit and looking back, wide ears spread, big, gray, white-striped, his horns a marvel, as he looked straight toward us over his shoulder. I thought I must make absolutely sure this time, now, with the dark coming and I held my breath and shot him a touch behind the fore-shoulder. We heard the bullet smack and saw him buck heavily with the shot. M'Cola shouted, "Piga! Piga! Piga!" as he went out of sight and as we ran again, like hounds, we almost fell over something. It was a huge, beautiful kudu bull, stone-dead, on his side, his horns in great dark spirals, wide-spread and unbelievable as he lay dead five yards from where we stood when I had just that instant shot. I looked at him, big, long-legged, a smooth gray with the white stripes and the great, curling, sweeping horns, brown as walnut meats, and ivory pointed, at the big ears and the great, lovely heavy-maned neck the white chevron between his eyes and the white of his muzzle and I stooped over and touched him to try to believe it. He was lying on the side where the bullet had gone in and there was not a mark on him and he smelled sweet and lovely like the breath of cattle and the odor of thyme after rain.

Then the Roman had his arms around my neck and M'Cola was shouting in a strange high sing-song voice and Wanderobo-Masai kept slapping me on the shoulder and jumping up and down and then one after the other they all shook hands in a strange way that I had never known in which they took your thumb in their fist and held it and shook it and pulled it and held it again, while they looked you in the eyes, fiercely.

We all looked at him and M'Cola knelt and traced the curve of his horns with his finger and measured the spread with his arms and kept crooning, "Oo-oo-eee-eee," making small high noises of ecstasy and stroking the kudu's muzzle and his mane.

I slapped the Roman on the back and we went through the thumb pulling again; me pulling his thumb too. I embraced the

Wanderobo-Masai and he, after a thumb-pulling of great intensity and feeling, slapped his chest and said very proudly, "Wanderobo-Masai wonderful guide."

"Wanderobo-Masai wonderful Masai," I said.

M'Cola kept shaking his head, looking at the kudu and making the strange small noises. Then he said, "Doumi, Doumi, Doumi! B'wana Kabor Kidogo, Kidogo." Meaning this was a bull of bulls. That Karl's had been a little one, a nothing.

We all knew we had killed the other kudu that I had mistaken for this one, while this first one was lying dead from the first shot, and it seemed of no importance beside the miracle of this kudu. But I wanted to see the other.

"Come on, kudu," I said.

"He's dead," said M'Cola, "Kufa!"

"Come on."

"This one best."

"Come on."

"Measure," M'Cola pleaded. I ran the steel tape around the curve of one horn, M'Cola holding it down. It was well over fifty inches. M'Cola looked at me anxiously.

"Big! Big!" I said. "Twice as big as B'wana Kabor."

"Eee-eee," he crooned.

"Come on," I said. The Roman was off already.

We cut for where we saw the bull when I shot and there were the tracks with blood breast high on the leaves in the brush from the start. In a hundred yards we came on him absolutely dead. He was not quite as big as the first bull. The horns were as long, but narrower, but he was as beautiful, and he lay on his side, bending down the brush where he fell.

We all shook hands again, using the thumb which evidently denoted extreme emotion.

"This askari," M'Cola explained. "This bull was the policeman or bodyguard for the bigger one. He had evidently been in the timber when we had seen the first bull, had run with him, and had looked back to see why the big bull did not follow.

I wanted pictures and told M'Cola to go back to camp with the Roman and bring the two cameras, the Graflex and the cinema camera and my flashlight. I knew we were on the same side of the stream and above the camp and I hoped the Roman could make a short cut and get back before the sun set.

They went off and now, at the end of the day, the sun came out brightly below the clouds and the Wanderobo-Masai and I looked at this kudu, measured his horns smelled the fine smell of him, sweeter than an eland, even, stroked his nose, his neck, and his shoulder, marvelling at the great ears, and the smoothness and cleanness of his hide, looked at his hooves, that were built long, narrow, and springy so he seemed to walk on tiptoe, felt under his shoulder for the bullet-hole and then shook hands again while the Wanderobo-Masai told what a man he was and I told him he was my pal and gave him my best four-bladed pocket knife.

"Let's go look at the first one, Wanderobo-Masai," I said in English.

The Wanderobo-Masai nodded, understanding perfectly, and we trailed back to where the big one lay in the edge of the little clearing. We circled him, looking at him and then the Wanderobo-Masai, reaching underneath while I held the shoulder up, found the bullet hole and put his finger in. Then he touched his forehead with the bloody finger and made the speech about "Wanderobo-Masai wonderful guide!"

"Wanderobo-Masai king of guides," I said. "Wanderobo-Masai my pal."

I was wet through with sweat and I put on my raincoat that M'Cola had been carrying and left behind and turned the collar up around my neck. I was watching the sun now and worrying about it being gone before they got up with the cameras. In a little while we could hear them coming in the brush and I shouted to let them know where we were. M'Cola answered and we shouted back and forth and I could hear them talking and crashing in the brush while I would shout and watch the sun which was almost down.

Finally I saw them and I shouted to M'Cola, "Run, run," and pointed to the sun, but there was no run left in them. They had made a fast trip uphill, through heavy brush, and when I got the camera, opened the lens wide and focused on the bull the sun was only lighting the tops of the trees. I took a half a dozen exposures and used the cinema while they all dragged the kudu to where there seemed to be a little more light, then the sun was down and, obligation to try to get a picture over, I put the camera into its case and settled, happily, with the darkness into the unresponsibility of victory; only emerging to direct M'Cola in where to cut to make a full enough cape when skinning out the head-skin. M'Cola used a knife beautifully and I liked to watch him skin-out, but tonight, after I had shown him where to make the first cut, well down on the legs, around the lower chest where it joined the belly and well back over the withers I did not watch him because I wanted to re-member the bull as I had first seen him, so I went, in the dusk, to the second kudu and waited there until they came, with the flash-light and then, remembering that I had skinned-out or seen skinned-out every animal that I had ever shot, yet remembered every one exactly as he was at every moment, that one memory does not destroy another, and that the not-watching idea was only laziness and a form of putting the dishes in the sink until morning, I held the flashlight for M'Cola while he worked on the second bull and, although tired, enjoyed as always his fast, clean, delicate scalpeling with the knife, until, the cape all clear and spread back he nocked through the connection of the skull and the spine and then, twisting with the horns, swung the head loose and lifted it, cape and all, free from the neck, the cape hanging heavy and wet in the light of the electric torch that shone on his red hands and on the dirty khaki of his tunic. We left the Wanderobo-Masai, Gar-rick, the Roman, and his brother with a lantern to skin out and pack in the meat and M'Cola with a head, the old man with a head, and me with the flashlight and the two guns, we started in the dark back for camp.

"A Good Country"

(from *Green Hills of Africa*)

It is easier to keep well in a good country by taking simple precautions than to pretend that a country which is finished is still good.

A continent ages quickly once we come. The natives live in harmony with it. But the foreigner destroys, cuts down the trees, drains the water, so that the water supply is altered and in a short time the soil, once the sod is turned under, is cropped out and, next, it starts to blow away as it has blown away in every old country and as I had seen it start to blow in Canada. The earth gets tired of being exploited. A country wears out quickly unless man puts back in it all his residue and that of all his beasts. When he quits using beasts and uses machines, the earth defeats him quickly. The machine can't reproduce, nor does it fertilize the soil, and it eats what he cannot raise. A country was made to be as we found it. We are the intruders and after we are dead we may have ruined it but it will still be there and we don't know what the next changes are. I suppose they all end up like Mongolia.

I would come back to Africa but not to make a living from it. I could do that with two pencils and a few hundred sheets of the cheapest paper. But I would come back to where it pleased me to live; to really live. Not just let my life pass. Our people went to America because that was the place to go then. It had been a good country and we had made a bloody mess of it and I would go, now, somewhere else as we had always had the right to go somewhere else and as we had always gone. You could always come back. Let the others come to America who did not know that they had come too late. Our people had seen it at its best and fought for it when it was well worth fighting for. Now I would go somewhere else. We always went in the old days and there were still good places to go.

I knew a good country when I saw one. Here there was game, plenty of birds, and I liked the natives. Here I could shoot and fish. That, and writing, and reading, and seeing pictures was all I cared about doing.

"Hunters versus Soldiers"

(from *For Whom the Bell Tolls*)

"Let us go," Robert Jordan said. He started up the hill, moving carefully and taking advantage of the cover until they were out of sight. Anselmo followed him at a hundred yards distance. When they were well out of sight of the bridge, he stopped and the old man came up and went into the lead and climbed steadily through the pass, up the steep slope in the dark.

"We have a formidable aviation," the old man said happily.

"Yes."

"And we will win."

"We have to win."

"Yes. And after we have won you must come to hunt."

"To hunt what?"

"The boar, the bear, the wolf, the ibex—"

"You like to hunt?"

"Yes, man. More than anything. We all hunt in my village. You do not like to hunt?"

"No," said Robert Jordan. "I do not like to kill animals."

"With me it is the opposite," the old man said. "I do not like to kill men."

"Nobody does except those who are disturbed in the head," Robert Jordan said. "But I feel nothing against it when it is necessary. When it is for the cause."

"It is a different thing, though," Anselmo said. "In my house, when I had a house, and now I have no house, there were the tusks of boar I had shot in the lower forest. There were the hides of wolves I had shot. In the winter, hunting them in the snow. One very big one, I killed at dusk in the outskirts of the village on my way home one night in November. There were four wolf hides on the floor of my house. They were worn by stepping on them but they were wolf hides. There were the horns of ibex that I had killed in the high Sierra, and there was an eagle stuffed by an embalmer of birds of Avila, with his wings spread, and eyes as yellow and real as the eyes of an eagle alive. It was a very beautiful thing and all of those things gave me great pleasure to contemplate."

"Yes," said Robert Jordan.

"On the door of the church of my village was nailed the paw of a bear that I killed in the spring, finding him on a hillside in the snow, overturning a log with this same paw."

"When was this?"

"Six years ago. And every time I saw that paw, like the hand of a man, but with those long claws, dried and nailed through the palm to the door of the church, I received a pleasure."

"Of pride?"

"Of pride of remembrance of the encounter with the bear on that hillside in the early spring. But of the killing of a man, who is a man as we are, there is nothing good that remains."

"You can't nail his paw to the church," Robert Jordan said.

"No. Such a barbarity is unthinkable. Yet the hand of a man is like the paw of a bear."

"So is the chest of a man like the chest of a bear," Robert Jordan said. "With the hide removed from the bear, there are many similarities in the muscles."

"Yes," Anselmo said. "The gypsies believe the bear to be a brother of man."

"So do the Indians in America," Robert Jordan said. "And when they kill a bear they apologize to him and ask his pardon. They put his skull in a tree and they ask him to forgive them before they leave it."

"The gypsies believe the bear to be a brother to man because he has the same body beneath his hide, because he drinks beer, because he enjoys music and because he likes to dance."

"So also believe the Indians."

"Are the Indians then gypsies?"

"No. But they believe alike about the bear."

"Clearly. The gypsies also believe he is a brother because he steals for pleasure."

"Have you gypsy blood?"

"No. But I have seen much of them and clearly, since the movement, more. There are many in the hills. To them it is not a sin to kill outside the tribe. They deny this but it is true."

"Like the Moors."

"Yes. But the gypsies have many laws they do not admit to having. In the war many gypsies have become bad again as they were in olden times."

"They do not understand why the war is made. They do not know for what we fight."

"No," Anselmo said. "They only know now there is a war and people may kill again as in the olden times without a surety of punishment."

"You have killed?" Robert Jordan asked in the intimacy of the dark and of their day together.

"Yes. Several times. But not with pleasure. To me it is a sin to kill a man. Even Fascists whom we must kill. To me there is a great difference between the bear and the man and I do not believe the wizardry of the gypsies about the brotherhood with animals. No. I am against all killing of men."

"Yet you have killed."

"Yes. And will again. But if I live later, I will try to live in such a way, doing no harm to any one, that it will be forgiven."

"By whom?"

"Who knows? Since we do not have God here any more, neither His Son nor the Holy Ghost, who forgives? I do not know."

"You have not God any more?"

"No. Man. Certainly not. If there were God, never would He have permitted what I have seen with my eyes. Let *them* have God."

"They claim Him."

"Clearly I miss Him, having been brought up in religion. But now a man must be responsible to himself."

"Then it is thyself who will forgive thee for killing."

"I believe so," Anselmo said. "Since you put it clearly in that way I believe that must be it. But with or without God, I think it is a sin to kill. To take the life of another is to me very grave. I will do it whenever necessary but I am not of the race of Pablo."

"To win a war we must kill our enemies. That has always been true."

"Clearly. In war we must kill. But I have very rare ideas," Anselmo said.

They were walking now close together in the dark and he spoke softly, sometimes turning his head as he climbed. "I would not kill even a Bishop. I would not kill a proprietor of any kind. I would make them work each day as we have worked in the fields and as we work in the mountains with the timber, all of the rest of their lives. So they would see what man is born to. That they should sleep where we sleep. That they should eat as we eat. But above all that they should work. Thus they would learn."

"And they would survive to enslave thee again."

"To kill them teaches nothing," Anselmo said. "You cannot exterminate them because from their seed comes more with greater hatred. Prison is nothing. Prison only makes hatred. That all our enemies should learn."

"But still thou hast killed."

"Yes," Anselmo said. "Many times and will again. But not with pleasure and regarding it as a sin."

"And the sentry. You joked of killing the sentry."

"That was in joke. I would kill the sentry. Yes. Certainly and with a clear heart considering our task. But not with pleasure."

"We will leave them to those who enjoy it," Robert Jordan said. "There are eight and five. That is thirteen for those who enjoy it."

"There are many of those who enjoy it," Anselmo said in the dark. "We have many of those. More of those than of men who would serve for a battle."

"Hast thou ever been in a battle?"

"Nay," the old man said. "We fought in Segovia at the start of the movement but we were beaten and we ran. I ran with the others. We did not truly understand what we were doing, nor how it should be done. Also I had only a shotgun with cartridges of large buckshot and the *guardia civil* had Mausers. I could not hit them with buckshot at a hundred yards, and at three hundred yards they shot us as they wished as though we were rabbits. They shot much and well and we were like sheep before them." He was silent. Then asked, "Thinkest thou there will be a battle at the bridge?"

"There is a chance."

"I have never seen a battle without running," Anselmo said. "I do not know how I would comport myself. I am an old man and I have wondered."

"I will respond for thee," Robert Jordan told him.

"And hast thou been in many battles?"

"Several."

"And what thinkest thou of this of the bridge?"

"First I think of the bridge. That is my business. It is not difficult to destroy the bridge. Then we will make the dispositions for the rest. For the preliminaries. It will all be written."

"Very few of these people read," Anselmo said.

"It will be written for every one's knowledge so that all know, but also it will be clearly explained."

"I will do that to which I am assigned," Anselmo said. "But remembering the shooting in Segovia, if there is to be a battle or even much exchanging of shots, I would wish to have it very clear what I must do under all circumstances to avoid running. I remember that I had a great tendency to run at Segovia."

"We will be together," Robert Jordan told him. "I will tell you what there is to do at all times."

"Then there is no problem," Anselmo said. "I can do anything that I am ordered."

"For us will be the bridge and the battle, should there be one," Robert Jordan said and saying it in the dark, he felt a little theatrical but it sounded well in Spanish.

"It should be of the highest interest," Anselmo said and hearing him say it honestly and clearly and with no pose, neither the English pose of understatement nor any Latin bravado, Robert Jordan thought he was very lucky to have this old man and having seen the bridge and worked out and simplified the problem it would have been to surprise the posts and blow it in a normal way, he resented Golz's orders, and the necessity for them. He resented them for what they could do to him and for what they could do to this old man. They were bad orders all right for those who would have to carry them out.

And that is not the way to think, he told himself, and there is not you, and there are no people that things must not happen to. Neither you nor this old man is anything. You are instruments to do your duty. There are necessary orders that are no fault of yours and there is a bridge and that bridge can be the point on which the future of the human race can turn. As it can turn on everything that happens in this war. You have only one thing to do and you must do it. Only one thing, hell, he thought. If it were one thing it was easy. Stop worrying, you windy bastard, he said to himself. Think about something else.

So he thought about the girl Maria, with her skin, the hair and the eyes all the same golden tawny brown, the hair a little darker than the rest but it would be lighter as her skin tanned deeper, the smooth skin, pale gold on the surface with a darkness underneath.

"Duck Hunting on the
Venetian Lagoon"

(from *Across the River and Into the Trees*)

1

They started two hours before daylight, and at first, it was not necessary to break the ice across the canal as other boats had gone on ahead. In each boat, in the darkness, so you could not see, but only hear him, the poler stood in the stern, with his long oar. The shooter sat on a shooting stool fastened to the top of a box that contained his lunch and shells, and the shooter's two, or more, guns were propped against the load of wooden decoys. Somewhere, in each boat, there was a sack with one or two live mallard hens, or a hen and a drake, and in each boat there was a dog who shifted and shivered uneasily at the sound of the wings of the ducks that passed overhead in the darkness.

Four of the boats went on up the main canal toward the big lagoon to the north. A fifth boat had already turned off into a side

145

canal. Now, the sixth boat turned south into a shallow lagoon, and there was no broken water.

It was all ice, new-frozen during the sudden, windless cold of the night. It was rubbery and bending against the thrust of the boatman's oar. Then it would break as sharply as a pane of glass, but the boat made little forward progress.

"Give me an oar," the shooter in the sixth boat said. He stood up and braced himself carefully. He could hear the ducks passing in the darkness, and feel the restless lurching of the dog. To the north he heard the sound of breaking ice from the other boats.

"Be careful," the poler in the stern said. "Don't tip the boat over."

"I am a boatman, too," the shooter said.

He took the long oar the boatman handed him and reversed it so he could hold it by the blade. Holding the blade he reached forward and punched the handle through the ice. He felt the firm bottom of the shallow lagoon, put his weight on the top of the wide oar-blade, and holding with both hands and, first pulling, then shoving, until the pole-hold was well to the stern, he drove the boat ahead to break the ice. The ice broke like sheets of plate glass as the boat drove into it, and onto it, and astern the boatman shoved them ahead into the broken passage.

After a while, the shooter, who was working hard and steadily and sweating in his heavy clothes, asked the boatman, "Where is the shooting barrel?"

"Off there to the left. In the middle of the next bay."

"Should I turn for it now?"

"As you wish."

"What do you mean, as I wish? You know the water. Is there water to carry us there?"

"The tide is low. Who knows?"

"It will be daylight before we get there if we don't hurry."

The boatman did not answer.

All right, you surly jerk, the shooter thought to himself. We are going to get there. We've made two-thirds of the way now and if you are worried about having to work to break ice to pick up birds, that is altogether too bad.

"Get your back in it, jerk," he said in English.

"What?" the boatman asked in Italian.

"I said let's go. It's going to be light."

It was daylight before they reached the oaken staved hogshead sunk in the bottom of the lagoon. It was surrounded by a sloping rim of earth that had been planted with sedge and grass, and the shooter swung carefully up onto this, feeling the frozen grasses break as he stepped on them. The boatman lifted the combination shooting stool and shell box out of the boat and handed it to the shooter, who leaned over and placed it in the bottom of the big barrel.

The shooter, wearing his hip boots and an old combat jacket, with a patch on the left shoulder that no one understood, and with the slight light places on the straps, where stars had been removed, climbed down into the barrel and the boatman handed him his two guns.

He placed them against the wall of the barrel and hung his other shell bag between them, hanging it on two hooks built into the wall of the sunken barrel. Then he leaned the guns against each side of the shell bag.

"Is there water?" he asked the boatman.

"No water," the boatman said.

"Can you drink the lagoon water?"

"No. It is unhealthy."

The shooter was thirsty from the hard work of breaking the ice and driving the boat in and he felt his anger rise, and then held it, and said, "Can I help you in the boat to break ice to put out the decoys?"

"No," the boatman said and shoved the boat savagely out onto the thin sheet ice that cracked and ripped as the boat drove up onto it. The boatman commenced smashing at the ice with the blade of his oar and then started tossing decoys out to the side and behind him.

He's in a beautiful mood, the shooter thought. He's a big brute, too. I worked like a horse coming out here. He just pulled his weight and that's all. What the hell is eating him? This is his trade isn't it?

He arranged the shooting stool so he would have the maximum swing to left and right, opened a box of shells, and filled his pockets and opened another of the boxes of shells in the shell bag so he could reach into it easily. In front of him, where the lagoon lay glazed in the first light, was the black boat and the tall, heavily built boatman smashing with his oar at the ice and tossing decoys overboard as though he were ridding himself of something obscene.

It was getting lighter now and the shooter could see the low line of the near point across the lagoon. Beyond that point he knew there were two other shooting posts and far beyond it there was much more marsh and then the open sea. He loaded both his guns and checked the position of the boat that was putting out decoys.

From behind him, he heard the incoming whisper of wings and he crouched, took hold of his right hand gun with his right hand as he looked up from under the rim of the barrel, then stood to shoot at the two ducks that were dropping down, their wings set to brake, coming down dark in the gray dim sky, slanting toward the decoys.

His head low, he swung the gun on a long slant, down, well and ahead of the second duck, then without looking at the result of his shot he raised the gun smoothly, up, up ahead and to the left of the other duck that was climbing to the left and as he pulled, saw it fold in flight and drop among the decoys in the broken ice. He looked to his right and saw the first duck a black patch on the same ice. He knew he had shot carefully on the first duck, far to the right of where the boat was, and on the second, high out and to the left, letting the duck climb far up and to the left to be sure the boat was out of any line of fire. It was a lovely double, shot exactly as he should have shot, with complete consideration and respect for the position of the boat, and he felt very good as he reloaded.

"Listen," the man in the boat called. "Don't shoot toward the boat."

I'll be a sad son of a bitch, the shooter said to himself. I will indeed.

"Get your decoys out," he called to the man in the boat. "But get them out fast. I won't shoot until they are all out. Except straight overhead."

The man in the boat said nothing that could be heard.

I can't figure it, the shooter thought to himself. He knows the game. He knows I split the work, or more, coming out. I never shot a safer or more careful duck in my life than that. What's the matter with him? I offered to put the dekes out with him. The hell with him.

Out on the right now, the boatman was still chopping angrily at the ice, and tossing out the wooden decoys in a hatred that showed in every move he made.

Don't let him spoil it, the shooter told himself. There won't be much shooting with this ice unless the sun should melt it later on. You probably will only have a few birds, so don't let him spoil it for you. You don't know how many more times you will shoot ducks and do not let anything spoil it for you.

He watched the sky lightening beyond the long point of marsh, and turning in the sunken barrel, he looked out across the frozen lagoon, and the marsh, and saw the snow-covered mountains a long way off. Low as he was, no foothills showed, and the mountains rose abruptly from the plain. As he looked toward the mountains he could feel a breeze on his face and he knew, then, the wind would come from there, rising with the sun, and that some birds would surely come flying in from the sea when the wind disturbed them.

The boatman had finished putting out the decoys. They were in two bunches, one straight ahead and to the left toward where the sun would rise, and the other to the shooter's right. Now he dropped over the hen mallard with her string and anchor, and the calling duck bobbed her head under water, and raising and dipping her head, splashed water onto her back.

"Don't you think it would be good to break more ice around the edges?" the shooter called to the boatman. "There's not much water to attract them."

The boatman said nothing but commenced to smash at the jagged perimeter of ice with his oar. This ice breaking was unnecessary and the boatman knew it. But the shooter did not know it and he thought, I do not understand him but I must not let him ruin it. I must keep it entire and not let him do it. Every time you shoot now can be the last shoot and no stupid son of a bitch should be allowed to ruin it. Keep your temper, boy, he told himself.

2

But he was not a boy. He was fifty and a Colonel of Infantry in the Army of the United States and to pass a physical examination that he had to take the day before he came down to Venice for this shoot, he had taken enough mannitol hexanitrate to, well he did not quite know what to—to pass, he said to himself.

The surgeon had been quite skeptical. But he noted the readings after taking them twice.

"You know, Dick," he said. "It isn't indicated; in fact it is definitely contra-indicated in increased intra-ocular and intra-cranial pressure."

"I don't know what you are talking about," the shooter, who was not a shooter, then, except potentially, and was a Colonel of Infantry in the Army of the United States, reduced from being a general officer, said.

"I have known you a long time, Colonel. Or maybe it just seems a long time," the surgeon told him.

"It's been a long time," the Colonel said.

"We sound like song writers," the surgeon said. "But don't you ever run into anything, or let any sparks strike you, when you're really souped up on nitroglycerin. They ought to make you drag a chain like a high-octane truck."

"Wasn't my cardiograph O.K.?" the Colonel asked.

"Your cardiograph was wonderful, Colonel. It could have been that of a man of twenty-five. It might have been that of a boy of nineteen."

"Then what are you talking about?" the Colonel asked.

That much mannitol hexanitrate produced a certain amount of nausea, sometimes, and he was anxious for the interview to terminate. He was also anxious to lie down and take a seconal. I ought to write the manual of minor tactics for the heavy pressure platoon, he thought. Wish I could tell him that. Why don't I just throw myself on the mercy of the court? You never do, he told himself. You always plead them non-guilty.

"How many times have you been hit in the head?" the surgeon asked him.

"You know," the Colonel told him. "It's in my 201."

"How many times have you been hit *on* the head?"

"Oh Christ." Then he said, "You are asking for the army or as my physician?"

"As your physician. You didn't think I'd try to wind your clock, did you?"

"No, Wes. I'm sorry. Just what was it you wanted to know?"

"Concussions."

"Real ones?"

"Any time you were cold or couldn't remember afterwards."

"Maybe ten," the Colonel said. "Counting polo. Give or take three."

"You poor old son of a bitch," the surgeon said. "Colonel, sir," he added.

"Can I go now?" the Colonel asked.

151

"Yes, sir," the surgeon said. "You're in good shape."

"Thanks," the Colonel said. "Want to go on a duck shoot down in the marshes at the mouth of the Tagliamento? Wonderful shoot. Some nice Italian kids I met up at Cortina own it."

"Is that where they shoot coots?"

"No. They shoot real ducks at this one. Good kids. Good shoot. Real ducks. Mallard, pin-tail, widgeon. Some geese. Just as good as at home when we were kids."

"I was kids in twenty-nine and thirty."

"That's the first mean thing I ever heard you say."

"I didn't mean it like that. I just meant I didn't remember when duck shooting was good. I'm a city boy, too."

"That's the only God-damn trouble with you, too. I never saw a city boy yet that was worth a damn."

"You don't mean that, do you, Colonel?"

"Of course not. You know damn well I don't."

"You're in good shape, Colonel," the surgeon said. "I'm sorry I can't go on the shoot. I can't even shoot."

"Hell," said the Colonel. "That doesn't make any difference. Neither can anybody else in this army. I'd like to have you around."

"I'll give you something else to back up what you're using."

"Is there anything?"

"Not really. They're working on stuff, though."

"Let 'em work," the Colonel said.

"I think that's a laudable attitude, sir."

"Go to hell," the Colonel said. "You sure you don't want to go?"

"I get my ducks at Longchamps on Madison Avenue," the surgeon said. "It's air-conditioned in the summer and it's warm in the winter and I don't have to get up before first light and wear long-horned underwear."

"All right, City Boy. You'll never know."

"I never wanted to know," the surgeon said. "You're in good shape, Colonel, sir."

"Thanks," said the Colonel and went out.

II

Dispatches from the Field

". . . outside of writing I have two well developed talents; for sea fishing where there is a current and migratory fish and shooting with a rifle on targets at unknown ranges where the vital spots are not marked but have to be understood to be hit . . ."

—To Arnold Gingrich, Key West,
July 15, 1934

". . . I have a Thompson Sub Machine gun and we shoot sharks with it. Shot 27 in two weeks. All over ten feet long. As soon as they put their heads out we give them a burst."

—To Sara Murphy, Bimini, British West Indies,
July 10, 1935

". . . Have been shooting driven pheasants twice a week with Ben Gallagher (all wild fast birds). Have gotten on to it now. Very tough, they come high like rockets and there is still so much foliage the shots are very hard. We killed 57 last day—45 before— Thing is to get on quickly and never stop your swing. You can't get too far ahead."

—To Arnold Gingrich, Paris,
October 22, 1938

Game-Shooting in Europe

THE TORONTO DAILY STAR
NOVEMBER 3, 1923

In a popular conception Europe is a very overcrowded, overcivilized, altogether decadent place where what shooting is done is committed by fashionably dressed languid members of the aristocracy who shoot hundreds of braces of protected grouse or woodcock driven past them by beaters, between pauses for cups of tea and snapshots by the photographers for the leading illustrated weeklies.

Hunting, to be never confused with shooting under pain of social ostracism, consists of these same popular social figures donning pink coats and remaining in an upright position on top of a horse as long as possible as near as practicable to the rear of a pack of dogs who pursue a fox across the fields and meadows of the loyal and cheering peasantry.

Not so on the continent. Hunting is the great national sport of France, Belgium, Italy, Germany, Czechoslovakia and points east.

155

It is called hunting, "*la chasse*," and it means shooting. And there is plenty to shoot. Right now you would have extreme difficulty getting inside of any local train leaving Paris in any direction on Saturday or Sunday because of the thousands of hunters, their shotguns slung over the shoulders, leaving for a weekend in the country.

There is probably more game within twenty miles of Paris, France, than within twenty miles of Toronto, Ontario. There is good deer hunting in Germany, good snipe and plover shooting in the Ruhr, good partridge and rabbit shooting in almost every department of France and dangerous big-game hunting in France, Belgium and Germany.

It is a moot question whether there is any dangerous big-game hunting in Ontario, excluding the skunk and porcupine. The hunter in the woods is in fully as much danger from the moose as though he were stationed in the members' enclosure at the Woodbine taking potshots at the favorite. The black bear wants just one thing from the hunter, distance. Wolves, I understand, are a tender subject.

But there is scattered all over Europe a really dangerous game animal. He is the wild boar and every year incautious hunters are killed by him. Last year there were two hunters killed in France alone by wild boars. During the war when there was almost no shooting game flourished unchecked all over Europe. One of the best little flourishers of them all was the wild boar.

In some districts, like the wild Auvergne country and parts of the wooded slopes of the Côte d'Or down below Dôle, boars became so numerous that they destroyed crops and were a public menace. One farmer last winter had shot eighteen on his place in less than a year. The nineteenth was a big, chunky, viciously built fellow that the farmer saw out of his window one snowy morning. He took down the old shotgun and fired from the back door. The boar went into a thicket. The farmer followed him and the boar charged with a squealing grunt of rage and bowling the farmer over, savaged him with his tusks. A wild boar's tusk is like a razor and

staghounds and I have a standing invitation to hunt any fall with Herr Bugler of Triberg.

There are lots of snipe, plover and woodcock all down through the Rhineland and around the Ruhr and good duck shooting along the Rhine in the spring. Last spring, coming down the river from Mayence to Cologna, we passed great rafts of ducks. The British officers in the garrison at Cologne had very good pheasant, grouse and quail shooting in the country within sight of the great cathedral towers.

Switzerland is the home of the chamois. I have never come any closer to the chamois than in the form of a gasoline strainer. He produces a very fine grade of celluloid horn, however, which is used to ornament the alpenstocks that are sold to tourists. So he cannot be regarded as extinct. But as a popular sporting animal he is about on the same plane as the wooden carved bears that are sold in Berne.

There are still chamois but they live very high and far off and are very rarely shot and only then by an expert mountaineer and climber who works with field glasses and a telescope sight. Switzerland is a good game country though. Full of rabbits, big snow hares, partridges and the giant black cock. Black cock, or capercailzie, are a sort of glorified partridge with glossy, iridescent plumage. They are larger than a big orpington chicken, terrific flyers, and live in the forests of Switzerland and nearly all central and western Europe.

Italy is probably the only country in the world where they not only shoot but eat foxes. In the fall in Milan you will see hanging outside the door of the butcher's shop two or three deer, a long line of pheasants and quail, and one or two red foxes. Everybody who can get a license and get out hunts in Italy. The shooting is probably poorer than in any other country in Europe, because no sorts of birds seem to be protected and all day long in the hills you hear the boom of the black-powder fowling pieces and in the evening see the hunters coming into town with their game bags full of thrushes, robins, warblers, finches, woodpeckers and only an occasional game bird. Next day in the marketplace you can see long lines of songbirds of every sort hung up for sale. Even sparrows are sold.

To get a license to shoot in Italy you must have a certificate that you have never been in jail signed by the chief of police and the mayor of your hometown. This gave me some difficulty when I first applied for a shooting license. In the Abruzzi, the wild, mountainous part of Italy lying up in the country from Naples, there are still bears. There are wolves too, in the wild wastes of the Campagna, within thirty miles of Rome. It is a safe statement that there will be wolves in Italy long after they are exterminated in Ontario. For the Roman wolves have existed since long before the Christian religion first came to Rome, while less than five hundred years ago the American continent was undiscovered.

Belgium is a good shooting country and the Ardennes forest is one of the greatest wild-boar-hunting parts of Europe.

In the Pyrenees, in the south of France and north of Spain, there is perhaps the wildest country of western Europe. Every year hunters kill dozens of bears in the Pyrenees mountain fastnesses.

What is the reason for the continued existence of game in good numbers in the most highly civilized and well-settled centers of the world while in many of the United States, like Indiana, Ohio and Illinois, game is rapidly being exterminated? It is careful protection, rigidly enforced closed seasons, and the fact of government-owned forests, which are really farmed for timber rather than cut over and denuded of trees. Indiana was once a timber country. So was the Lower Peninsula of Michigan. Today there is hardly a patch of virgin timber in the Upper Peninsula of Michigan. Michigan deer hunters are already going north into Ontario. Ontario's supply of game seems inexhaustible. But wait until the steady hunting, the destruction of timber and the forest fires have kept up for fifty years. See the result that has been obtained in the States by the motorcar that allows a party to hunt over a hundred miles where they used to be able to hunt over five. The prairie chicken, one of the finest game birds, has been practically wiped out. Quail have been practically exterminated in many states. The curlew has gone. The wild turkey has gone.

But France will always be a game country. For there are forests in France that were here in Caesar's time. More important still, there are new forests in France that were not there in Napoleon's time. Even more important, there will be new forests, a hundred years from now, where today M. Poincaré has looked on only scarred hillsides. And all the forests will be full of game.

The Frenchman likes to hunt. If the game falls off he wants to know the reason why.

A. D. in Africa: A Tanganyika Letter

Esquire
APRIL, 1934

To write this sort of thing you need a typewriter. To describe, to narrate, to make funny cracks you need a typewriter. To fake along, to stall, to make light reading, to write a good piece, you need luck, two or more drinks and a typewriter. Gentlemen, there is no typewriter.

The air-mail leaves tomorrow night. Your amœbic dysentery correspondent is in bed, fully injected with emetine, having flown four hundred miles to Nairobi via Arusha from where the outfit is camped on the Serenea river on the far side of the Serengeti plain. Cause of flight, a. d. Cause of a. d. unknown. Symptoms of a. d. run from weakly insidious through spectacular to phenomenal. I believe the record is held by a Mr. McDonald with 232 movements in the twenty-four hours although many old a. d. men claim the McDonald record was never properly audited.

According to Dr. Anderson the difficulty about a. d. is to diagnose it. My own diagnosis was certainly faulty. Leaning against a tree two days ago shooting flighting sand-grouse as they came into a water hole near camp after ten days of what Dr. Anderson says was a. d. all the time, I became convinced that though an unbeliever I had been chosen as the one to bear our Lord Buddha when he should be born again on earth. While flattered at this, and wondering how much Buddha at that age would resemble Gertrude Stein, I found the imminence of the event made it difficult to take high incoming birds and finally compromised by reclining against the tree and only accepting crossing shots. This, the coming-of-Buddha symptom, Dr. Anderson describes as prolapsus.

Anyway, no matter how you get it, it is very easily cured. You feel the good effects of the emetine within six hours and the remedy, continued, kills the amœba the way quinine kills the malarial parasite. Three days from now we'll fly back to join the outfit in the country to the south of Ngocongoro where we are going to hunt greater Kuda. But, as stated, there is no typewriter; they won't let you drink with this; and if the reader finds this letter more dysenteric than the usual flow, lay it to the combination of circumstances.

The general run of this highland country is the finest I have ever seen. When there has been rain the plains roll green against the blue hills the way the western end of Nebraska lifts as you approach Wyoming when it has gone too long without rain. It is a brown land like Wyoming and Montana but with greater roll and distance. Much of the upland bush country that you hunt through looks exactly like an abandoned New England orchard until you top a hill and see the orchard runs on for fifty miles. Nothing that I have ever read has given any idea of the beauty of the country or the still remaining quantity of game.

On the Serengeti we struck the great migration of the wildebeeste. Where they were grazing the plain was green after a nine months' drought and it was black with the bison shaped antelope as far as you could see in all directions during a full day in the truck. The Game Department of Tanganyika estimates the herd at three million. Following them and living on the fringe of the herd were the lions, the spotted hyenas and the jackals.

Going out at sunrise every morning we would locate lions by the vultures circling above a kill. Approaching you would see the jackals trotting away and hyenas going off in that drag belly obscene gallop, looking back as they ran. If the birds were on the ground you knew the lions were gone.

Sometimes we met them in the open plain on their way toward a gully or shallow water course to lie up for the day. Sometimes we saw them on a high knoll in the plain with the herd grazing not half a mile away, lying sleepy and contemptuous looking over the country. More often we saw them under the shade of a tree or saw their great round heads lift up out of the grass of a shallow donga as they heard the noise of the truck. In two weeks and three days in lion country we saw 84 lions and lionesses. Of these twenty were maned lions.

We shot the twenty-third, the forty-seventh, the sixty-fourth and the seventy-ninth. All were shot on foot, three were killed in bush country to the west of the Serengeti and one on the plain itself. Three were full black maned lions and one was a lioness. She was in heat and when the big lion she was with was hit and had gotten into cover the lioness took up her position outside the thick bush. She wanted to charge and it was impossible to go after the lion without killing her first. I broke her neck with a 220 grain .30-06 solid at thirty yards.

At this point Dr. Anderson just came in and administered another injection of emetine and offered the information that when you take emetine you can't think coherently. So this may be a good place to knock off. Had been feeling that too for some time.

In the next letter I will attempt to discuss whether lion shooting in Tanganyika is a sport or not; go into the difference between lion and leopard hunting, have a few remarks on the buffalo and try to get in a lot of facts. This letter has been pretty well emetined.

As far as bag goes, if anyone is interested, we have good heads of Eland, Waterbuck, Grant Robertsi and other gazelles. A fine roan antelope, two big leopard, and excellent, if not record, impalla; also the limit all around on cheetah. They are much too nice an animal to shoot and I will never kill another.

On the other hand we shot thirty-five hyena out of the lot that follow the wildebeeste migration to keep after the cows that are about to calve and wish we had ammunition to kill a hundred.

In three days we start out for rhino, buffalo again, lesser and greater Kudu, and sable antelope.

Dr. Anderson, a little emetine please.

Shootism versus Sport:
The Second Tanganyika Letter

Esquire
JUNE, 1934

There are two ways to murder a lion. One is to shoot him from a motor car, the other, to shoot him at night with a flashlight from a platform or the shelter of a thorn boma, or blind, as he comes to feed on a bait placed by the shootist or his guide. (Tourists who shoot in Africa are called shootists to distinguish them from sportsmen.) These two ways to murder lion rank, as sport, with dynamiting trout or harpooning swordfish. Yet many men who go to Africa and return to think of themselves as sportsmen and big game hunters, have killed lions from motor cars or from blinds.

The Serengeti plain is the great lion country of present day Africa and the Serengeti is a motor car proposition. The distances between water are too great for it to have been reached and hunted in the old foot safari days, and that was what preserved it. The

167

game migrations, which are determined by the food which is produced by an often casual and unpredictable rainfall, are movements over hundreds of miles, and you may drive seventy-five or a hundred miles over a brown, dry, parched, dusty waste without seeing a herd of game, to come suddenly onto a rise of green horizon broken and edged with the black of wildebeeste as far as you can see. It is because of these distances that you must use the motor car in hunting the Serengeti, since your camp must be on a water hole and the game may be over half a day's march away on the plain.

Now a lion, when you locate him in the morning after he has fed, will have only one idea if he sees a man, to get away into cover where the man will not trouble him. Until he is wounded, that lion will not be dangerous unless you come on him unexpectedly, so closely that you startle him, or unless he is on a kill and does not want to leave it.

If you approach the lion in a motor car, the lion will not see you. His eyes can only distinguish the outline or silhouette of objects, and, because it is illegal to shoot from a motor car, this object means nothing to him. If anything, since the practice of shooting a zebra and dragging it on a rope behind the motor car as a bait for lion in order to take photographs, the motor car may seem a friendly object. For a man to shoot at a lion from the protection of a motor car, where the lion cannot even see what it is that is attacking him, is not only illegal but is a cowardly way to assassinate one of the finest of all game animals.

But supposing, unexpectedly, as you are crossing the country, you see a lion and a lioness say a hundred yards from the car. They are under a thorn tree and a hundred yards behind them is a deep donga, or dry, reed-filled water course, that winds across the plain for perhaps ten miles and gives perfect cover in the daytime to all the beasts of prey that follow the game herds.

You sight the lions from the car; you look the male over and decide he is shootable. You have never killed a lion. You are allowed to kill only two lions on the Serengeti and you want a lion with a full mane, as black as possible. The white hunter says quietly:

"I believe I'd take him. We might beat him but he's a damned fine lion."

You look at the lion under the tree. He looks very close, very calm, very, very big and proudly beautiful. The lioness has flattened down on the yellow grass and is swinging her tail parallel to the ground.

"All right," says the white hunter.

You step out of the car from beside the driver on the side away from the lion, and the white hunter gets out on the same side from the seat behind you.

"Better sit down," he says. You both sit down and the car drives away. As the car starts to move off you have a very different feeling about lions than you have ever had when you saw them from the motor car.

As the end of the car is past, you see that the lioness has risen and is standing so that you cannot see the lion clearly.

"Can't see him," you whisper. As you say it you see that the lions have seen you. He has turned away and is trotting off and she is still standing, the tail swinging wide.

"He'll be in the donga," the white hunter says.

You stand up to shoot and the lioness turns. The lion stops and looks back. You see his great head swing toward you, his mouth wide open and his mane blowing in the wind. You hold on his shoulder, start to flinch, correct, hold your breath and squeeze off. You don't hear the gun go off but you hear a crack like the sound of a policeman's club on a rioter's head and the lion is down.

"You've got him. Watch the lioness."

She has flattened down facing you so that you see her head, the ears back, the long yellow of her is flat out along the ground and her tail is now flailing straight up and down.

"I think she's going to come," the white hunter says. "If she comes, sit down to shoot."

"Should I bust her?" you say.

"No. Maybe she won't come. Wait till she starts to come."

You stand still and see her and beyond her the bulk of the big lion, on his side now, and finally she turns slowly and goes off and out of sight into the donga.

"In the old days," the white hunter said, "the rule was to shoot the lioness first. Damned sensible rule."

The two of you walk toward the lion with your guns ready. The car comes up and the gunbearers join you. One of them throws a stone at the lion. He doesn't move. You lower the guns and go up to him.

"You got him in the neck," the white hunter says. "Damned good shooting." There is blood coming from the thick hair of his mane where the camel flies are crawling. You regret the camel flies.

"It was a lucky one," you say.

You say nothing about having squeezed off from his shoulder, and then, suddenly, a strain is over and people are shaking your hand.

"Better keep an eye out for the old lady," the white hunter says. "Don't wander over too far that way."

You are looking at the dead lion; at his wide head and the dark shag of his mane and the long, smooth, yellow sheathed body, the muscles still twitching and running minutely under the skin. He is a fine hide and all that but he was a damned wonderful looking animal when he was alive—it was a shame he should always have had the camel flies, you think.

All right. That is the nearest to a sporting way to use a motor car after lion. Once you are on the ground and the car is gone, lion hunting is the same as it always was. If you wound the lion in any but a vital spot he will make for the shelter of the donga and then you will have to go after him. At the start, if you can shoot carefully and accurately and know where to shoot, the odds are ten to one in your favor against anything untoward happening, provided you do not have to take a running shot at first. If you wound the lion and he gets into cover it is even money you will be mauled when you go in after him. A lion can still cover one hundred yards so fast toward you that there is barely time for two aimed shots before he is on you. After he has the first bullet, there is no nervous shock to further wounds, and you have to kill him stone dead or he will keep coming.

If you shoot as you should on the Serengeti, having the car drive off as you get out, the chances are that the first shot will be a moving shot, as the lions will move off when they see the man on foot. That means that unless you are a good or a very lucky shot there will be a wounded lion and a possible charge. So do not let anyone tell you that lion shooting, if you hunt big maned lions, who, being super-fine trophies, will obviously have been hunted before and be adept at saving their hides, is no longer a sporting show. It will be exactly as dangerous as you choose to make it. The only way the danger can be removed or mitigated is by your ability to shoot, and that is as it should be. You are out to kill a lion, on foot and cleanly, not to be mauled. But you will be more of a sportsman to come back from Africa without a lion than to shoot one from the protection of a motor car, or from a blind at night when the lion is blinded by a light and cannot see his assailant.

Clarence Hemingway, EH's father, on a hunting trip in the Great Smoky Mountains, North Carolina, 1891. He holds a musket in his right hand; trophies, a black bear skin, and deer antlers hang in the background.

Clarence with Ernest in Northern Michigan, 1900.

EH "The Little Hunter," 1903.

Ernest, age 4, standing in front of a tent holding a large owl.

Ernest Hall, grandfather and namesake of Ernest, with EH (with gun) and his sisters, Ursula and Marcelline, 1904.

Ernest at Walloon Lake, about 1913, with his father's lever-action shotgun and willow grouse.

Ernest (at left) and his friend, Harold Sampson, with the 14-pound porcupine they killed in Bacon's woods, 1913. EH holds his first gun, a 20-gauge shotgun.

Ernest and his younger brother, Leicester, in Oak Park, ca. 1920.

Ernest and his second wife, Pauline Pfeiffer, ca. 1927.

Ernest with his elk and grizzly bear trophies outside the main lodge at the Nordquist ranch, 1932.

Ernest with his lion on the Serengeti Plain, 1933–1934 safari.

Pauline (P.O.M.) with her lion on the Serengeti Plain, 1933–1934 safari.

EH with a cape buffalo, 1933–1934 safari.

EH beaming with his kudu and roan antelope trophies, 1933–1934 safari.

From left to right: Pauline, Tommy Shevlin, Patrick, Mrs. Shevlin and EH with Ernest's grizzly bear, 1936.

From left to right: Gregory, Jack, EH, Martha Gellhorn and Patrick embarking on a pheasant shoot in Sun Valley, 1940. (Photo by Lloyd Arnold. Used by permission of Lloyd Arnold/Hutton Archives/Getty Images)

EH takes aim for a publicity shoot (he always shot with his glasses) in Sun Valley. (Photo by Lloyd Arnold. Used by permission of Lloyd Arnold/Hutton Archives/Getty Images)

EH with a large pheasant, Sun Valley, 1940. (Photo by Robert Capa. Used by permission of Robert Capa & Magnum Photos)

EH with Pauline's 6.5 Mannlicher rifle in Sun Valley, ca. 1940. (Photo by Lloyd Arnold. Used by permission of Lloyd Arnold/Hutton Archives/Getty Images)

EH teaching Patrick (at left) and Gregory to shoot birds, Sun Valley. (Photo by Lloyd Arnold. Used by permission of Lloyd Arnold/Hutton Archives/Getty Images)

EH and Martha Gellhorn (third and fourth from left) returning from a successful antelope hunt, Sun Valley, 1940. (Photo by Lloyd Arnold. Used by permission of Lloyd Arnold/Hutton Archives/ Getty Images)

EH bird shooting in Sun Valley, 1941. (Photo by Robert Capa. Used by permission of Robert Capa & Magnum Photos)

EH with Gregory and the antelope from "The Shot," 1941. (Photo by Lloyd Arnold. Used by permission of Lloyd Arnold/Hutton Archives/Getty Images)

EH and Gregory taking a break on Silver Creek, 1941. (Photo by Robert Capa. Used by permission of Robert Capa & Magnum Photos)

"General Hemingway" and his troops rabbit hunting on the Freer Farm. (Photo by Lloyd Arnold. Used by permission of Lloyd Arnold/Hutton Archives/Getty Images)

Gregory shooting flying fish from the bow of the *Pilar*, 1943.

EH returning from a round at his shooting club in Cuba.

Papa measures the antler spread of Patrick's first big game kill - an Idaho mule deer buck, October 1946. (Photo by Lloyd Arnold. Used by permission of Lloyd Arnold/Hutton Archives/Getty Images)

EH (kneeling) and Gary Cooper receiving birds from their dogs at
Sun Valley, fall of 1940. (Photo by Lloyd Arnold. Used by permission of Lloyd Arnold/Hutton Archives/Getty Images)

EH and Jane Russell "shooting" in Sun Valley, ca. 1947–1948.
(Photo by Lloyd Arnold. Used by permission of Lloyd Arnold/
Hutton Archives/Getty Images)

From left to right: Philip Percival, EH, and Denis Zaphiro on the African safari of 1953–1954.

EH setting out to hunt with his tracker and his gun bearer, 1953–1954 safari.

EH readies himself to shoot a charging rhino, 1953–1954 safari. (Photo by Earl Theisen. Used by permission of Earl Theisen Archives & Roxann E. Livingston)

EH stands over the fallen rhino, 1953–1954 safari. (Photo by Earl Theisen. Used by permission of Earl Theisen Archives & Roxann E. Livingston)

EH tracking lion spoor, 1953–1954 safari.

Miss Mary and her lion, 1953–1954 safari.

Patrick, Mary, and EH look towards Mount Kilimanjaro, 1953–1954 safari. (Used by permission of the Estate of Ernest Hemingway)

EH with a fine impala, 1953–1954 safari. (Used by permission of the Estate of Ernest Hemingway)

EH throws clay pigeons for a friend, Idaho, late 1950s.

EH, a solitary hunter in the woods near Ketchum, in the final year
of his life. (Used by permission of John Bryson)

Notes on Dangerous Game:
The Third Tanganyika Letter

Esquire
JULY, 1934

In the ethics of shooting dangerous game is the premise that the trouble you shoot yourself into you must be prepared to shoot yourself out of. Since a man making his first African shoot will have a white hunter, as a non-native guide is called, to counsel him and aid him when he is after dangerous animals, and since the white hunter has the responsibility of protecting him no matter what trouble he gets into, the shooter should do exactly what the white hunter tells him to do.

If you make a fool of yourself all that you get is mauled but the white hunter who has a client wounded or killed loses, or seriously impairs, his livelihood. So when the white hunter begins to trust you and let you take chances, that is a mark of confidence and you should not abuse it. For any good man would rather take chances

173

any day with his life than his livelihood and that is the main point about professionals that amateurs seem never to appreciate.

There are two white hunters in Africa who not only have never had a client mauled—there are many such, but these two have never been mauled themselves; and there are very few of these. It is true that Philip Percival had a buffalo die with his head in the now ample Percival lap, and that Baron von Blixen, if there were any justice for elephants, would have been trampled to death at least twice. But the point is that they do not get mauled and that their clients get record heads, record tusks and super lions year after year. They simply happen to be super hunters and super shots. (*There are too many supers in these last two sentences. Re-write them yourselves lads and see how easy it is to do better than Papa. Thank you. Exhilarating feeling, isn't it?*)

Both mask their phenomenal skill under a pose of nervous incapacity which serves as an effective insulation and cover for their truly great pride in the reserve of deadliness that they live by. (*All right now, better that one. Getting harder, what? Not too hard you say? Good. Perhaps you're right.*) Blix, who can shoot partridges flying with a .450 No. 2 Express rifle will say, "I use the hair trigger because my hand is always shaking so, what?" Or, stopping a charging rhino at ten yards, remarking apologetically to his client who happened to have his rifle already started back to camp by the gun-bearer, "I could not let him come forever, what?"

(*You see, this is where Papa scores. Just as you learn to better one of those awful sentences, with too many supers or too many verys in it and you think he's gone wa-wa on you, you find that it is the thing he is writing about that is interesting. Not the way it's written. Any of you lads can go out there and write twice as good a piece, what?*)

Philip, who swears by the .450 No. 2 as the only, or at least lightest, stopper for a man to use on animals that will "come," killed all his own lions with a .256 Mannlicher when he had only his own life to look after. I have seen him, careful, cautious, as wary about procedure as Saleri, Marcial Lalanda, or any of the old masters of chance controlling, light up like a schoolboy at the approach of vacation, when all the safe and sane methods were finally exhausted or rendered impractical and there was no choice but to go in after him as he went in after them in the old days before it was a matter of the safety of the client. (*Excuse me, Mr. P. You see I do this for a living. We all have to do a lot of things for a living. But we're still drinking their whiskey, aren't we?*)

Many people want not to shoot but to have shot dangerous game. These people, regardless of their means, usually make the African shoot only once, and their white hunter usually fires as many or more shots than his client does. A very good standard by which to judge your real effectiveness against buffalo, rhino, elephant, lion and leopard is to keep track of how many times your white hunter shot on the safari. (*You shot twice, Mr. P. Correct me if I'm wrong. Once at that leopard's mate when she broke back and you spun her over like a rabbit, and the other time when we caught the bull in the open and had two down and the third bull with four solids in him going at that same gallop, all one solid piece, the neck a part of the shoulders, dusty black and the horns blacker, the head not tossing in the gallop. You figured he would make the bush so you shot and the gallop changed into a long slide forward on his nose.*)

Philip Percival ranks leopard as more dangerous than lion for these reasons. They are nearly always met unexpectedly, usually when you are hunting impala or buck. They usually give you only a running shot which means more of a chance of wounding than killing. They will charge nine times out of ten when wounded, and they come so fast that no man can be sure of stopping them with a rifle. They use their claws, both fore and hind when mauling and make for the face so that the eyes are endangered, whereas the lion grabs with the claws and bites, usually for the arm, shoulders or thigh. The most effective stopper for a leopard is a shotgun and you should not fire until the animal is within ten yards. It does not matter what size shot is used at that range. Birdshot is even more effective than buckshot as it hangs together to blow a solid hole.

(Mr. P. took the top of the head off one once with a load of number sevens and the leopard came right on by and on for fifteen yards. Didn't know he was dead it seems. Tripped on a blade of grass or something finally.)

Personally, so far, and it is from a very minute quantity of experience indeed—the killing of four of them—I cannot see the buffalo as comparing in dangerous possibilities to either lion or leopard. We twice saw lion catch and kill wildebeeste. This is a very rare thing. Philip Percival had seen lion kill only once before in all his years of hunting. It was while he was out with Mr. Prentice Gray, who recorded the occurrence, I believe. The sight of that speed, that unbelievable smooth rush the lioness made to close the gap between herself and the fast galloping, though ungainly, antelope made me see what a charge from a slightly wounded lion could be if allowed to get under way. The buffalo, on the other hand, seemed unbelievably slow compared to a Spanish fighting bull, and I see no reason why a man who could wait for him as he came could not be sure of blowing the front of his head in if he let him get close and shot carefully with a heavy enough rifle. Certainly a tunnel in thick bush, or high reeds, or any dense cover can make the wounded buffalo dangerous, but that is a case of circumstances rather than the animal, and in the same circumstances a lion would be much more deadly. In the open a lion or leopard is a hundred times more dangerous.

The buffalo has courage, vindictiveness and an incredible ability to absorb punishment but I believe that in the bull ring he would be more like the big truck that comes charging in during the intermission to water the dusty sand than like the light hoofed, quick whirling, fast charging fighting bull.

Of course, he is not an animal of the open and you must take him where you find him and follow him where he goes, and he goes into bad places, but the point was to compare the inherent danger in the actual animals on an equal terrain—not in the peculiar circumstances under which he must be dealt with. *(There won't be any more asides you will be glad to hear. Am going to write Mr. P. a let-*

ter instead. The asides were put in when I read this over on the boat. Got to missing him.)

To me, also, and the experience it must be again stated is profoundly limited, the rhino is a joke. He may be a bad joke, too, but his atrociously poor eyesight gives the hunter an advantage over him that his bulk, his really remarkable speed and agility, and his sometimes idiotic pugnacity cannot overcome unless aided by advantage of terrain. Many times the rhino will have this advantage which will usually consist in encountering him on one of the paths or tunnels he has made through otherwise impossible tall grass and bush, and then he is as dangerous as a vindictive, horned, locomotive. He is, too, very fast. I believe he is faster than a buffalo. But fundamentally, to me, he seems a dangerous practical joke let loose by nature and armed with a horn which the Chinese pay high prices for to grind up and use as an aphrodisiac, and the pursuit of which by white and native hunters has made him shy and furtive in his habits and driven him from the plains to the broken hills and high mountain forests—where he can grow his horn and browse in peace, and where, incidentally, he is much better hunting.

Elephant I have never shot so I cannot write of them even to give the questionable impressions of the greenhorn. We plan to go out again to Kenya for six months next year to try to get a really good one, to hunt buffalo and rhino, and to see how far wrong first impressions of these were, and to try to get a good bull sable. Meantime, I know nothing about elephant from personal experience, and since notes on dangerous game by a man who has never hunted elephant are like campaign impressions of a bloke who has never seen a major engagement, that is the sort of notes these notes will have to be.

(There turns out to be one more of these. One night when we were eating supper at Mombasa after fishing, A. V. and Mr. P. and I were talking about writing these letters and I suggested Alfred write one about hunting elephant with Blix before he started to write on racing. I was writing on rhino and buffalo, etc., I said. Mr. P., who was on his first deep sea fishing

trip, didn't say much, but the next day we got into a big school of large dol-
phin and caught about 15 before the lousy boat broke down. Mr. P. got so
excited that his legs shook, he screwed the reel brake backwards until it
stuck, he had dolphin jumping into, out of, and over the boat. Sometimes
he jerked the bait out of their mouths; occasionally he let them swallow it,
but always he had a dolphin jumping on his line.

"How do you like it, Pop?" I asked him.

"God," he said, "I haven't had so much fun since the day you shot
the buffalo." Then, a little later, "I'm going to write an article on it for
Esquire. Call it Dolphin Fishing by One Who Knows.")

Remembering Shooting-Flying:
A Key West Letter

Esquire
FEBRUARY, 1935

There is a heavy norther blowing; the gulf is too rough to fish and there is no shooting now. When you are through work it is nearly dark and you can ride out on the boulevard by the sea and throw clay targets with a hand trap against this gale and they will dip and jump and rise into strange angles like a jacksnipe in the wind. Or you can throw them out with the gale behind them and they will go like a teal over the water. Or you can get down below the sea wall and have some one throw them out high over your head riding the wind, but if you puff one into black dust you can not pretend it was an old cock pheasant unless you are a better pretender than I am. The trouble is there isn't any thud, nor is there the line of bare trees, nor are you standing on a wet, leaf-strewn road, nor do you hear the beaters, nor the racket when a cock gets up and, as he tops

179

the trees, you are on him, then ahead of him, and at the shot he turns over and there is that thump when he lands. Shooting driven pheasants is worth whatever you pay for it.

But when you cannot shoot you can remember shooting and I would rather stay home, now, this afternoon and write about it than go out and sail clay saucers in the wind, trying to break them and wishing they were what they're not.

When you have been lucky in your life you find that just about the time the best of the books run out (and I would rather read again for the first time *Anna Karenina, Far Away and Long Ago, Buddenbrooks, Wuthering Heights, Madame Bovary, War and Peace, A Sportsman's Sketches, The Brothers Karamazov, Hail and Farewell, Huckleberry Finn, Winesburg, Ohio, La Reine Margot, La Maison Tellier, Le Rouge et le Noire, La Chartreuse de Parme, Dubliners*, Yeats's *Autobiographies* and a few others than have an assured income of a million dollars a year) you have a lot of damned fine things that you can remember. Then when the time is over in which you have done the things that you can now remember, and while you are doing other things, you find that you can read the books again and, always, there are a few, a very few, good new ones. Last year there was *La Condition Humaine* by André Malraux. It was translated, I do not know how well, as *Man's Fate*, and sometimes it is as good as Stendhal and that is something no prose writer has been in France for over fifty years.

But this is supposed to be about shooting, not about books, although some of the best shooting I remember was in Tolstoi and I have often wondered how the snipe fly in Russia now and whether shooting pheasants is counter-revolutionary. When you have loved three things all your life, from the earliest you can remember; to fish, to shoot and, later, to read; and when, all your life, the necessity to write has been your master, you learn to remember and, when you think back you remember more fishing and shooting and reading than anything else and that is a pleasure.

You can remember the first snipe you ever hit walking on the prairie with your father. How the jacksnipe rose with a jump and you hit him on the second swerve and had to wade out into a slough after him and brought him in wet, holding him by the bill, as proud as a bird dog, and you can remember all the snipe since in many places. You can remember the miracle it seemed when you hit your first pheasant when he roared up from under your feet to top a sweet briar thicket and fell with his wings pounding and you had to wait till after dark to bring him into town because they were protected, and you can feel the bulk of him still inside your shirt with his long tail up under your armpit, walking in to town in the dark along the dirt road that is now North Avenue where the gypsy wagons used to camp when there was prairie out to the Des Plaines river where Wallace Evans had a game farm and the big woods ran along the river where the Indian mounds were.

I came by there five years ago and where I shot that pheasant there was a hot dog place and filling station and the north prairie, where we hunted snipe in the spring and skated on the sloughs when they froze in the winter, was all a subdivision of mean houses, and in the town, the house where I was born was gone and they had cut down the oak trees and built an apartment house close out against the street. So I was glad I went away from there as soon as I did. Because when you like to shoot and fish you have to move often and always further out and it doesn't make any difference what they do when you are gone.

The first covey of partridges I ever saw, they were ruffed grouse but we called them partridges up there, was with my father and an Indian named Simon Green and we came on them dusting and feeding in the sun beside the grist mill on Horton's Creek in Michigan. They looked as big as turkeys to me and I was so excited with the whirr of the wings that I missed both shots I had, while my father, shooting an old lever action Winchester pump, killed five out of the covey and I can remember the Indian picking them up and laughing. He was an old fat Indian, a great admirer of my father, and when I look back at that shooting I am a great admirer of my father too. He was a beautiful shot, one of the fastest I have ever seen; but he was too nervous to be a great money shot.

Then I remember shooting quail with him when I do not think I could have been more than ten years old, and he was showing me off, having me shoot pigeons that were flying around a barn, and some way I broke the hammer spring in my single barrel 20 gauge, and the only gun down there at my Uncle's place in Southern Illinois that no one was shooting was a big old L. C. Smith double that weighed, probably, about nine pounds. I could not hit anything with it and it kicked me so it made my nose bleed. I was afraid to shoot it and I got awfully tired carrying it and my father had left me standing in a thickety patch of timber while he was working out the singles from a covey we had scattered. There was a red bird up in a tree and then I looked down and under the tree was a quail, freshly dead. I picked it up and it was still warm. My father had evidently hit it when the covey went up with a stray pellet and it had flown this far and dropped. I looked around to see nobody was in sight and then, laying the quail down by my feet, shut both my eyes and pulled the trigger on that old double barrel. It kicked me against the tree and when I opened it up I found it had doubled and fired both barrels at once and my ears were ringing and my nose was bleeding. But I picked the quail up, reloaded the gun, wiped my nose and set out to find my father. I was sick of not hitting any.

"Did you get one, Ernie?"

I held it up.

"It's a cock," he said. "See his white throat? It's a beauty."

But I had a lump in my stomach that felt like a baseball from lying to him and that night I remember crying with my head under the patchwork quilt after he was asleep because I had lied to him. If he would have waked up I would have told him, I think. But he was tired and sleeping heavily. I never told him.

So I won't think any more about that but I remember now how I broke the spring in the 20 gauge. It was from snapping the hammer on an empty chamber practicing swinging on the pigeons after they wouldn't let me shoot any more. And some older boys came along the road when I was carrying the pigeons from the barn to the house and one of them said I didn't shoot those pigeons. I called him a liar and the smaller of the two whipped hell out of me. That was an unlucky trip.

On a day as cold as this you can remember duck shooting in the blind, hearing their wings go whichy-chu-chu-chu in the dark before daylight. That is the first thing I remember of ducks; the whistly, silk tearing sound the fast wingbeats make; just as what you remember first of geese is how slow they seem to go when they are traveling, and yet they are moving so fast that the first one you ever killed was two behind the one you shot at, and all that night you kept waking up and remembering how he folded up and fell. While the woodcock is an easy bird to hit, with a soft flight like an owl, and if you do miss him he will probably pitch down and give you another shot. But what a bird to eat flambé with armagnac cooked in his own juice and butter, a little mustard added to make a sauce, with two strips of bacon and pommes soufflé and Corton, Pommard, Beaune, or Chambertin to drink.

Now it is colder still and we found ptarmigan in the rocks on a high plain above and to the left of the glacier by the Madelenerhaus in the Vorarlberg with it blowing a blizzard and the next day we followed a fox track all day on skis and saw where he had caught a ptarmigan underneath the snow. We never saw the fox.

There were chamois up in that country too and black cock in the woods below the timber-line and big hares that you found sometimes at night when we were coming home along the road. We ate them jugged and drank Tyroler wine. And why, today, remember misses?

There were lots of partridges outside of Constantinople and we used to have them roasted and start the meal with a bowl of caviar, the kind you never will be able to afford again, pale grey, the grains as big as buck shot and a little vodka with it, and then the partridges, not overdone, so that when you cut them there was the

juice, drinking Caucasus burgundy, and serving French fried potatoes with them and then a salad with roquefort dressing and another bottle of what was the number of that wine? They all had
numbers. Sixty-one I think it was.

And did you ever see the quick, smooth-lifting, reaching flight
the lesser bustard has, or make a double on them, right and left, or
shoot at flighting sand grouse coming to water early in the morning
and see the great variety of shots they give and hear the cackling
sound they make when flighting, a little like the noise of prairie
chickens on the plains when they go off, fast beat of wings and
soar, fast beat of wings and soar stiff-winged, and see a coyote
watching you a long way out of range and see an antelope turn and
stare and lift his head when he hears the shotgun thud? Sand
grouse, of course, fly nothing like a prairie chicken. They have a
cutting, swooping flight like pigeons but they make that grouse-
like cackle, and with the lesser bustard and the teal, there is no
bird to beat them for pan, the griddle or the oven.

So you recall a curlew that came in along the beach one time in
a storm when you were shooting plover, and jumping teal along a
water course that cut a plain on a different continent, and having
a hyena come out of the grass when you were trying to stalk up on a
pool and see him turn and look at ten yards and let him have it with
the shotgun in his ugly face, and standing, to your waist in water,
whistling a flock of golden plover back, and then, back in the winter woods, shooting ruffed grouse along a trout stream where only
an otter fished now, and all the places and the different flights of
birds, jumping three mallards now, down where the beavers cut
away the cottonwoods, and seeing the drake tower, white-breasted,
green-headed, climbing and get above him and splash him in the
old Clark's Fork, walking along the bank watching him until he
floated onto a pebbly bar.

Then there are sage hens, wild as hawks that time, the biggest
grouse of all, getting up out of range, and out of range, until you
came around an alfalfa stack and four whirred up one after the

other at your feet almost and, later walking home, in your hunting coat they seemed to weigh a ton.

I think they all were made to shoot because if they were not why did they give them that whirr of wings that moves you suddenly more than any love of country? Why did they make them all so good to eat and why did they make the ones with silent flight like wood-cock, snipe, and lesser bustard, better eating even than the rest?

Why does the curlew have that voice, and who thought up the plover's call, which takes the place of noise of wings, to give us that catharsis wing shooting has given to men since they stopped flying hawks and took to fowling pieces? I think that they were made to shoot and some of us were made to shoot them and if that is not so well, never say we did not tell you that we liked it.

My Pal the Gorilla Gargantua

Ken,
JULY 28, 1938

Gene Tunney, you know, really believes he can beat that gorilla. In his public statements he suggests that any good heavyweight who is in training be given the chance to fight Gargantua. But in private you get the impression it's Gene that can beat him. And he beats him with left and right hooks to the body.

You ought to see him turn those demonstration punches loose in the washroom of the Stork or in the wine cellar of the St. Regis. If that gorilla is smart he will get out of the country now before Gene catches up with him.

If he is not that smart, at least he should be smart enough to keep out of the washroom at the Stork, so Gene can't back him up against one of those marble wash basins before he tears him in two with a left hook to the liver. And somebody should tell that gorilla under no circumstances to let Gene ever get him down into the wine cellar at the St. Regis where Gene can bull him back and crowd him up against one of those bins full of bottles before he doubles him up with a savage two-handed body attack and then knocks his head right back in there among the magnums.

We were having lunch down there in the wine cellar and Grantland Rice and I were sort of ribbing Gene about that gorilla. But Gene does not rib about that gorilla. For years he has resented Brisbane's often published edict that a gorilla could whip both Dempsey and Tunney in the same ring at the same time and, although some of us have a feeling that it is just a little late, and that Brisbane is dead anyhow, Gene is now out to clear the honor of the human race.

I had a good friend who killed many gorillas in the Kameruns in what was then German West Africa. He told me that when you shoot a gorilla in the belly at 25 yards with a Springfield 30-06 (which, shooting a 220 grain bullet, has a muzzle striking energy of 2,940 foot pounds) the gorilla will grab his belly and moan and cry like a man. Even if he has been coming toward you he will stop, if you gut-shoot him, and go through that moaning and groaning act. Then, my friend explained, you could shoot him in a vulnerable place such as the heart, the neck, or the head, and kill him. I told this to Gene and he was delighted.

"He can't take it in the body, Ernest," he said. "That's very interesting."

Of course the difficulty in establishing a line of comparative performances here is that we have no record of how Gene himself would act if you shot him in the belly at 25 yards with a Springfield 30-06 throwing a 220 grain bullet with a muzzle energy of 2,940 foot pounds. Partisan though I am of the human race, sincere admirer that I am of Gene, I am afraid that he would go down. I have seen several people gut-shot at greater range than that and they usually went down, while the gorilla, that yellow animal, just beat his stomach and moaned and groaned.

Maybe Gene can beat that gorilla. If any man could, Gene could, because he would not be afraid, because he can hit to the body and because he is intelligent. But if he did beat him, then, in our progress back toward the gladiatorial combats of Rome, the next opponent for Gene, if he is really going to represent the human race as an all around champion, should be a local animal; the grizzly.

Now standing in one corner of a boxing ring with a .22 caliber Colt automatic pistol, shooting a bullet weighing only 40 grains and with a striking energy of only 51 foot pounds at 25 feet from the muzzle, I will guarantee to kill either Gene or Joe Louis before they can get to me from the opposite corner. This is the smallest caliber pistol cartridge made; but it is also one of the most accurate and easy to hit with, since the pistol has no recoil. I have killed many horses with it, cripples and for bear baits, with a single shot, and what will kill a horse will kill a man. I have hit six duelling silhouettes in the head with it at regulation distance in five seconds. It was this type pistol that the Millen boys' colleague, Abe Faber, did all his killings with. Yet this same pistol bullet fired at point blank range will not even dent a grizzly's skull, and to shoot at a grizzly with a .22 caliber pistol would simply be one way of committing suicide.

Stanley Ketchell, who could beat several chimpanzees, died from a .22 caliber bullet fired from a cheap Flobert rifle belonging to the hired man on a farm in the Ozarks. The rifle and the pistol are still the equalizer when one man is more of a man than another, and if that gorilla is really smart, he will not only keep away from the washroom of the Stork and the wine cellar of the St. Regis, he will get a permit to carry one and then drop around to Abercrombie and Fitch and buy himself a .22 caliber Colt automatic pistol, Woodsman model, with a five-inch barrel and a box of shells. I advise him to get lubricated hollow points to avoid jams and to ensure a nice expansion on the bullet. He might even get several boxes and practice a little.

Then if any representative of the human race, even Tony Galento, say, comes around to pick on Grantland Rice's and my little jungle comrade, let the gorilla shoot the representative a couple of times in the body to bring his guard down and see if he would moan, and then give him the rest of the clip in the head. And listen, Gargantua, old pal, don't let them try to play dead on you. Those human beings are tough. After whoever it is goes down, just push the pistol against the back of the neck, in the center, where the haircut stops, and give him one more for luck, for Grantland and for me. That will teach those human racers to pick on us gorillas.

The Louis-Schmeling thing was not pretty to watch. Louis stood in his corner, nervous and jumpy as a doped race horse. He came out fast, his hands high, hooked Schmeling twice with lefts and smashed a right against the German's jaw. The fight was over then before it had started, but with Schmeling hung helpless on the ropes, glassy-eyed, unable to go down because the top strand was under his right armpit, swung half sideways toward Louis, the Negro swung, hooked, swung and hooked at him as though he were the big bag.

Donovan finally pushed Louis away and Schmeling staggered out to be dropped with a right in the first clean shot Louis had at his jaw since the first right that drove him against the ropes. Schmeling got up at three, still absolutely glassy-eyed, and Louis left hooked him, then put him down again with a right before the German ever knew where he was or what he was doing. This time Max got up without a count. He was unable to lift his left hand and Louis moved in on him, jabbed him with the left, hooked him with the left, hooked him again, feinted with his right, and then threw it against Schmeling's jaw. The German went down on his face and you knew he would never get up.

Max Machon threw the towel in as Donovan was counting three. Donovan did not see it at first. Then as the count reached five, Donovan spread his arms wide and signalled that the fight was over. As a fight it had been over since the first right hand punch Louis landed.

Schmeling threw only three punches in the entire fight. One was a glancing right Louis ducked inside of. The other two were pitiful right hands that Schmeling pushed out of the fog.

There was no foul in the fight. The injury to Schmeling's spine could have come from a punch Louis landed on his side as the German went sideways into the ropes after the first and decisive right, or from any one of half a dozen body punches Louis smashed in as Max leaned and hung helpless on the ropes. It was up to Donovan to push Louis away if he did not want him to keep on punching.

The foul was committed by those people who kept Schmeling from a chance to fight for the heavyweight title for two years while age caught up with him and his legs went. They got close to a million dollar gate out of it and Louis got a chance at the man who had beaten him when that man, who was past a fighter's best age when he beat him, was a full two years older.

The wise boys say that Schmeling is from three to five years older than his official fighting age. That has often been true of foreign fighters. Try to find out how old Tom Heeney really was when he first hit New York for what he thought was to be a single fight on his way home across the country to New Zealand, a fight to get passage money home, but which turned out to be the first in a series which led to a chance to fight for the championship of the world.

The wise boys say there was a training camp secret about Louis' change from a phlegmatic, nerveless, slow starter into a nervous, sweating, rageing attacker. Some of the secrets they suggest are too silly to mention. It is no secret that he worked two rounds in his dressing room to heat him up before he came in.

The wise boys all knew Schmeling's legs were gone. They bet two to one on it and they were right.

Louis is still the fastest and hardest hitting heavyweight I have ever seen. Probably he punches faster and harder than any heavyweight that ever lived. But he still has that weak jaw although Schmeling could not tag it. If he goes out to kill the way he did against Schmeling every time he fights, and if he carries his left hand as high as he did on the night of June 22, few people will ever tag him. They will not have time.

He is in a position to tell Tunney's gorilla, if he should ever challenge him, to go out and get a reputation. But if I were that gorilla I'd still go get me a gun.

The Clark's Fork Valley, Wyoming

Vogue
FEBRUARY, 1939

At the end of summer, the big trout would be out in the centre of the stream; they were leaving the pools along the upper part of the river and dropping down to spend the winter in the deep water of the canyon. It was wonderful fly-fishing then in the first weeks of September. The native trout were sleek, shining, and heavy, and nearly all of them leaped when they took the fly. If you fished two flies, you would often have two big trout on and the need to handle them very delicately in that heavy current.

The nights were cold, and, if you woke in the night, you would hear the coyotes. But you did not want to get out on the stream too early in the day because the nights were so cold they chilled the water, and the sun had to be on the river until almost noon before the trout would start to feed.

You could ride in the morning, or sit in front of the cabin, lazy in the sun, and look across the valley where the hay was cut so the meadows were cropped brown and smooth to the line of quaking aspens along the river, now turning yellow in the fall. And on the hills rising beyond, the sage was silvery grey.

Up the river were the two peaks of Pilot and Index, where we would hunt mountain-sheep later in the month, and you sat in the sun and marvelled at the formal, clean-lined shape mountains can have at a distance, so that you remember them in the shapes they show from far away, and not as the broken rockslides you crossed, the jagged edges you pulled up by, and the narrow shelves you sweated along, afraid to look down, to round that peak that looked so smooth and geometrical. You climbed around it to come out on a clear space to look down to where an old ram and three young rams were feeding in the juniper bushes in a high, grassy pocket cupped against the broken rock of the peak.

The old ram was purple-grey, his rump was white, and when he raised his head you saw the great heavy curl of his horns. It was the white of his rump that had betrayed him to you in the green of the junipers when you had lain in the lee of a rock, out of the wind, three miles away, looking carefully at every yard of the high country through a pair of good Zeiss glasses.

Now as you sat in front of the cabin, you remembered that down-hill shot and the young rams standing, their heads turned, staring at him, waiting for him to get up. They could not see you on that high ledge, nor wind you, and the shot made no more impression on them than a boulder falling.

You remembered the year we had built a cabin at the head of Timber Creek, and the big grizzly that tore it open every time we were away. The snow came late that year, and this bear would not hibernate, but spent his autumn tearing open cabins and ruining a trap-line. But he was so smart you never saw him in the day. Then you remembered coming on the three grizzlies in the high country at the head of Crandall Creek. You heard a crash of timber and thought it was a cow elk bolting, and then there they were, in the broken shadow, running with an easy, lurching smoothness, the afternoon sun making their coats a soft, bristling silver.

You remembered elk bugling in the fall, the bull so close you could see his chest muscles swell as he lifted his head, and still not see his head in the thick timber; but hear that deep, high mounting whistle and the answer from across another valley. You thought of all the heads you had turned down and refused to shoot, and you were pleased about every one of them.

You remembered the children learning to ride; how they did with different horses; and how they loved the country. You remembered how this country had looked when you first came into it, and the year you had to stay four months after you had brought the first car ever to come in for the swamp roads to freeze solid enough to get the car out. You could remember all the hunting and all the fishing and the riding in the summer sun and the dust of the pack-train, the silent riding in the hills in the sharp cold of fall going up after the cattle on the high range, finding them wild as deer and as quiet, only bawling noisily when they were all herded together being forced along down into the lower country.

Then there was the winter; the trees bare now, the snow blowing so you could not see, the saddle wet, then frozen as you came down-hill, breaking a trail through the snow, trying to keep your legs moving, and the sharp, warming taste of whiskey when you hit the ranch and changed your clothes in front of the big open fireplace. It's a good country.

The Shot

(an excerpt)

True
APRIL, 1951

There are two ways to hunt pronghorn antelope; maybe three is juster. One is to shoot the buck that has been hanging around the back pasture and who believes himself to be a member of the family. He is shot on the opening day of the season by some dude who has been enticed to Wyoming by an outfit that advertises "Antelope Guaranteed" and has scouted the country closely for guaranteeable antelope. Oftentimes he is gut-shot and makes an effort to get away with a hole in his belly or a broken leg. But he is in that pasture, gentlemen, and what a trophy his head must make.

Then they hunt them on the flats and in that broken country between Casper and Rawlins, Wyoming, with the aid of command cars, these carry more hunters; jeeps, out of which only a few can hunt; weapons carriers, plenty hunters, Jack, but just about as un-comfortable as a weapon carrier always was. But you are after antelope, men, and shots are guaranteed. These vehicles will put you in range of the ferocious beasts and your marksmanship can be proved or unproved. Hold your breath a little bit; put the peak, or the spike, or the cross hairs of the reticule low down on the shoulder and squeeze off. It's a trophy, men, if you glassed them right and took the biggest buck and didn't shoot a doe mistaking ears for horns. It is probably shot through both shoulders too and is still living and will try to get up, looking at you, as you come with the knife. From the eyes you can tell that the buck is thinking, "What the hell did I do to deserve this?"

Then there is the third way where you hunt them in high country on foot or on horseback and no antelope are guaranteed. The author of this article, after taking a long time to make up his mind, and admitting his guilt on all counts, believes that it is a sin to kill any non-dangerous game animal except for meat. Now, with low-temperature refrigeration, you can keep meat properly and the amount of hunters has greatly increased. It has increased to such a point that you are lucky if some character does not loose off at you or your horse at least once in any three days of shooting. There is only one answer when this starts. Loose off quick yourself, shooting low. Because antelope, deer, elk and moose never shoot back and the character who opens fire, however undeveloped he may be in a sporting way, understands this basic principle. And if you should hit the son of a bitch it is only a hunting accident anyway. Shoot back if they shoot at you.

Don't run up any white flags. They might take you for a bald eagle. Or, if you waved your red bandanna that we wear around a Stetson since shooters became really at large, they might think it was a fox maybe or even a subversive element. But so far I have never seen one return the fire when you shot back. Especially if you shoot back at where you figure their feet will be.

Of course a hunter could go into the hills with a megaphone strapped to his back, and when shot at simply shout through his megaphone, "Please cease firing, brother shooter and fellow sportsman. I am the animal that walks on two legs and pays income tax and there is no open season on us this year . . . You fooled yourself there, boy."

Or he might make it shorter and more sporting and say, "Desist, brother sportsman. It is I."

But until they issue us with the proper megaphones at the time we purchase the licenses, I figure to shoot back quick if any brother sportsman shoots at me. Because he might not even be a brother sportsman. He might be an old friend or some companion of early youth or childhood.

Now about antelope in the hills.

This was a funny hunt. Three of my kids were along and one, Jack, who is a captain of infantry in Berlin, is a fisherman; so he wanted to fish the Pahsimeroi for salmon. (No salmon.) Of the other two boys one stayed the pace all the way and the other joined Jack in Operation No Salmon.

We figured to find the big bucks high up in the draws above timberline. Somebody had spooked them. Anyway there was something wrong and for keeps wrong. They were in broken country; could see you for a mile and were nervous and watching.

We were sleeping, down on the Pahsimeroi, in the cabin of a character known as the Old-timer. This was before the days of DDT or of bug bombs and the Old-timer had been raising the more hardy insects instead of cattle. He called Taylor Williams who was then in his later fifties "Young Man" and he called me "Kid." He said, "Kid, you're going to make a rider and you can shoot pretty good and I'll be proud if you get some place."

He said, "Kid, if these are really your boys they ought to have something to drink." Then he added, "What have you got?"

We had come from Sun Valley, Idaho, and were a little softened up by the swimming pool, nights in The Ram, and the wheels of Ketchum; but the Old-timer fixed that. We rode to the top of the range where we could look over all the way into the Middle Fork of the Salmon, across the loveliest mountains that I know. We rode down the mountain, across the mountain, back across the broken ground and down into the foothills and flats. All the time there were antelope; but they watched you from a mile away and moved. Taylor was mounted on a white horse and the Old-timer started to refer to him as "The young fellow on the white horse. Scares antelope to death."

The night of the first day was Saturday and that was a big night at Goldburg where they had some sort of a mine and always a big Saturday night. The children slept in the car and Taylor Williams and I and a boy named Wild Bill, who could hit like Stan Ketchell with either hand, went to Goldburg. The Old-timer stayed home to care for his insects.

It was a rough night although I bypassed all the fights. You might have fought ten or twelve times if you weren't pacific. Taylor never fights because he does not have to anymore and I try never to fight. Wild Bill, however, who was horse wrangling for us, spotted the Sheriff's boy from one of the nearest towns who had turned King's Evidence or something corresponding to that, one time versus Wild Bill. Wild Bill asked him outside and demolished him. Wild Bill could certainly hit. Every time he hit Sheriff's boy you could hear something go. Sheriff's boy fought well; but it wasn't any courtroom. Finally Sheriff's boy went just like the things you had been hearing go. We gentled down Wild Bill and gave first aid to Sheriff's boy and drove home. The fight had, in a way, quieted down the happiness in Goldburg.

The next day was like the first day. Only now they looked back over their lovely brown shoulders at a mile and a half and then you would see the white ruff on their rumps when they would take off. We rode to the top of the range. We blocked several draws and turned them. We crisscrossed the mountain, staying in dead ground and coming up on the ridges dismounted, and crawling to the edge of high ground and glassing the country.

The Shot

We rode downhill, uphill and around hill. By this time there was only Gigi, my youngest boy, who rides a horse as though his mother had dropped him into the saddle; Taylor Williams, the old Kentucky Colonel who will kill you dead at 300 yards with a borrowed rifle; the Old-timer who you had to keep to windward of, and whose scent was possibly driving the antelope out of the country; and me, on a nice mare with more brains than I had. She was an old rope horse.

So that was the second day and when we hit the shale and then the pebbles and rode over the wooden bridge and through the cottonwoods the moon was up. It was a nice night at the Old-timer's to be off-horse and hear the no-salmon fisher's stories and we had brought some lemons and made whisky sours. The Old-timer said he had never tasted a mixed drink but he would try it this once.

"How old are you, Old-timer?" I asked him.

"Son," he said, "when they killed General George Armstrong Custer on the Little Big Horn, I was getting along in years."

This was obviously impossible so I asked the Old-timer how old he thought Taylor was.

"He's a boy," he said.

"What about me?" I asked.

"You're just starting."

"What about the boys?"

"They're all false except that one was poured into a saddle and stuck there."

"Where you come from, Old-timer?"

"God knows. I forgot."

"Were you ever around Montana way?"

"Sure."

"Were you in Wyoming?"

"I was there for the Wagon Box fight when we were snaking timber to the Fort."

This was impossible so I asked him if he knew Tom Horn.

"Tom? I heard him say, standing up there before they put the hood over him; no; they didn't put any hood over Tom. What he

201

said was, 'Gentlemen, all I want in this life is a pair of heavy shoes and a long drop. And I forgive all my enemies. Amen!' Everybody was crying but Tom never cried. He stood there looking sort of distinguished but he wanted a heavy pair of shoes and a decent drop so he wouldn't resist the rope. That's the worst thing can happen to a man, to resist the rope. I seen them hang since I was a boy and it ain't no good. Not for him that is hung nor for anybody. It's just a sort of legal vengeance."

The next day we were out at daylight with the horses saddled and our guns in the gun buckets and Wild Bill's hands sore and him sort of ashamed. We knew the Sheriff's boy couldn't really fight a lick and he remembered that in the middle of the night. It made him feel bad because he was a fighter and would have fought anybody. Besides, he broke the Sheriff's boy's jaw and we all heard it go. And he had his sore hands to remind him. He wasn't riding with us. He was just staying at the shack and corrals with break-jaw remorse.

So we start early and there is a little mist over the flat and then we start to climb in the sage.

"How does it look to you, Colonel?" I asked Taylor.

Gigi is asleep in the saddle letting the horse do the work.

"I think we've got them," Taylor said. "We haven't shot at them and this is the third day and they are getting used to us and some of the big bucks will stand. They don't know what we are now and they have curiosity and want to find out."

We did the usual; gained our altitude, worked the draws, the pockets, and the ridges and then started to move down and across.

Then we jumped a bunch that were sleeping, or feeding, in a draw and there was only one way for them to go. I got off the horse and pulled the old .30-06 out of the bucket. We hang them forward. Then I started to run for where they would have to pass. It was about 200 or 250 yards. I picked the biggest buck when they came streaming over the edge of the hump and swung ahead of him and squeezed gently and the bullet broke his neck. It was a very lucky shot.

The Old-timer said, "You no-good kid. I knew you would amount to something sometime."

Taylor said, "Do you know how far you ran and how far you shot him at? I'm going to pace it."

I didn't care, because nobody ever believes shooting stories ever, and the pleasure had been in the run and trying to hold your heart in when you swing and hold your breath, sweet and clean, and swing ahead and squeeze off lightly with the swing.

So end of antelope story.

Safari

(an excerpt)

Look,
JANUARY 26, 1954

The never-ending monsoon was breaking the sea white over the roof outside Mombasa as we came in through the channel. The hills rose green beyond the harbor and the white town and that night the rain beat on the roof of the hotel and there were pools of water in half-finished streets when we started out in the morning for the upper country.

But when the hunting car had climbed the red road through the green of the coastal hills we were in a thorn scrub desert and after the desert was the high plateau where the rains had failed for two years. This had been a green or tawny land when I had known it in the old days. Now it was gray or red with dust that dragged in clouds behind the cars or trucks that moved along the road and soon our faces were masked by it.

Across the plains were hills that were blue from the timber on their slopes. It looked like Wyoming west of Cheyenne. But over the land dust devils whirled and rose in high flat-topped pillars that moved across the plains and around the foothills. The wind never stopped blowing and no living thing, not even a bird, could change position without showing its movement by a rising dust. I watched a partridge run with dust rising from his feet and when he flushed, whirring, you could not see him in the dust he raised.

"I know how you feel, Pop," Philip Percival said, "but we'll find some places."

"I think it's lovely," Mary said. "It's rather like the Bible in the part where Lot's wife looked back and they turned her into a pillar of salt."

"Don't think about Mombasa," Philip said, "nor about Paris nor Gomorrah."

"Look," Mary said, "look at that odd formation. It looks exactly like a giraffe."

"It is a giraffe," Philip said.

"I'm sorry," said Miss Mary, "but I'm new here."

"Dust gets in your eyes," Mister P. said. "Ruined mine years ago."

It was not all dust although there was dust every day. There was Nairobi with certain bars as self-consciously heroic as Tombstone, Arizona. There was a war on upcountry where it was necessary to bear arms. Often it was necessary for people to be armed in Nairobi. But in Nairobi many people were bearing arms at high noon in bars which seemed highly defensible and whose defense already appeared to be entrusted to the competent authorities. You go to prison for six months, quite properly, if you lose a pistol or have it stolen. So it is an excellent idea to keep your weapon firmly attached to your person. There is no law, however, as far as I know against concealed weapons and I saw one very well turned out lady, definitely the very social type, who was prominently displaying on her person two pistols of the type which was designed to be worn up your sleeve and only displayed in the event of the production of five aces or some other such error of taste.

No visitor need bring a pistol to Nairobi. In spite of anything you have read it is still not good form to shoot your way into or out of either Torrs or the New Stanley. It is even frowned upon in Woolworths and it might be misinterpreted in Barclay's Bank.

Someone asked me why we were studying the animals rather than the Mau Mau. I answered that something might happen to the animals but that I believed the Mau Mau might be going on for a considerable time. I hoped, I said, to return to study them. If I were unable to return I would entrust their study to my second eldest son who is a settler in the country.

Nairobi and the basic long-term problem of the Kikuyu war, the upcountry war and the war in the passes, the borders and the marches are no part of this picture story. The war which is being fought each day is a long complicated and ugly story and we know something of it. You may be sure that it will continue for a long time. But know truly that no one coming to Africa who is interested in the kingdom of the animals need worry about it personally except as it affects the Bongo, Giant Forest Hog, and the big Forest Rhino and Buffalo of the north where the Mau Mau have gone into the hills. Nairobi for a foreigner with no one with a grudge against him is safer than New York, five times safer than parts of Memphis, West Memphis or Jacksonville, infinitely safer than many parts of Chicago and most certainly safer than Brooklyn, the Bronx, Central Park at night or Cooke City, Montana, on the date of the celebration of the Old Timers Fish Fry.

The bush is perfectly safe with a white hunter. He has to belong to the White Hunters Association and after being apprenticed and qualified he is licensed and disciplined by them. After that he must present himself personally to the Game Department who can issue him a license or refuse it without explanation. If he ever had anything happen to you he'd never work again. (Interruption by

Mary: "This seems to be excessive emphasis on safety, a fickle friend.")

If you should ever hunt without a white hunter you are just as safe as the degree to which your knowledge, your experience, your speed when it is needed, your ability to track, to size up a bad situation, and your absolute ability to shoot cold when the chips are down protects you. I do not advise hunting without a white hunter. To photograph dangerous game at close range without a white hunter is doubly dangerous.

The pictures in these pages show where Philip Percival our white hunter took us when the country was blowing away in the drought and he said, "Don't worry, Pop. We'll find something better." We found it and this is a small part of the oases we found in the different deserts and a little about the animals and people who had the right to live there.

Philip Percival took us to the dry sand river camp where the elephant came every second night to drink at the Masai watering hole. You could lie in bed and hear them blowing water with their trunks. Mary said that when they came through camp they sounded like men walking very softly in rubber waders.

There was a flock of more than six thousand guinea fowl and we shot only what we needed for meat. The sand grouse came to drink at the water in the mornings in pairs, singly, and in scattered bunches. They also came in flocks that were dense as the passenger pigeons around Petoskey before Michigan ever was a state.

He and our best friend, a game ranger who according to the traditions of that service does not wish his name used, took us to the swamp camp where one hundred and fifty, counted, buffalo lived in the papyrus and fed out at night. It was there that Mary saw them all looking at us in a most unfriendly way when it was too late to take pictures and heard the ranger, whom we call GC, say, "Don't let them cut us off from the river, Pop."

Safari

People have written that herds of 150 buffalo can stampede over you with no risk at all. Neither to you nor to them. But I do not think these people ever stood on their own two feet and looked at the buff head-on when the tick birds have flown and thought that truly. It is a very beautiful theory, though, and photographers who fake or photograph from armored trucks in national parks love to state it.

The Christmas Gift

Look
APRIL 20, MAY 4, 1954

As you most probably know, the night in Africa is completely different from the day. Very few people see the night without the benefit of the headlights of a car which distort it since the headlights terrify or occasionally anger the animals. After the sun has set and the fire is built in camp, the usual thing is for you to sit for a time and with your white hunter and companions discuss the events of the day and the plans for the following day.

You have a moderate amount of drinks and then bathe in a canvas tub with water which has been warmed at the cook fire. After that, you put on pajamas and mosquito boots and over them a dressing gown and go out to the fire where you have one more drink and wait for dinner to be served. After dinner, you go to bed which is covered by a mosquito net, and sleep or lie awake listening to the sound of the animals until half an hour before first light when you are roused by your personal boy bringing tea, known locally as *chai*. If you have no white hunter and consequently no need to observe rituals nor to be under anyone's discipline except your own, you are at liberty to do what you wish with the night, which is the loveliest time in Africa.

In the night, the animals are quite transformed. The lion, who is nearly always silent in the daytime, hunts by himself and from time to time coughs, grunts or roars. I have not been able yet to discover if he is communicating with his mates who are also hunting, or whether he is trying to make the game which sleeps quietly at night move and thus disclose its position. It may be that he roars much as Irishmen do in public drinking places occasionally. It may also be that he coughs from dyspepsia and grunts from irascibility due to the difficulty of procuring a meal.

The hyenas follow the lion and when he kills or when his women folk kill you can hear the talking of the hyenas among themselves. This is the time when you hear the so-called laughter of the hyena. His normal note at night is quite pleasant and I believe he gives it as communication to the other hyenas.

In hunting at night with a spear, you hear many other sounds. The wildebeest, which is a big antelope which was designed to try to look like a buffalo or bison, gives off terrifying noises in the effort to seem a dangerous beast. You can in the night, if you sight the silhouette on the ground and approach the wildebeest, or gnu, with extreme caution, tap him on the rump with the butt end of your spear. He will spring to his feet and emit this terrifying sound. At this point, you may say, "Had you there, wildebeest, old boy."

In the night, you will see many bat-eared foxes. These are lovely animals which live in burrows and are almost never seen in broad daylight and live on insects and other small deer. This does not refer to actual deer but to the animals on which Poor Tom in *King Lear* existed. Mr. Gene Tunney, the Shakespearean scholar, can provide the quotation. The bat-eared fox looks like a real fox except for his ears, which are at least three times the size of those of Clark Gable, the actor, but are in no way to be compared to those of the elephant.

You will probably hear the voice of Mr. Chui, the leopard. He is about on his beat giving short coughing grunts. These are given in such a deep bass voice that they cannot be confused with the voice of the other beasts. At night if you hear Mr. Chui on your left, you make a smart right turn. Mr. Chui is a very serious beast. He has his defects but he has great and terrible qualities as a beast.

If you hear Mr. Chui and he is working along a stream or wooded area you may mark his progress by the speech of the baboons who respond to his grunts with what I take in baboon to be imprecations, insults and warnings to all other baboons to seek the highest part of the treetops. At daylight, coming home from the night out with the spear, I have noted the tops of the fig trees along the creek loaded as though these trees bore fruit of baboons rather than figs. They had been placed in this difficult position by the passage of Mr. Chui.

Thinking about these times and about how fine the night could be when you were allowed to roam freely, I skipped further dreams and decided to think about the past.

This past was never my past life which truly bores me to think about and is often very distasteful due to the mistakes that I have made and the casualties to various human beings involved in that sad affair. I tried to think instead of other people, of the fine deeds of people and animals I have known, and I thought a long time about my dog Black Dog and what the two winters must have been when he had no master in Ketchum, Idaho, having been lost or abandoned by some summer motorist. Any small hardships we had encountered seemed to me to be dwarfed by Blackie's odyssey.

We encountered Blackie when we were living in a log cabin in Ketchum and had two deer, killed, respectively, by Mary and

Patrick, hung up in the open door of the barn. There was also a string of mallard ducks hung out of the reach of cats and there were also hung up Hungarian partridges, different varieties of quail and other fine eating birds. It seeming that we were people of such evident solidarity, Blackie abandoned promiscuous begging and attached himself to us as our permanent dog. His devotion was exemplary and his appetite enormous. He slept by the fireplace and he had perfect manners.

III

A Hunter's Return to the Good Country

"Any gun that you're used to, and throws a good heavy bullet that won't go to pieces, ought to be all right. . . . But the principle is that foot ball players aren't made by fancy pants, nor baseball players by eight dollar catcher mits, and shots are made by shooting; but a Springfield made to fit you, and heavy enough so it doesn't kick is sure a lovely gun."
—To Archibald MacLeish, Billings, Montana, November 22, 1930

"Did you know Joyce? He was terrible with his admirers; really insupportable. With idolators: worse. But he was the best companion and finest friend I ever had. I remember one time he was feeling fairly gloomy and he asked me if I didn't think that his books were too suburban. He said that was what got him down sometimes. Mrs. Joyce said, 'Ah Jim could do with a spot of that lion hunting.' And Joyce said, 'The thing we must face is I couldn't see the lion.' Mrs. Joyce said, 'Hemingway'd describe him to you Jim and afterwards you could go up and touch him and smell of him. That's all you'd need.' "
—To Bernard Berenson, La Finca Vigia, October 14, 1952

"I have to kill the beasts that kill their stock or molest and destroy their crops. So as long as I go OK on that I have a certain popularity. The beasts are no dopes by the time they take up marauding. . . . It is like knowing every day you are going to pitch in big league ball. Pitching you have to do with your arm so you could never start every day but I am a relief pitcher in this. You never come on until it's no good. Have gone back to chewing tobacco to have confidence."
—To Harvey Breit, near Magadi, Kenya, January 3, 1954

The Last Good Country

(two excerpts)

"Nickie," his sister said to him. "Listen to me, Nickie."

"I don't want to hear it."

He was watching the bottom of the spring where the sand rose in small spurts with the bubbling water. There was a tin cup on a forked stick that was stuck in the gravel by the spring and Nick Adams looked at it and at the water rising and then flowing clear in its gravel bed beside the road.

He could see both ways on the road and he looked up the hill and then down to the dock and the lake, the wooded point across the bay and the open lake beyond where there were white caps running. His back was against a big cedar tree and behind him there was a thick cedar swamp. His sister was sitting on the moss beside him and she had her arm around his shoulders.

"They're waiting for you to come home to supper," his sister said. "There's two of them. They came in a buggy and they asked where you were."

"Did anybody tell them?"

"Nobody knew where you were but me. Did you get many, Nickie?"

"I got twenty-six."

"Are they good ones?"

"Just the size they want for the dinners."

"Oh, Nickie, I wish you wouldn't sell them."

"She gives me a dollar a pound," Nick Adams said.

His sister was tanned brown and she had dark brown eyes and dark brown hair with yellow streaks in it from the sun. She and Nick loved each other and they did not love the others. They always thought of everyone else in the family as the others.

"They know about everything, Nickie," his sister said hopelessly. "They said they were going to make an example of you and send you to the reform school."

"They've only got proof on one thing," Nick told her. "But I guess I have to go away for a while."

"Can I go?"

"No. I'm sorry, Littless. How much money have we got?"

"Fourteen dollars and sixty-five cents. I brought it."

"Did they say anything else?"

"No. Only that they were going to stay till you came home."

"Our mother will get tired of feeding them."

"She gave them lunch already."

"What were they doing?"

"Just sitting around on the screen porch. They asked our mother for your rifle but I'd hid it in the woodshed when I saw them by the fence."

"Were you expecting them?"

"Yes. Weren't you?"

"I guess so. Goddam them."

"Goddam them for me, too," his sister said. "Aren't I old enough to go now? I hid the rifle. I brought the money."

"I'd worry about you," Nick Adams told her. "I don't even know where I'm going."

"Sure you do."

"If there's two of us they'd look harder. A boy and a girl show up."

"I'd go like a boy," she said. "I always wanted to be a boy anyway. They couldn't tell anything about me if my hair was cut."

"No," Nick Adams said. "That's true."

"Let's think something out good," she said. "Please, Nick, please. I could be lots of use and you'd be lonely without me. Wouldn't you be?"

"I'm lonely now thinking about going away from you."

"See? And we may have to be away for years. Who can tell? Take me, Nickie. Please take me." She kissed him and held onto him with both her arms. Nick Adams looked at her and tried to think straight. It was difficult. But there was no choice.

"I shouldn't take you. But then I shouldn't have done any of it," he said. "I'll take you. Maybe only for a couple of days, though."

"That's all right," she told him. "When you don't want me I'll go straight home. I'll go home anyway if I'm a bother or a nuisance or an expense."

"Let's think it out," Nick Adams told her. He looked up and down the road and up at the sky where the big high afternoon clouds were riding and at the white caps on the lake out beyond the point.

"I'd go through the woods down to the inn beyond the point and sell her the trout," he told his sister. "She ordered them for dinners tonight. Right now they want more trout dinners than chicken dinners. I don't know why. The trout are in good shape. I gutted them and they're wrapped in cheesecloth and they'll be cool and fresh. I'll tell her I'm in some trouble with the game wardens and that they're looking for me and I have to get out of the country for a while. I'll get her to give me a small skillet and some salt and pepper and some bacon and some shortening and some corn meal. I'll get her to give me a sack to put everything in and I'll get some dried apricots and some prunes and some tea and plenty of matches and a hatchet. But I can only get one blanket. She'll help me because buying trout is just as bad as selling them."

"I can get a blanket," his sister said. "I'll wrap it around the rifle and I'll bring your moccasins and my moccasins and I'll change to different overalls and a shirt and hide these so they'll think I'm wearing them and I'll bring soap and a comb and a pair of scissors and something to sew with and *Lorna Doone* and *Swiss Family Robinson.*"

"Bring all the .22's you can find," Nick Adams said. Then quickly, "Come on back. Get out of sight." He had seen a buggy coming down the road.

Behind the cedars they lay flat against the springy moss with their faces down and heard the soft noise of the horses' hooves in the sand and the small noise of the wheels. Neither of the men in the buggy was talking but Nick Adams smelled them as they went past and he smelled the sweated horses. He sweated himself until they were well past on their way to the dock because he thought they might stop to water at the spring or to get a drink.

"Is that them, Littless?" he asked.

"Yeah," she said.

"Crawl way back in," Nick Adams said. He crawled back into the swamp, pulling his sack of fish. The swamp was mossy and not muddy there. Then he stood up and hid the sack behind the trunk of a cedar and motioned the girl to come further in. They went into the cedar swamp, moving as softly as deer.

"I know the one," Nick Adams said. "He's a no good son of a bitch."

"He said he'd been after you for four years."

"I know."

"The other one, the big one with the spit tobacco face and the blue suit, is the one from down state."

"Good," Nick said. "Now we've had a look at them I better get going. Can you get home all right?"

"Sure. I'll cut up to the top of the hill and keep off the road. Where will I meet you tonight, Nickie?"

"I don't think you ought to come, Littless."

"I've got to come. You don't know how it is. I can leave a note for our mother and say I went with you and you'll take good care of me."

"All right," Nick Adams said. "I'll be where the big hemlock is that was struck by lightning. The one that's down. Straight up from the cove. Do you know the one? On the short cut to the road."

"That's awfully close to the house."

"I don't want you to have to carry the stuff too far."

"I'll do what you say. But don't take chances, Nickie."

"I'd like to have the rifle and go down now to the edge of the timber and kill both of those bastards while they're on the dock and wire a piece of iron on them from the old mill and sink them in the channel."

"And then what would you do?" his sister asked. "Somebody sent them."

"Nobody sent that first son of a bitch."

"But you killed the moose and you sold the trout and you killed what they took from your boat."

"That was all right to kill that."

He did not like to mention what that was, because that was the proof they had.

"I know. But you're not going to kill people and that's why I'm going with you."

"Let's stop talking about it. But I'd like to kill those two sons of bitches."

"I know," she said. "So would I. But we're not going to kill people, Nickie. Will you promise me?"

"No. Now I don't know whether it's safe to take her the trout."

"I'll take them to her."

"No. They're too heavy. I'll take them through the swamp and to the woods in back of the hotel. You go straight to the hotel and see if she's there and if everything's all right. And if it is you'll find me there by the big basswood tree."

"It's a long way there through the swamp, Nicky."

"It's a long way back from reform school, too."

"Can't I come with you through the swamp? I'll go in then and see her while you stay out and come back out with you and take them in."

"All right," Nick said. "But I wish you'd do it the other way."

"Why, Nickie?"

"Because you'll see them maybe on the road and you can tell me where they've gone. I'll see you in the second-growth wood lot in back of the hotel where the big basswood is."

Nick waited more than an hour in the second-growth timber and his sister had not come. When she came she was excited and he knew she was tired.

"They're at our house," she said. "They're sitting out on the screen porch and drinking whiskey and ginger ale and they've un-hitched and put their horses up. They say they're going to wait till you come back. It was our mother told them you'd gone fishing at the creek. I don't think she meant to. Anyway I hope not."

"What about Mrs. Packard?"

"I saw her in the kitchen of the hotel and she asked me if I'd seen you and I said no. She said she was waiting for you to bring her some fish for tonight. She was worried. You might as well take them in."

"Good," he said. "They're nice and fresh. I repacked them in ferns."

"Can I come in with you?"

"Sure," Nick said.

The hotel was a long wooden building with a porch that fronted on the lake. There were wide wooden steps that led down to the pier that ran far out into the water and there were natural cedar railings alongside the steps and natural cedar railings around the porch. There were chairs made of natural cedar on the porch and in them sat middle-aged people wearing white clothes. There were three pipes set on the lawn with spring water bubbling out of them, and little paths led to them. The water tasted like rotten eggs because these were mineral springs and Nick and his sister used to drink from them as a matter of discipline. Now coming toward the rear of the hotel, where the kitchen was, they crossed a plank bridge over a small brook running into the lake beside the hotel, and slipped into the back door of the kitchen.

"Wash them and put them in the ice box, Nickie," Mrs. Packard said. "I'll weigh them later."

"Mrs. Packard," Nick said. "Could I speak to you a minute?"

"Speak up," she said. "Can't you see I'm busy?"

"If I could have the money now."

Mrs. Packard was a handsome woman in a gingham apron. She had a beautiful complexion and she was very busy and her kitchen help were there as well.

"You don't mean you want to sell trout. Don't you know that's against the law?"

"I know," Nick said. "I brought you the fish for a present. I mean my time for the wood I split and corded."

"I'll get it," she said. "I have to go to the annex."

Nick and his sister followed her outside. On the board sidewalk that led to the icehouse from the kitchen she stopped and put her hands in her apron pocket and took out a pocketbook.

"You get out of here," she said quickly and kindly. "And get out of here fast. How much do you need?"

"I've got sixteen dollars," Nick said.

"Take twenty," she told him. "And keep that tyke out of trouble. Let her go home and keep an eye on them until you're clear."

"When did you hear about them?"

She shook her head at him.

"Buying is as bad or worse than selling," she said. "You stay away until things quiet down. Nickie, you're a good boy no matter

223

what anybody says. You see Packard if things get bad. Come here nights if you need anything. I sleep light. Just knock on the window."

"You aren't going to serve them tonight are you, Mrs. Packard? You're not going to serve them for the dinners?"

"No," she said. "But I'm not going to waste them. Packard can eat half a dozen and I know other people that can. Be careful, Nickie, and let it blow over. Keep out of sight."

"Littless wants to go with me."

"Don't you dare take her," Mrs. Packard said. "You come by tonight and I'll have some stuff made up for you."

"Could you let me take a skillet?"

"I'll have what you need. Packard knows what you need. I don't give you any more money so you'll keep out of trouble."

"I'd like to see Mr. Packard about getting a few things."

"He'll get you anything you need. But don't you go near the store, Nick."

"I'll get Littless to take him a note."

"Anytime you need anything," Mrs. Packard said. "Don't you worry. Packard will be studying things out."

"Good-bye, Aunt Halley."

"Good-bye," she said and kissed him. She smelt wonderful when she kissed him. It was the way the kitchen smelled when they were baking. Mrs. Packard smelled like her kitchen and her kitchen always smelled good.

"Don't worry and don't do anything bad."

"I'll be all right."

"Of course," she said. "And Packard will figure out something."

They were in the big hemlocks on the hill behind the house now. It was evening and the sun was down beyond the hills on the other side of the lake.

"I've found everything," his sister said. "It's going to make a pretty big pack, Nickie."

"I know it. What are they doing?"

"They ate a big supper and now they're sitting out on the porch and drinking. They're telling each other stories about how smart they are."

"They aren't very smart so far."

"They're going to starve you out," his sister said. "A couple of nights in the woods and you'll be back. You hear a loon holler a couple of times when you got an empty stomach and you'll be back."

"What did our mother give them for supper?"

"Awful," his sister said.

"Good."

"I've located everything on the list. Our mother's gone to bed with a sick headache. She wrote our father."

"Did you see the letter?"

"No. It's in her room with the list of stuff to get from the store tomorrow. She's going to have to make a new list when she finds everything is gone in the morning."

"How much are they drinking?"

"They've drunk about a bottle, I guess."

"I wish we could put knockout drops in it."

"I could put them in if you'll tell me how. Do you put them in the bottle?"

"No. In the glass. But we haven't got any."

"Would there be any in the medicine cabinet?"

"No."

"I could put paregoric in the bottle. They have another bottle. Or calomel. I know we've got those."

"No," said Nick. "You try to get me about half the other bottle when they're asleep. Put it in any old medicine bottle."

"I better go and watch them," his sister said. "My, I wish we had knockout drops. I never even heard of them."

"They aren't really drops," Nick told her. "It's chloral hydrate. Whores give it to lumberjacks in their drinks when they're going to jack roll them."

"It sounds pretty bad," his sister said. "But we probably ought to have some for in emergencies."

"Let me kiss you," her brother said. "Just for in an emergency. Let's go down and watch them drinking. I'd like to hear them talk sitting in our own house."

"Will you promise not to get angry and do anything bad?"

"Sure."

"Nor to the horses. It's not the horses' fault."

"Not the horses either."

"I wish we had knockout drops," his sister said loyally.

"Well, we haven't," Nick told her. "I guess there aren't any this side of Boyne City."

They sat in the woodshed and they watched the two men sitting at the table on the screen porch. The moon had not risen and it was dark, but the outlines of the men showed against the lightness that the lake made behind them. They were not talking now but were both leaning forward on the table. Then Nick heard the clink of ice against a bucket.

"The ginger ale's gone," one of the men said.

"I said it wouldn't last," the other said. "But you were the one said we had plenty."

"Get some water. There's a pail and a dipper in the kitchen."

"I've drunk enough. I'm going to turn in."

"Aren't you going to stay up for that kid?"

"No. I'm going to get some sleep. You stay up."

"Do you think he'll come in tonight?"

"I don't know. I'm going to get some sleep. You wake me when you get sleepy."

"I can stay up all night," the local warden said. "Many's the night I've stayed up all night for jack lighters and never shut an eye."

"Me, too," the down-state man said. "But now I'm going to get a little sleep."

Nick and his sister watched him go in the door. Their mother had told the two men they could sleep in the bedroom next to the living room. They saw when he struck a match. Then the window was dark again. They watched the other warden sitting at the table until he put his head on his arms. Then they heard him snoring.

"We'll give him a little while to make sure he's solid asleep. Then we'll get the stuff," Nick said.

"You get over outside the fence," his sister said. "It doesn't matter if I'm moving around. But he might wake up and see you."

"All right," Nick agreed. "I'll get everything out of here. Most of it's here."

"Can you find everything without a light?"

"Sure. Where's the rifle?"

"Flat on the back upper rafter. Don't slip or make the wood fall down, Nick."

"Don't you worry."

She came out to the fence at the far corner where Nick was making up his pack beyond the big hemlock that had been struck by lightning the summer before and had fallen in a storm that autumn. The moon was just rising now behind the far hills and enough moonlight came through the trees for Nick to see clearly what he was packing. His sister put down the sack she was carrying and said, "They're sleeping like pigs, Nickie."

"Good."

"The down-state one was snoring, just like the one outside. I think I got everything."

"You good old Littless."

"I wrote a note to our mother and told her I was going with you to keep you out of trouble and not to tell anybody and that you'd take good care of me. I put it under her door. It's locked."

"Oh, shit," Nick said. Then he said, "I'm sorry, Littless."

"Now it's not your fault and I can't make it worse for you."

"You're awful."

"Can't we be happy now?"

"Sure."

"I brought the whiskey," she said hopefully. "I left some in the bottle. One of them can't be sure the other didn't drink it. Anyway they have another bottle."

"Did you bring a blanket for you?"

"Of course."

"We better get going."

"We're all right if we're going where I think. The only thing that makes the pack bigger is my blanket. I'll carry the rifle."

"All right. What kind of shoes have you?"

"I've got my work-moccasins."

"What did you bring to read?"

"*Lorna Doone* and *Kidnapped* and *Wuthering Heights*."

"They're all too old for you but *Kidnapped*."

"*Lorna Doone* isn't."

"We'll read it out loud," Nick said. "That way it lasts longer. But, Littless, you've made things sort of hard now and we better go. Those bastards can't be as stupid as they act. Maybe it was just because they were drinking."

Nick had rolled the pack now and tightened the straps and he sat back and put his moccasins on. He put his arm around his sister. "You sure you want to go?"

"I have to go, Nickie. Don't be weak and indecisive now. I left the note."

"All right," Nick said. "Let's go. You can take the rifle until you get tired of it."

"I'm all ready to go," his sister said. "Let me help you strap the pack."

"You know you haven't had any sleep at all and that we have to travel?"

"I know. I'm really like the snoring one at the table says he was."

"Maybe he was that way once, too," Nick said. "But what you have to do is keep your feet in good shape. Do the moccasins chafe?"

"No. And my feet are tough from going barefoot all summer."

"Mine are good, too," said Nick. "Come on. Let's go."

They started off walking on the soft hemlock needles and the trees were high and there was no brush between the tree trunks. They walked uphill and the moon came through the trees and showed Nick with the very big pack and his sister carrying the .22 rifle. When they were at the top of the hill they looked back and saw the lake in the moonlight. It was clear enough so they could see the dark point, and beyond were the high hills of the far shore.

"We might as well say good-bye to it," Nick Adams said.

"Good-bye, lake," Littless said. "I love you, too."

They went down the hill and across the long field and through the orchard and then through a rail fence and into a field of stubble. Going through the stubble field they looked to the right and saw the slaughterhouse and the big barn in the hollow and the old log farmhouse on the other high land that overlooked the lake. The long road of Lombardy poplars that ran to the lake was in the moonlight.

"Does it hurt your feet, Littless?" Nick asked.

"No," his sister said.

"I came this way on account of the dogs," Nick said. "They'd shut up as soon as they knew it was us. But somebody might hear them bark."

"I know," she said. "And as soon as they shut up afterwards they'd know it was us."

Ahead they could see the dark of the rising line of hills beyond the road. They came to the road of one cut field of grain and crossed the little sunken creek that ran down to the springhouse. Then they climbed across the rise of another stubble field and there was another rail fence and the sandy road with the second-growth timber solid beyond it.

"Wait till I climb over and I'll help you," Nick said. "I want to look at the road."

From the top of the fence he saw the roll of the country and the dark timber by their own house and the brightness of the lake in the moonlight. Then he was looking at the road.

"They can't track us the way we've come and I don't think they would notice tracks in this deep sand," he said to his sister. "We can keep to the two sides of the road if it isn't too scratchy."

"Nickie, honestly I don't think they're intelligent enough to track anybody. Look how they just waited for you to come back and then practically got drunk before supper and afterwards."

"They came down to the dock," Nick said. "That was where I was. If you hadn't told me they would have picked me up."

"They didn't have to be so intelligent to figure you would be on the big creek when our mother let them know you might have gone fishing. After I left they must have found all the boats were there and that would make them think you were fishing the creek. Everybody knows you usually fish below the grist mill and the cider mill. They were just slow thinking it out."

"All right," Nick said. "But they were awfully close then."

His sister handed him the rifle through the fence, butt toward him, and then crawled between the rails. She stood beside him on the road and he put his hand on her head and stroked it.

"Are you awfully tired, Littless?"

"No. I'm fine. I'm too happy to be tired."

"Until you're too tired you walk in the sandy part of the road where their horses made holes in the sand. It's so soft and dry tracks won't show and I'll walk on the other side where it's hard."

"I can walk on the side, too."

"No. I don't want you to get scratched."

They climbed, but with constant small descents, toward the height of land that separated the two lakes. There was close, heavy, second-growth timber on both sides of the road and blackberry and raspberry bushes grew from the edge of the road to the timber. Ahead they could see the top of each hill as a notch in the timber. The moon was well on its way down now.

"How do you feel, Littless?" Nick asked his sister.

"I feel wonderful. Nickie, is it always this nice when you run away from home?"

"No. Usually it's lonesome."

"How lonesome have you ever been?"

"Bad black lonesome. Awful."

"Do you think you'll get lonesome with me?"

"No."

"You don't mind you're with me instead of going to Trudy?"

"What do you talk about her for all the time?"

"I haven't been. Maybe you were thinking about her and you thought I was talking."

"You're too smart," Nick said. "I thought about her because you told me where she was and when I knew where she was I wondered what she would be doing and all that."

"I guess I shouldn't have come."

"I told you that you shouldn't have come."

"Oh, hell," his sister said. "Are we going to be like the others and have fights? I'll go back now. You don't have to have me."

"Shut up," Nick said.

"Please don't say that, Nickie. I'll go back or I'll stay just as you want. I'll go back whenever you tell me to. But I won't have fights. Haven't we seen enough fights in families?"

"Yes," said Nick.

"I know I forced you to take me. But I fixed it so you wouldn't get in trouble about it. And I did keep them from catching you."

They had reached the height of land and from here they could see the lake again although from here it looked narrow now and almost like a big river.

"We cut across country here," Nick said. "Then we'll hit that old logging road. Here's where you go back from if you want to go back."

He took off his pack and put it back into the timber and his sister leaned the rifle on it."

"Sit down, Littless, and take a rest," he said. "We're both tired."

Nick lay with his head on the pack and his sister lay by him with her head on his shoulder.

"I'm not going back, Nickie, unless you tell me to," she said. "I just don't want fights. Promise me we won't have fights?"

"Promise."

"I won't talk about Trudy."

"The hell with Trudy."

"I want to be useful and a good partner."

"You are. You won't mind if I get restless and mix it up with being lonesome?"

"No. We'll take good care of each other and have fun. We can have a lovely time."

"All right. We'll start to have it now."

"I've been having it all the time."

"We just have one pretty hard stretch and then a really hard stretch and then we'll be there. We might as well wait until it gets light to start. You got to sleep, Littless. Are you warm enough?"

"Oh, yes, Nickie, I've got my sweater."

She curled up beside him and was asleep. In a little while Nick was sleeping, too. He slept for two hours until the morning light woke him.

Nick had circled around through the second-growth timber until they had come onto the old logging road.

"We couldn't leave tracks going into it from the main road," he told his sister.

The old road was so overgrown that he had to stoop many times to avoid hitting branches.

"It's like a tunnel," his sister said.

"It opens up after a while."

"Have I ever been here before?"

"No. This goes up way beyond where I ever took you hunting."

"Does it come out on the secret place?"

"No, Littless. We have to go through some long bad slashings. Nobody gets in where we're going."

They kept on along the road and then took another road that was even more overgrown. Then they came out into a clearing. There was fireweed and brush in the clearing and the old cabins of the logging camp. They were very old and some of the roofs had fallen in. But there was a spring by the road and they both drank at it. The sun wasn't up yet and they both felt hollow and empty in the early morning after the night of walking.

"All this beyond was hemlock forest," Nick said. "They only cut it for the bark and they never used the logs."

"But what happens to the road?"

"They must have cut up at the far end first and hauled and piled the bark by the road to snake it out. Then finally they cut everything right to the road and piled the bark here and then pulled out."

"Is the secret place beyond all this slashing?"

"Yes. We go through the slashing and then some more road and then another slashing and then we come to virgin timber."

"How did they leave it when they cut all this?"

"I don't know. It belonged to somebody that wouldn't sell, I guess. They stole a lot from the edges and paid stumpage on it. But the good part's still there and there isn't any passable road into it."

"But why can't people go down the creek? The creek has to come from somewhere?"

They were resting before they started the bad traveling through the slashing and Nick wanted to explain.

"Look, Littless. The creek crosses the main road we were on and it goes through a farmer's land. The farmer has it fenced for a pasture and he runs people off that want to fish. So they stop at the bridge on his land. On the section of the creek where they would hit if they cut across his pasture on the other side from his house he runs a bull. The bull is mean and he really runs everybody off. He's the meanest bull I ever saw and he just stays there, mean all the time, and hunts for people. Then after him the farmer's land ends and there's a section of cedar swamp with sink holes and you'd have to know it to get through. And then, even if you know it, it's bad. Below that is the secret place. We're going in over the hills and sort of in the back way. Then below the secret place there's real swamp. Bad swamp that you can't get through. Now we better start the bad part."

The bad part and the part that was worse were behind them now. Nick had climbed over many logs that were higher than his head and others that were up to his waist. He would take the rifle and lay it down on the top of the log and pull his sister up and then she would slide down on the far side or he would lower himself down and take the rifle and help the girl down. They went over and around piles of brush and it was hot in the slashing, and the pollen from the ragweed and the fireweed dusted the girl's hair and made her sneeze.

"Damn slashings," she said to Nick. They were resting on top of a big log ringed where they sat by the cutting of the barkpeelers. The ring was gray in the rotting gray log and all around were other long gray trunks and gray brush and branches with the brilliant and worthless seeds growing.

"This is the last one," Nick said.

"I hate them," his sister said. "And the damn weeds are like flowers in a tree cemetery if nobody took care of it."

"You see why I didn't want to try to make it in the dark."

"We couldn't."

"No. And nobody's going to chase us through here. Now we come into the good part."

They came from the hot sun of the slashings into the shade of the great trees. The slashings had run up to the top of a ridge and over and then the forest began. They were walking on the brown forest floor now and it was springy and cool under their feet. There was no underbrush and the trunks of the trees rose sixty feet high before there were any branches. It was cool in the shade of the trees and high up in them Nick could hear the breeze that was rising. No sun came through as they walked and Nick knew there would be no sun through the high top branches until nearly noon. His sister put her hand in his and walked close to him.

"I'm not scared, Nickie. But it makes me feel very strange."

"Me, too," Nick said. "Always."

"I never was in woods like these."

"This is all the virgin timber left around here."

"Do we go through it very long?"

"Quite a way."

"I'd be afraid if I were alone."

"It makes me feel strange. But I'm not afraid."

"I said that first."

"I know. Maybe we say it because we are afraid."

"No. I'm not afraid because I'm with you. But I know I'd be afraid alone. Did you ever come here with anyone else?"

"No. Only by myself."

"And you weren't afraid?"

"No. But I always feel strange. Like the way I ought to feel in church."

"Nickie, where we're going to live isn't as solemn as this, is it?"

"No. Don't you worry. There it's cheerful. You just enjoy this, Littless. This is good for you. This is the way forests were in the olden days. This is about the last good country there is left. Nobody gets in here ever."

"I love the olden days. But I wouldn't want it all this solemn."

"It wasn't all solemn. But the hemlock forests were."

"It's wonderful walking. I thought behind our house was wonderful. But this is better. Nickie, do you believe in God? You don't have to answer if you don't want to."

"I don't know."

"All right. You don't have to say it. But you don't mind if I say my prayers at night?"

"No. I'll remind you if you forget."

"Thank you. Because this kind of woods makes me feel awfully religious."

"That's why they build cathedrals to be like this."

"You've never seen a cathedral, have you?"

"No. But I've read about them and I can imagine them. This is the best one we have around here."

"Do you think we can go to Europe some time and see cathedrals?"

"Sure we will. But first I have to get out of this trouble and learn how to make some money."

"Do you think you'll ever make money writing?"

"If I get good enough."

"Couldn't you maybe make it if you wrote cheerfuller things? That isn't my opinion. Our mother said everything you write is morbid."

"It's too morbid for the *St. Nicholas*," Nick said. "They didn't say it. But they didn't like it."

"But the *St. Nicholas* is our favorite magazine."

"I know," said Nick. "But I'm too morbid for it already. And I'm not even grown-up."

"When is a man grown-up? When he's married?"

"No. Until you're grown-up they send you to reform school. After you're grown-up they send you to the penitentiary."

"I'm glad you're not grown-up then."

"They're not going to send me anywhere," Nick said. "And let's not talk morbid even if I write morbid."

"I didn't say it was morbid."

"I know. Everybody else does, though."

"Let's be cheerful, Nickie," his sister said. "These woods make us too solemn."

"We'll be out of them pretty soon," Nick told her. "Then you'll see where we're going to live. Are you hungry, Littless?"

"A little."

"I'll bet," Nick said. "We'll eat a couple of apples."

They were coming down a long hill when they saw sunlight ahead through the tree trunks. Now, at the edge of the timber, there was wintergreen growing and some partridgeberries and the forest floor began to be alive with growing things. Through the tree trunks they saw an open meadow that sloped to where white birches grew along the stream. Below the meadow and the line of the birches there was the dark green of a cedar swamp and far beyond the swamp there were dark blue hills. There was an arm of the lake between the swamp and the hills. But from here they could not see it. They only felt from the distances that it was there.

"Here's the spring," Nick said to his sister. "And here's the stones where I camped before."

"It's a beautiful, beautiful place, Nickie," his sister said. "Can we see the lake, too?"

"There's a place where we can see it. But it's better to camp here. I'll get some wood and we'll make breakfast."

"The firestones are very old."

"It's a very old place," Nick said. "The firestones are Indian."

"How did you come to it straight through the woods with no trail and no blazes?"

"Didn't you see the direction sticks on the three ridges?"

"No."

"I'll show them to you sometime."

"Are they yours?"

"No. They're from the old days."

"Why didn't you show them to me?"

"I don't know," Nick said. "I was showing off I guess."

"Nickie, they'll never find us here."

"I hope not," Nick said.

*   *   *

In the night he was cold and he spread his Mackinaw coat over his sister and rolled his back over closer to her so that there was more of his side of the blanket under him. He felt for the gun and tucked it under his leg again. The air was cold and sharp to breathe and he smelled the cut hemlock and balsam boughs. He had not realized how tired he was until the cold had waked him. Now he lay comfortable again feeling the warmth of his sister's body against his back and he thought, I must take good care of her and keep her happy and get her back safely. He listened to her breathing and to the quiet of the night and then he was asleep again.

It was just light enough to see the far hills beyond the swamp when he woke. He lay quietly and stretched the stiffness from his body. Then he sat up and pulled on his khaki trousers and put on his moccasins. He watched his sister sleeping with the collar of the warm Mackinaw coat under her chin and her high cheek-bones and brown freckled skin light rose under the brown, her chopped-off hair showing the beautiful line of her head and emphasizing her straight nose and her close-set ears. He wished he could draw her face and he watched the way her long lashes lay on her cheeks.

She looks like a small wild animal, he thought, and she sleeps like one. How would you say her head looks, he thought. I guess the nearest is that it looks as though someone had cut her hair off on a wooden block with an ax. It has a sort of a carved look. He loved his sister very much and she loved him too much. But, he thought, I guess those things straighten out. At least I hope so.

There's no sense waking anyone up, he thought. She must have been really tired if I'm as tired as I am. If we were all right here we are doing just what we should do: staying out of sight until things quiet down and that down-state man pulls out. I've got to feed her better, though. It's a shame I couldn't have outfitted really good.

We've got a lot of things, though. The pack was heavy enough. But what we want to get today is berries. I better get a partridge or a couple if I can. We can get good mushrooms, too. We'll have to be careful about the bacon but we won't need it with the shortening. Maybe I fed her too light last night. She's used to lots of milk, too, and sweet things. Don't worry about it. We'll feed good. It's a good thing she likes trout. They were really good. Don't worry about her. She'll eat wonderfully. But, Nick, boy, you certainly didn't feed her too much yesterday. Better to let her sleep than to wake her up now. There's plenty for you to do.

He started to get some things out of the pack very carefully and his sister smiled in her sleep. The brown skin came taut over her cheekbones when she smiled and the undercolor showed. She did not wake and he started to prepare to make breakfast and get the fire ready. There was plenty of wood cut and he built a very small fire and made tea while he waited to start breakfast. He drank his tea straight and ate three dried apricots and he tried to read in *Lorna Doone*. But he had read it and it did not have magic any more and he knew it was a loss on this trip.

Late in the afternoon, when they had made camp, he had put some prunes in a tin pail to soak and he put them on the fire now to stew. In the pack he found the prepared buckwheat flour and he put it out with an enameled saucepan and a tin cup to mix the flour with water to make a batter. He had the tin of vegetable shortening and he cut a piece off the top of an empty flour sack and wrapped it around a cut stick and tied it tight with a piece of fish line. Littless had brought four old flour sacks and he was proud of her.

He mixed the batter and put the skillet on the fire, greasing it with the shortening which he spread with the cloth on the stick. First it made the skillet shine darkly, then it sizzled and spat and he greased again and poured the batter smoothly and watched it bubble and then start to firm around the edges. He watched the rising and the forming of the texture and the gray color of the cake. He loosened it from the pan with a fresh clean chip and flipped it and caught it, the beautiful browned side up, the other sizzling. He could feel its weight but see it growing in buoyancy in the skillet.

"Good morning," his sister said. "Did I sleep awfully late?"

"No, devil."

She stood up with her shirt hanging down over her brown legs.

"You've done everything."

"No. I just started the cakes."

"Doesn't that one smell wonderful? I'll go to the spring and wash and come and help."

"Don't wash in the spring."

"I'm not white man," she said. She was gone behind the lean-to.

"Where did you leave the soap?" she asked.

"It's by the spring. There's an empty lard bucket. Bring the butter, will you. It's in the spring."

"I'll be right back."

There was half a pound of butter and she brought it wrapped in the oiled paper in the empty lard bucket.

They ate the buckwheat cakes with butter and Log Cabin syrup out of a tin Log Cabin can. The top of the chimney unscrewed and the syrup poured from the chimney. They were both very hungry and the cakes were delicious with the butter melting on them and running down into the cut places with the syrup. They ate the prunes out of the tin cups and drank the juice. Then they drank tea from the same cups.

"Prunes taste like a celebration," Littless said. "Think of that. How did you sleep, Nickie?"

"Good."

"Thank you for putting the Mackinaw on me. Wasn't it a lovely night, though?"

"Yes. Did you sleep all night?"

"I'm still asleep. Nickie, can we stay here always?"

"I don't think so. You'd grow up and have to get married."

"I'm going to get married to you anyway. I want to be your common-law wife. I read about it in the paper."

"That's where you read about the Unwritten Law."

"Sure. I'm going to be your common-law wife under the Unwritten Law. Can't I, Nickie?"

"No."

"I will. I'll surprise you. All you have to do is live a certain time as man and wife. I'll get them to count this time now. It's just like homesteading."

"I won't let you file."

"You can't help yourself. That's the Unwritten Law. I've thought it out lots of times. I'll get cards printed Mrs. Nick Adams, Cross Village, Michigan—common-law wife. I'll hand these out to a few people openly each year until the time's up."

"I don't think it would work."

"I've got another scheme. We'll have a couple of children while I'm a minor. Then you have to marry me under the Unwritten Law."

"That's not the Unwritten Law."

"I get mixed up on it."

"Anyway, nobody knows yet if it works."

"It must," she said. "Mr. Thaw is counting on it."

"Mr. Thaw might make a mistake."

"Why Nickie, Mr. Thaw practically invented the Unwritten Law."

"I thought it was his lawyer."

"Well, Mr. Thaw put in the action anyway."

"I don't like Mr. Thaw," Nick Adams said.

"That's good. There's things about him I don't like either. But he certainly made the paper more interesting reading, didn't he?"

"He gives the others something new to hate."

"They hate Mr. Stanford White, too."

"I think they're jealous of both of them."

"I believe that's true, Nickie. Just like they're jealous of us."

"Think anybody is jealous of us now?"

"Not right now maybe. Our mother will think we're fugitives from justice steeped in sin and iniquity. It's a good thing she doesn't know I got you that whiskey."

"I tried it last night. It's very good."

"Oh, I'm glad. That's the first whiskey I ever stole anywhere. Isn't it wonderful that it's good? I didn't think anything about those people could be good."

"I've got to think about them too much. Let's not talk about them," Nick said.

"All right. What are we going to do today?"

"What would you like to do?"

"I'd like to go to Mr. John's store and get everything we need."

"We can't do that."

"I know it. What do you plan to really do?"

"We ought to get some berries and I ought to get a partridge or some partridges. We've always got trout. But I don't want you to get tired of trout."

"Were you ever tired of trout?"

"No. But they say people get tired of them."

"I wouldn't get tired of them," Littless said. "You get tired of pike right away. But you never get tired of trout nor of perch. I know, Nickie. True."

"You don't get tired of walleyed pike either," Nick said. "Only of shovelnose. Boy, you sure get tired of them."

"I don't like the pitchfork bones," his sister said. "It's a fish that surfeits you."

"We'll clean up here and I'll find a place to cache the shells and we'll make a trip for berries and try to get some birds."

"I'll bring two lard pails and a couple of the sacks," his sister said.

"Littless," Nick said. "You remember about going to the bathroom, will you please?"

"Of course."

"That's important."

"I know it. You remember, too."

"I will."

Nick went back into the timber and buried the carton of .22 long-rifles and the loose boxes of .22 shorts under the brown-needled floor at the base of a big hemlock. He put back the packed needles he had cut with his knife and made a small cut as far up as he could reach on the heavy bark of the tree. He took a bearing on the tree and then came out onto the hillside and walked down to the lean-to.

It was a lovely morning now. The sky was high and clear blue and no clouds had come yet. Nick was happy with his sister and he thought, no matter how this thing comes out we might as well have a good happy time. He had already learned there was only one day at a time and that it was always the day you were in. It would be today until it was tonight and tomorrow would be today again. This was the main thing he had learned so far.

Today was a good day and coming down to the camp with his rifle he was happy although their trouble was like a fishhook caught in his pocket that pricked him occasionally as he walked. They left the pack inside the lean-to. There were great odds against a bear bothering it in the daytime because any bear would be down below feeding on berries around the swamp. But Nick buried the bottle of whiskey up behind the spring. Littless was not back yet and Nick sat down on the log of the fallen tree they were using for firewood and checked his rifle. They were going after partridges so he pulled out the tube of the magazine and poured the long-rifle cartridges into his hand and then put them into a chamois pouch and filled the magazine with .22 shots. They made less noise and would not tear the meat up if he could not get head shots.

He was all ready now and wanted to start. Where's that girl any-way, he thought. Then he thought, don't get excited. You told her to take her time. Don't get nervous. But he was nervous and it made him angry at himself.

"Here I am," his sister said. "I'm sorry that I took so long. I went too far away, I guess."

"You're fine," Nick said. "Let's go. You have the pails?"

"Uh huh, and covers, too."

They started down across the hill to the creek. Nick looked carefully up the stream and along the hillside. His sister watched him. She had the pails in one of the sacks and carried it slung over her shoulder by the other sack.

"Aren't you taking a pole, Nickie?" she asked him.

"No. I'll cut one if we fish."

He moved ahead of his sister, holding the rifle in one hand, keeping a little way away from the stream. He was hunting now.

"It's a strange creek," his sister said.

"It's the biggest small stream I've ever known," Nick told her.

"It's deep and scary for a little stream."

"It keeps having new springs," Nick said. "And it digs under the bank and it digs down. It's awful cold water, Littless. Feel it."

"Gee," she said. It was numbing cold.

"The sun warms it a little," Nick said. "But not much. We'll hunt along easy. There's a berry patch down below."

They went along down the creek. Nick was studying the banks. He had seen a mink's track and shown it to his sister and they had seen tiny ruby-crowned kinglets that were hunting insects and let the boy and girl come close as they moved sharply and delicately in the cedars. They had seen cedar waxwings so calm and gentle and distinguished moving in their lovely elegance with the magic wax touches on their wing coverts and their tails, and Littless had said, "They're the most beautiful, Nickie. There couldn't be more simply beautiful birds."

"They're built like your face," he said.

"No, Nickie. Don't make fun. Cedar waxwings make me so proud and happy that I cry."

"When they wheel and light and then move so proud and friendly and gently," Nick said.

They had gone on and suddenly Nick had raised the rifle and shot before his sister could see what he was looking at. Then she heard the sound of a big bird tossing and beating its wings on the ground. She saw Nick pumping the gun and shoot twice more and each time she heard another pounding of wings in the willow brush. Then there was the whirring noise of wings as large brown birds burst out of the willows and one bird flew only a little way and lit in the willows and with its crested head on one side looked down, bending the collar of feathers on his neck where the other birds were still thumping. The bird looking down from the red willow brush was beautiful, plump, heavy and looked so stupid with his head turned down and as Nick raised his rifle slowly, his sister whispered, "No, Nickie. Please no. We've got plenty."

"All right," Nick said. "You want to take him?"

"No, Nickie. No."

Nick went forward into the willows and picked up the three grouse and batted their heads against the butt of the rifle stock and laid them out on the moss. His sister felt them, warm and full-breasted and beautifully feathered.

"Wait till we eat them," Nick said. He was very happy.

"I'm sorry for them now," his sister said. "They were enjoying the morning just like we were."

She looked up at the grouse still in the tree.

"It does look a little silly still staring down," she said.

"This time of year the Indians call them fool hens. After they've been hunted they get smart. They're not the real fool hens. Those never get smart. They're willow grouse. These are ruffled grouse."

"I hope we'll get smart," his sister said. "Tell him to go away, Nickie."

"You tell him."

"Go away, partridge."

The grouse did not move.

Nick raised the rifle and the grouse looked at him. Nick knew he could not shoot the bird without making his sister sad and he made a noise blowing out so his tongue rattled and lips shook like a grouse bursting from cover and the bird looked at him fascinated.

"We better not annoy him," Nick said.

"I'm sorry, Nickie," his sister said. "He *is* stupid."

"Wait till we eat them," Nick told her. "You'll see why we hunt them."

"Are they out of season, too?"

"Sure. But they are full grown and nobody but us would ever hunt them. I kill plenty of great horned owls and a great horned owl will kill a partridge every day if he can. They hunt all the time and they kill all the good birds."

"He certainly could kill that one easy," his sister said. "I don't feel bad any more. Do you want a bag to carry them in?"

"I'll draw them and then pack them in the bag with some ferns. It isn't so far to the berries now."

They sat against one of the cedars and Nick opened the birds and took out their warm entrails and feeling the inside of the birds hot on his right hand he found the edible parts of the giblets and cleaned them and then washed them in the stream. When the birds were cleaned he smoothed their feathers and wrapped them in ferns and put them in the flour sack. He tied the mouth of the flour sack and two corners with a piece of fish line and slung it over his shoulder and then went back to the stream and dropped the entrails in and tossed some bright pieces of lung in to see the trout rise in the rapid heavy flow of the water.

"They'd make good bait but we don't need bait now," he said. "Our trout are all in the stream and we'll take them when we need them."

"This stream would make us rich if it was near home," his sister said.

"It would be fished out then. This is the last really wild stream there is except in another awful country to get to beyond the foot of the lake. I never brought anybody here to fish."

"Who ever fishes it?"

"Nobody I know."

"Is it a virgin stream?"

"No. Indians fish it. But they're gone now since they quit cutting hemlock bark and the camps closed down."

"Does the Evans boy know?"

"Not him," Nick said. But then he thought about it and it made him feel sick. He could see the Evans boy.

"What're you thinking, Nickie?"

"I wasn't thinking."

"You were thinking. You tell me. We're partners."

"He might know," Nick said. "Goddam it. He might know."

"But you don't know that he knows?"

"No. That's the trouble. If I did I'd get out."

"Maybe he's back at camp now," his sister said.

"Don't talk that way. Do you want to bring him?"

"No," she said. "Please, Nickie, I'm sorry I brought it up."

"I'm not," Nick said. "I'm grateful. I knew it anyway. Only I'd stopped thinking about it. I have to think about things now the rest of my life."

"You always thought about things."

"Not like this."

"Let's go down and get the berries anyway," Littless said. "There isn't anything we can do now to help, is there?"

"No," Nick said. "We'll pick the berries and get back to camp."

But Nick was trying to accept it now and think his way all the way through it. He must not get in a panic about it. Nothing had changed. Things were just as they were when he had decided to come here and let things blow over. The Evans boy could have followed him here before. But it was very unlikely. He could have followed him one time when he had gone in from the road through the Hodges' place, but it was doubtful. Nobody had been fishing the stream. He could be sure of that. But the Evans boy did not care about fishing.

"All that bastard cares about is trailing me," he said.

"I know it, Nickie."

"This is three times he's made trouble."

"I know it, Nickie. But don't you kill him."

That's why she came along, Nick thought. That's why she's here. I can't do it while she's along.

"I know I mustn't kill him," he said. "There's nothing we can do now. Let's not talk about it."

"As long as you don't kill him," his sister said. "There's nothing we can't get out of and nothing that won't blow over."

"Let's get back to camp," Nick said.

"Without the berries?"

"We'll get the berries another day."

"Are you nervous, Nickie?"

"Yes. I'm sorry."

"But what good will we be back at camp?"

"We'll know quicker."

"Can't we just go along the way we were going?"

"Not now. I'm not scared, Littless. And don't you be scared. But something's made me nervous."

Nick had cut up away from the stream into the edge of the timber and they were walking in the shade of the trees. They would come onto the camp now from above.

From the timber they approached the camp carefully. Nick went ahead with the rifle. The camp had not been visited.

"You stay here," Nick told his sister. "I'm going to have a look beyond." He left the sack with the birds and the berry pails with Littless and went well upstream. As soon as he was out of sight of his sister he changed the .22 shorts in the rifle for the long-rifles. I won't kill him, he thought, but anyway it's the right thing to do. He made a careful search of the country. He saw no sign of anyone and he went down to the stream and then downstream and back up to the camp.

"I'm sorry I was nervous, Littless," he said. "We might as well have a good lunch and then we won't have to worry about a fire showing at night."

"I'm worried now, too," she said.

"Don't you be worried. It's just like it was before."

"But he drove us back from getting the berries without him even being here."

"I know. But he's not been here. Maybe he's never even been to this creek ever. Maybe we'll never see him again."

"He makes me scared, Nickie, worse when he's not here than when he's here."

"I know. But there isn't any use being scared."

"What are we going to do?"

"Well, we better wait to cook until night."

"Why did you change?"

"He won't be around here at night. He can't come through the swamp in the dark. We don't have to worry about him early in the mornings and late in the evening nor in the dark. We'll have to be like the deer and only be out then. We'll lay up in the daytime."

"Maybe he'll never come."

"Sure. Maybe."

"But I can stay though, can't I?"

"I ought to get you home."

"No. Please, Nickie. Who's going to keep you from killing him then?"

"Listen, Littless, don't ever talk about killing and remember I never talked about killing. There isn't any killing nor ever going to be any."

"True?"

"True."

"I'm so glad."

"Don't even be that. Nobody ever talked about it."

"All right. I never thought about it nor spoke about it."

"Me either."

"Of course you didn't."

"I never even thought about it."

No, he thought. You never even thought about it. Only all day and all night. But you mustn't think about it in front of her because she can feel it because she is your sister and you love each other.

"Are you hungry, Littless?"

"Not really."

"Eat some of the hard chocolate and I'll get some fresh water from the spring."

"I don't have to have anything."

They looked across to where the big white clouds of the eleven o'clock breeze were coming up over the blue hills beyond the swamp. The sky was a high clear blue and the clouds came up white and detached themselves from behind the hills and moved high in the sky as the breeze freshened and the shadows of the clouds moved over the swamp and across the hillside. The wind blew in the trees now and was cool as they lay in the shade. The water from the spring was cold and fresh in the tin pail and the chocolate was not quite bitter but was hard and crunched as they chewed it.

"It's as good as the water in the spring where we were when we first saw them," his sister said. "It tastes even better after the chocolate."

"We can cook if you're hungry."

"I'm not if you're not."

"I'm always hungry. I was a fool not to go on and get the berries."

"No. You came back to find out."

"Look, Littless. I know a good place back by the slashing we came through where we can get berries. I'll cache everything and we can go in there through the timber all the way and pick a couple of pails full and then we'll have them ahead for tomorrow. It isn't a bad walk."

"All right. But I'm fine."

"Aren't you hungry?"

"No. Not at all now after the chocolate. I'd love to just stay and read. We had a nice walk when we were hunting."

"All right," Nick said. "Are you tired from yesterday?"

"Maybe a little."

"We'll take it easy. I'll read *Wuthering Heights*."

"Is it too old to read out loud to me?"

"No."

"Will you read it?"

"Sure."

An African Story

(from *The Garden of Eden*)

He was waiting for the moon to rise and he felt Kibo's hair rise under his hand as he stroked him to be quiet and they both watched and listened as the moon came up and gave them shadows. His arm was around the dog's neck now and he could feel him shivering. All of the night sounds had stopped. They did not hear the elephant and David did not see him until the dog turned his head and seemed to settle into David. Then the elephant's shadow covered them and he moved past making no noise at all and they smelled him in the light wind that came down from the mountain. He smelled strong but old and sour and when he was past David saw that the left tusk was so long it seemed to reach the ground.

They waited but no other elephants came by and then David and the dog started off running in the moonlight. The dog kept close behind him and when David stopped the dog pressed his muzzle into the back of his knee.

David had to see the bull again and they came up on him at the edge of the forest. He was traveling toward the mountain and slowly moving into the steady night breeze. David came close enough to see him cut off the moon again and to smell the sour oldness but he could not see the right tusk. He was afraid to work closer with the dog and he took him back with the wind and pushed him down against the base of a tree and tried to make him understand. He thought the dog would stay and he did but when David moved up toward the bulk of the elephant again he felt the wet muzzle against the hollow of his knee.

The two of them followed the elephant until he came to an opening in the trees. He stood there moving his huge ears. His bulk was in the shadow but the moonlight would be on his head. David reached behind him and closed the dog's jaws gently with his hand and then moved softly and unbreathing to his right along the edge of the night breeze, feeling it on his cheek, edging with it, never letting it get between him and the bulk until he could see the elephant's head and the great ears slowly moving. The right tusk was as thick as his own thigh and it curved down almost to the ground.

He and Kibo moved back, the wind on his neck now, and they backtracked out of the forest and into the open park country. The dog was ahead of him now and he stopped where David had left the two hunting spears by the trail when they had followed the elephant. He swung them over his shoulder in their thong and leather cup harness and, with his best spear that he had kept with him all the time in his hand, they started on the trail for the shamba. The moon was high now and he wondered why there was no drumming from the shamba. Something was strange if his father was there and there was no drumming.

David had felt the tiredness as soon as they had picked up the trail again.

For a long time he had been fresher and in better shape than the two men and impatient with their slow trailing and the regular halts his father made each hour on the hour. He could have moved ahead much faster than Juma and his father but when he started to tire they were the same as ever and at noon they took only the usual five-minute rest and he had seen that Juma was increasing the pace a little. Perhaps he wasn't. Perhaps it had only seemed faster but the elephant dung was fresher now although it was not warm yet to the touch. Juma gave him the rifle to carry after they came upon the last pile of dung but after an hour he looked at him and took it back. They had been climbing steadily across a slope of the mountain but now the trail went down and from a gap in the forest he saw broken country ahead. "Here's where the tough part starts, Davey," his father said.

It was then he knew that he should have been sent back to the shamba once he had put them on the trail. Juma had known it for a long time. His father knew it now and there was nothing to be done. It was another of his mistakes and there was nothing to do now except gamble.

David looked down at the big flattened circle of the print of the elephant's foot and saw where the bracken had been pressed down and where a broken stem of a weed was drying. Juma picked it up and looked at the sun. Juma handed the broken weed to David's father and his father rolled it in his fingers. David noticed the white flowers that were drooped and dying. But they still had not dried in the sun nor shed their petals.

"It's going to be a bitch," his father said. "Let's get going."

Late in the afternoon they were still tracking through the broken country. He had been sleepy now for a long time and as he watched the two men he knew that sleepiness was his real enemy and he followed their pace and tried to move through and out of the sleep that deadened him. The two men relieved each other tracking on the hour and the one who was in second place looked back at him at regular intervals to check if he was with them. When they made a dry camp at dark in the forest he went to sleep as soon as he sat down and woke with Juma holding his moccasins and feeling his bare feet for blisters. His father had spread his coat over him and was sitting by him with a piece of cold cooked meat and two biscuits. He offered him a water bottle with cold tea.

"He'll have to feed, Davey," his father said. "Your feet are in good shape. They're as sound as Juma's. Eat this slowly and drink some tea and go to sleep again. We haven't any problems."

"I'm sorry I was so sleepy."

"You and Kibo hunted and traveled all last night. Why shouldn't you be sleepy? You can have a little more meat if you want it."

"I'm not hungry."

"Good. We're good for three days. We'll hit water again tomorrow. Plenty of creeks come off the mountain."

"Where's he going?"

"Juma thinks he knows."

"Isn't it bad?"

"Not too bad, Davey."

"I'm going back to sleep," David had said. "I don't need your coat."

"Juma and I are all right," his father said. "I always sleep warm you know."

David was asleep even before his father said good night. Then he woke once with the moonlight on his face and he thought of the elephant with his great ears moving as he stood in the forest, his head hung down with the weight of the tusks. David thought then in the night that the hollow way he felt as he remembered him was from waking hungry. But it was not and he found that out in the next three days.

The next day was very bad because long before noon he knew that it was not just the need for sleep that made the difference between a boy and men. For the first three hours he was fresher than they were and he asked Juma for the .303 rifle to carry but Juma shook his head. He did not smile and he had always been David's best friend and had taught him to hunt. He offered it to me yesterday, David thought, and I'm in better shape today than I was then. He was, too, but by ten o'clock he knew the day would be as bad or worse than the day before.

It was as silly for him to think that he could trail with his father as to think he could fight with him. He knew too that it was not just that they were men. They were professional hunters and he knew now that was why Juma would not even waste a smile. They knew everything the elephant had done, pointed out the signs of it to each other without speaking, and when the tracking became difficult his father always yielded to Juma. When they stopped to fill the water bottles at a stream his father said, "Just last the day out, Davey." Then when they were past the broken country and climbing toward the forest the tracks of the elephant turned off to the right onto an old elephant trail. He saw his father and Juma talking and when he got up to them Juma was looking back over the way they had come and then at a far distant stony island of hills in the dry country and seemed to be taking a bearing of this against the peaks of three far blue hills on the horizon.

"Juma knows where he's going now," his father explained. "He thought he knew before but then he dropped down into this stuff." He looked back at the country they had come through all day. "Where he's headed now is pretty good going but we'll have to climb."

They climbed until it was dark and then made another dry camp. David killed two spur fowl with his slingshot out of a small flock that had walked across the trail just before the sunset. The birds had come into the old elephant trail to dust, walking neatly and plumply, and when the pebble broke the back of one and the bird began to jerk and toss with its wings thumping, another bird ran forward to peck at it and David pouched another pebble and pulled it back and sent it against the ribs of the second bird. As he ran forward to put his hand on it the other birds whirred off. Juma had looked back and smiled this time and David picked up the two birds, warm and plump and smoothly feathered, and knocked their heads against the handle of his hunting knife.

Now where they were camped for the night his father said, "I've never seen that type of francolin quite so high. You did very well to get a double on them."

257

Juma cooked the birds spitted on a stick over the coals of a very small fire. His father drank a whiskey and water from the cup top on his flask as they lay and watched Juma cook. Afterward Juma gave them each a breast with the heart in it and ate the two necks and backs and the legs himself.

"It makes a great difference, Davey," his father said. "We're very well off on rations now."

"How far are we behind him?" David asked.

"We're quite close," his father said. "It depends on whether he travels when the moon comes up. It's an hour later tonight and two hours later than when you found him."

"Why does Juma think he knows where he's going?"

"He wounded him and killed his *askari* not too far from here."

"When?"

"Five years ago, he says. That may mean anytime. When you were still a *toto* he says."

"Has he been alone since then?"

"He says so. He hasn't seen him. Only heard of him."

"How big does he say he is?"

"Close to two hundred. Bigger than anything I've ever seen. He says there's only been one greater elephant and he came from near here too."

"I'd better get to sleep," David said. "I hope I'll be better tomorrow."

"You were splendid today," his father said. "I was very proud of you. So was Juma."

In the night when he woke after the moon was up he was sure they were not proud of him except perhaps for his dexterity in killing the two birds. He had found the elephant at night and followed him to see that he had both of his tusks and then returned to find the two men and put them on the trail. David knew they were proud of that. But once the deadly following started he was useless to them and a danger to their success just as Kibo had been to him when he had gone up close to the elephant in the night, and he

258

knew they must each have hated themselves for not having sent him back when there was time. The tusks of the elephant weighed two hundred pounds apiece. Ever since these tusks had grown beyond their normal size the elephant had been hunted for them and now the three of them would kill him for them.

David was sure that they would kill him now because he, David, had lasted through the day and kept up after the pace had destroyed him by noon. So they probably were proud of him doing that. But he had brought nothing useful to the hunt and they would have been far better off without him. Many times during the day he had wished that he had never betrayed the elephant and in the afternoon he remembered wishing that he had never seen him. Awake in the moonlight he knew that was not true.

The next morning they were following the spoor of the elephant on an old elephant trail that was a hard-packed worn road through the forest. It looked as though elephants had traveled it ever since the lava had cooled from the mountain and the trees had first grown tall and close.

Juma was very confident and they moved fast. Both his father and Juma seemed very sure of themselves and the going on the elephant road was so easy that Juma gave him the .303 to carry as they went on through the broken light of the forest. Then they lost the trail in smoking piles of fresh dung and the flat round prints of a herd of elephants that had come onto the elephant road from the heavy forest on the left of the trail. Juma had taken the .303 from David angrily. It was afternoon before they worked up to the herd and around it, seeing the gray bulks through the trees and the movement of the big ears and the searching trunks coiling and uncoiling, hearing the crash of branches broken, the crash of trees pushed over, the rumbling in the bellies of the elephants and the slap and thud of the dung falling.

They had found the trail of the old bull finally and when it turned off onto a smaller elephant road Juma had looked at David's father and grinned showing his filed teeth and his father had nodded his head. They looked as though they had a dirty secret, just as they had looked when he had found them that night at the shamba.

It was not very long before they came on the secret. It was off to the right in the forest and the tracks of the old bull led to it. It was a skull as high as David's chest and white from the sun and the rain. There was a deep depression in the forehead and a ridge ran from between the bare white eye sockets and flared out in empty broken holes where the tusks had been chopped away.

Juma pointed out where the great elephant they were trailing had stood while he looked down at the skull and where his trunk had moved it a little way from the place it had rested on the ground and where the points of his tusks had touched the ground beside it. He showed David the single hole in the big depression in the white bone of the forehead and then the four holes close together in the bone around the earhole. He grinned at David and at his father and took a .303 solid from his pocket and fitted the nose into the hole in the bone of the forehead.

"Here is where Juma wounded the big bull," his father said. "This was his *askari*. His friend, really, because he was a big bull too. He charged and Juma knocked him down and finished him in the ear."

Juma was pointing out the scattered bones and how the big bull had walked among them. Juma and David's father were both very pleased with what they had found.

"How long do you suppose he and his friend had been together?" David asked his father.

"I haven't the faintest idea," his father said. "Ask Juma."

"You ask him, please."

His father and Juma spoke together and Juma had looked at David and laughed.

"Probably four or five times your life, he says," David's father told him. "He doesn't know or care really."

I care, David thought. I saw him in the moonlight and he was alone but I had Kibo. Kibo has me too. The bull wasn't doing any harm and now we've tracked him to where he came to see his dead friend and now we're going to kill him. It's my fault. I betrayed him.

Now Juma had worked out the trail and motioned to his father and they started on.

My father doesn't need to kill elephants to live, David thought. Juma would not have found him if I had not seen him. He had his chance at him and all he did was wound him and kill his friend. Kibo and I found him and I never should have told them and I should have kept him secret and had him always and let them stay drunk at the beer shamba. Juma was so drunk we could not wake him. I'm going to keep everything a secret always. I'll never tell them anything again. If they kill him Juma will drink his share of the ivory or just buy himself another goddamn wife. Why didn't you help the elephant when you could? All you had to do was not go on the second day. No, that wouldn't have stopped them. Juma would have gone on. You never should have told them. Never, never tell them. Try and remember that. Never tell anyone anything ever. Never tell anyone anything again.

His father waited for him to come up and said very gently, "He rested here. He's not traveling as he was. We'll be up on him anytime now."

"Fuck elephant hunting," David had said very quietly.

"What's that?" his father asked.

"Fuck elephant hunting," David said softly.

"Be careful you don't fuck it up," his father had said to him and looked at him flatly.

That's one thing, David had thought. He's not stupid. He knows all about it now and he will never trust me again. That's good. I don't want him to because I'll never ever tell him or anybody anything again, never anything again. Never ever never.

* * *

In the morning he was on the far slope of the mountain again. The elephant was no longer traveling as he had been but was moving aimlessly now, feeding occasionally and David had known they were getting close to him.

He tried to remember how he had felt. He had no love for the elephant yet. He must remember that. He had only a sorrow that had come from his own tiredness that had brought an understanding of age. Through being too young, he had learned how it must be to be too old.

He was lonesome for Kibo and thinking of how Juma killing the elephant's friend had turned him against Juma and made the elephant his brother. He knew then how much it meant to him to have seen the elephant in the moonlight and to have followed him and come close to him in the clearing so that he had seen the great tusks. But he did not know that nothing would ever be as good as that again. Now he knew they would kill the elephant and there was nothing he could do about it. He had betrayed the elephant when he had gone back to tell them at the shamba. They would kill me and they would kill Kibo if we had ivory, he had thought, and known it was untrue.

Probably the elephant is going to find where he was born and they'll kill him there. That's all they'd need to make it perfect. They'd like to have killed him where they killed his friend. That would be a big joke. That would have pleased them. The goddamned friend killers.

They had moved to the edge of thick cover now and the elephant was close ahead. David could smell him and they could all hear him pulling down branches and the snapping that they made. His father put his hand on David's shoulder to move him back and have him wait outside and then he took a big pinch of ashes from the pouch in his pocket and tossed it in the air. The ash barely slanted toward them as it fell and his father nodded at Juma and bent down to follow him into the thick cover. David watched their backs and their asses go in and out of sight. He could not hear them move.

David had stood still and listened to the elephant feeding. He could smell him as strongly as he had the night in the moonlight when he had worked up close to him and had seen his wonderful tusks. Then as he stood there it was silent and he could not smell the elephant. Then there had been a high squealing and smashing and a shot by the .303, then the heavy rocking double report of his father's .450, then the smashing and crashing had gone on going steadily away and he had gone into the heavy growth and found Juma shaken and bleeding from his forehead all down over his face and his father white and angry.

"He went for Juma and knocked him over," his father had said. "Juma hit him in the head."

"Where did you hit him?"

"Where I fucking well could," his father had said. "Get on the blood spoor."

There was plenty of blood. One stream as high as David's head that had squirted bright on trunks and leaves and vines and another much lower that was dark and foul with stomach content.

"Lung and gut shot," his father said. "We'll find him down or anchored—I hope the hell," he added.

They found him anchored, in such suffering and despair that he could no longer move. He had crashed through the heavy cover where he had been feeding and crossed a path of open forest and David and his father ran along the heavily splashed blood trail. Then the elephant had gone on into thick forest and David had seen him ahead standing gray and huge against the trunk of a tree. David could only see his stern and then his father moved ahead and he followed and they came alongside the elephant as though he was a ship and David saw the blood coming from his flanks and running down his sides and then his father raised his rifle and fired and the elephant turned his head with the great tusks moving heavy and slow and looked at them and when his father fired the second barrel the elephant seemed to sway like a felled tree and came smashing down toward them. But he was not dead. He had been anchored and now he was down with his shoulder broken. He did not move but his eye was alive and looked at David. He had very long eyelashes and his eye was the most alive thing David had ever seen.

"Shoot him in the earhole with the three oh three," his father said. "Go on."

"You shoot him," David had said.

Juma had come up limping and bloody, the skin of his forehead hanging down over his left eye, the bone of his nose showing and one ear torn and had taken the rifle from David without speaking and pushed the muzzle almost into the earhole and fired twice, jerking the bolt and driving it forward angrily. The eye of the elephant had opened wide on the first shot and then started to glaze and blood came out of the ear and ran in two bright streams down the wrinkled gray hide. It was different colored blood and David had thought I must remember that and he had but it had never been of any use to him. Now all the dignity and majesty and all the beauty were gone from the elephant and he was a huge wrinkled pile.

"Well, we got him, Davey, thanks to you," his father had said. "Now we'd better get a fire going so I can put Juma back together again. Come here, you bloody Humpty Dumpty. Those tusks will keep."

Juma had come to him grinning, bringing the tail of the elephant that had no hairs on it at all. They had made a dirty joke and then his father had begun to speak rapidly in Swahili. How far to water? How far will you have to go to get people to get those tusks out of here? How are you, you worthless old pig fucker? What have you broken?

With the answers known his father had said, "You and I will go back to get the packs where we dropped them. Juma can get wood and have the fire ready. The medical kit is in my pack. We have to get the packs before it's dark. He won't infect. It's not like claw wounds. Let's go."

That evening as David had sat by the fire he had looked at Juma with his stitched-up face and his broken ribs and wondered if the elephant had recognized him when he had tried to kill him. He hoped he had. The elephant was his hero now as his father had been for a long time and he had thought, I didn't believe he could do it when he was so old and tired. He would have killed Juma, too. But he didn't look at me as though he wanted to kill me. He only looked sad the same way I felt. He visited his old friend on the day he died.

David remembered how the elephant lost all dignity as soon as his eye had ceased to be alive and how when his father and he had returned with the packs the elephant had already started to swell, even in the cool evening. There was no more true elephant; only the gray wrinkled swelling dead body and the huge mottled brown and yellow tusks that they had killed him for. The tusks were stained with dried blood and he scraped some off with his thumbnail like a dried piece of sealing wax and put it in the pocket of his shirt. That was all he took from the elephant except the beginning of the knowledge of loneliness.

After the butchery his father tried to talk to him that night by the fire.

"He was a murderer you know, Davey," he had said. "Juma says nobody knows how many people he has killed."

"They were all trying to kill him, weren't they?"

"Naturally," his father had said, "with that pair of tusks."

"How could he be a murderer then?"

"Just as you like," his father had said. "I'm sorry you got so mixed up about him."

"I wish he'd killed Juma," David said.

"I think that's carrying it a little far," his father said. "Juma's your friend, you know."

"Not any more."

"No need to tell him so."

"He knows it," David had said.

"I think you misjudge him," his father said and they had left it there.

Then when they were finally back safely with the tusks after all the things that had happened and the tusks were propped against the wall of the stick and mud house, leaning there with their points touching, the tusks so tall and thick that no one could believe them even when they touched them and no one, not even his father, could reach to the top of the bend where they curved in for the points to meet, there when Juma and his father and he were heroes and Kibo was a hero's dog and the men who had carried the tusks were heroes, already slightly drunk heroes and to be drunker, his father had said, "Do you want to make peace, Davey?"

"All right," he said because he knew this was the start of the never telling that he had decided on.

"I'm so glad," his father said. "It's so much simpler and better."

Then they sat on old men's stools under the shade of the fig tree with the tusks against the wall of the hut and drank beer from gourd cups that were brought by a young girl and her younger brother, the servant of heroes, sitting in the dust by the heroic dog of a hero who held an old cockerel, newly promoted to the standing of the heroes' favorite rooster. They sat there and drank beer while the big drum started and the *ngoma* began to build.

"Miss Mary's Lion"

(from *True at First Light*)

"In Africa a thing is true at first light and a lie by noon and you have no more respect for it than for the lovely, perfect weed-fringed lake you see across the sun-baked salt plain. You have walked across that plain in the morning and you know that no such lake is there. But now it is there absolutely true, beautiful and believable."

—Ernest Hemingway

The day that Miss Mary shot her lion was a very beautiful day. That was about all that was beautiful about it. White flowers had blossomed in the night so that with the first daylight before the sun had risen all the meadows looked as though a full moon was shining on new snow through a mist. Mary was up and dressed long before first light. The right sleeve of her bush jacket was rolled up and she had checked all the rounds in her Mannlicher .256. She said she did not feel well and I believed her. She acknowledged

267

G.C.'s and my greetings briefly and we were careful not to make any jokes. I did not know what she had against G.C. except his tendency to lightheartedness in the face of undeniably serious work. Her being angry at me was a sound reaction, I thought. If she were in a bad mood I thought she might feel mean and shoot as deadly as I knew she knew how to shoot. This agreed with my last and greatest theory that she had too kind a heart to kill animals. Some people shoot easily and loosely; others shoot with a dreadful speed that is still so controlled that they have all the time they need to place the bullet as carefully as a surgeon would make his first incision; others are mechanical shots who are very deadly unless something happens to interfere with the mechanics of the shooting. This morning it looked as though Miss Mary was going out to shoot with grim resolution, contemptuous of all those who did not take things with appropriate seriousness, armored in her bad physical condition, which provided an excuse if she missed, and full of rigid, concentrated do-or-die deadliness. It seemed fine to me. It was a new approach.

We waited by the hunting car for it to be light enough to start and we were all solemn and deadly. Ngui nearly always had an evil temper in the very early morning so he was solemn, deadly and sullen. Charo was solemn, deadly but faintly cheerful. He was like a man going to a funeral who did not really feel too deeply about the deceased. Mthuka was happy as always in his deafness watching with his wonderful eyes for the start of the lightening of the darkness.

We were all hunters and it was the start of that wonderful thing, the hunt. There is much mystic nonsense written about hunting but it is something that is probably much older than religion. Some are hunters and some are not. Miss Mary was a hunter and a brave and lovely one but she had come to it late instead of as a child and many of the things that had happened to her in hunting came as unexpectedly as being in heat for the first time to the

kitten when she becomes a cat. She grouped all these new knowl-
edges and changes as things we know and other people don't.

The four of us who had seen her go through these changes and
had seen her now, for months, hunting something grimly and seriously against every possible sort of odds were like the cuadrilla of a
very young matador. If the matador was serious the cuadrilla would
be serious. They knew all the matador's defects and they were all
well paid in different ways. All had lost completely any faith in the
matador and all had regained it many times. As we sat in the car or
moved around it waiting for it to be light enough to set out I was reminded very much of how it is before a bullfight. Our matador was
solemn; so we were solemn, since as is unusual, we loved our matador. Our matador was not well. This made it even more necessary
that he be protected and given even a better chance in everything
he chose to do. But as we sat and leaned and felt sleep drain from us
we were as happy as hunters. Probably no one is as happy as hunters
with the always new, fresh, unknowing day ahead and Mary was a
hunter too. But she had set herself this task and being guided and
trained and indoctrinated into absolute purity and virtue of killing a
lion by Pop who had made her his last pupil and given her ethics he
had never been able to impose on other women so that her killing of
her lion must not be the way such things are done but the way such
things should ideally be done; Pop finding finally in Mary the spirit
of a fighting cock embodied in a woman; a loving and belated killer
with the only defect that no one could say where the shot would go.
Pop had given her the ethics and then it was necessary that he go
away. She had the ethics now but she only had G.C. and me and
neither of us was to be really trusted as Pop was. So now she was
going out again to her corrida that always was postponed.

Mthuka nodded to me that the light was beginning to be possible and we started off through the fields of white flowers where
yesterday all the meadows had been green. As we came even with
the trees of the forest with the high dead yellow grass on our left

Mthuka slid the car to a quiet stop. He turned his head and I saw the arrow-shaped scar on his cheek and the slashes. He said nothing and I followed his eyes. The great black-maned lion, his head huge above the yellow grass, was coming out toward us. Only his head showed above the stiff tall yellow grass.

"What do you say we circle easy back to camp?" I whispered to G.C.

"I quite agree," he whispered.

As we spoke the lion turned and moved back toward the forest. All you could see of him was the movements of the high grass.

When we got back to camp and had breakfast Mary understood why we had done what we did and agreed that it was right and necessary. But the corrida had been called off again when she was all set and tense for it and we were not popular. I felt so sorry that she felt ill and I wanted her to let down in tension if she could. There was no use going on talking about how the lion had made a mistake finally. Both G.C. and I were sure we had him now. He had not fed during the night and had come out to look for the bait in the morning. He had gone back into the forest again. He would lie up hungry and, if he were not disturbed, he should be out early in the evening; that is he should be. If he was not G.C. had to leave the next day no matter what happened and he would revert back to Mary and me on our own. But the lion had broken his pattern of behavior and made a very grave mistake and I did not worry anymore about our getting him. I might have been happier to hunt him with Mary without G.C. but I loved to hunt with G.C. too and I was not so stupid as to want any sort of bad show to happen with me alone with Mary. G.C. had pointed out too well how it could be. I always had the great illusion of Mary hitting the lion exactly where she should and the lion rolling over like anything else I had seen them do so many times and be as dead as only a lion can be. I was going to drive two into him if he rolled over alive and that was that. Miss Mary would have killed her lion and been happy about it always and I would only have given him the puntilla and she would know it and love me very much forever world without end amen. It was now the sixth month that we had looked forward to this.

*   *   *

Mary went to sleep almost as soon as she lay down on her cot. The back of the tent was propped open and a good cool breeze blew down from the Mountain and through the tent. We ordinarily slept facing the open door of the tent but I took the pillows and placed them at opposite ends of the cot and doubling them over and with the balsam pillow under my neck lay on the cot with my boots and trousers off and read with the good light behind me. I was reading a very good book by Gerald Hanley, who had written another good book called *The Consul at Sunset.* This book was about a lion who made much trouble and killed practically all the characters in the book. G.C. and I used to read this book in the mornings on the latrine to inspire us. There were a few characters the lion did not kill but they were all headed for some other sort of bad fate so we did not really mind. Hanley wrote very well and it was an excellent book and very inspiring when you were in the lion-hunting business. I had seen a lion come, at speed, once and I had been very impressed and am still impressed. On this afternoon I was reading the book very slowly because it was such a good book and I did not want to finish it. I was hoping the lion would kill the hero or the Old Major because they were both very noble and nice characters and I had gotten very fond of the lion and wanted him to kill some upper-bracket character. The lion was doing very well though and he had just killed another very sympathetic and important character when I decided it would be better to save the rest and got up and pulled on my trousers and put my boots on without zipping them up and went over to see if G.C. was awake. I coughed outside his tent the way the Informer always did outside the mess tent.

"Come in, General," G.C. said.

"No," I said. "A man's home is his castle. Are you feeling up to facing the deadly beasts?"

"It's too early yet. Did Mary sleep?"

"She's still sleeping. What are you reading?"

"Lindbergh. It's damned good. What were you reading?"

"*The Year of the Lion*. I'm sweating out the lion."

"You've been reading that for a month."

"Six weeks. How are you coming with the mysticism of the air?"

That year we were both, belatedly, full of the mysticism of the air. I had given up on the mysticism of the air finally in 1945 when flying home in an overaged unreconditioned flight-weary B-17.

When it was time I got Mary up while the gun bearers got her rifle and my big gun from under the beds and checked the solids and the soft-nosed.

"He's there, honey. He's there and you'll get him."

"It's late."

"Don't think about anything. Just get out in the car."

"I have to put my boots on, you know that."

I was helping her on with them.

"Where's my damned hat?"

"Here's your damned hat. Walk, don't run, to the nearest Land Rover. Don't think about anything but hitting him."

"Don't talk to me so much. Leave me alone."

Mary and G.C. were in the front seats with Mthuka driving. Ngui, Charo and I were in the open back with the Game Scout. I was checking the cartridges in the barrel and the magazine of the 30-06, checking those in my pockets and checking and cleaning the rear sight aperture of any dust with a toothpick. Mary was holding her rifle straight up and I had a fine view of the new wiped dark barrel and the Scotch tape that held her rear sight leaves down, of the back of her head and her disreputable hat. The sun was just above the hills now and we were out of the flowers and going north on the old track that ran parallel to the woods. Somewhere on the right was the lion. The car stopped and everyone got out except

Mthuka, who stayed at the wheel. The lion's tracks went off to the right toward a clump of trees and brush on our side of the lone tree where the bait was covered by a pile of brush. He was not on the bait and there were no birds on it either. They were all up in the trees. I looked back at the sun and it did not have more than ten minutes before it would be behind the far hills to the west. Ngui had climbed the anthill and looked carefully over the top. He pointed with his hand held close by his face so that you could hardly see it move and then came fast down from the mound.

"Hiko huko," he said. "He's out there. Mzuri motocah."

G.C. and I both looked at the sun again and G.C. waved his arm for Mthuka to come up. We climbed into the car and G.C. told Mthuka how he wanted him to go.

"But where is he?" Mary asked G.C.

G.C. put his hand on Mthuka's arm and he stopped the car.

"We leave the car back here," G.C. told Mary. "He must be in that far clump of trees and brush. Papa will take the left flank and block him off from breaking back to the forest. You and I will move straight in on him."

The sun was still above the hills as we moved up toward where the lion must be. Ngui was behind me and on our right Mary was walking a little ahead of G.C. Charo was behind G.C. They were walking straight toward the trees with the thin brush at their base. I could see the lion now and I kept working to the left, walking sideways and forward. He was watching us and I thought what a bad place he had gotten himself into now. Every step I made I was blocking him worse from his safety that he had retreated into so many times. He had no choice now except to break toward me, to come out toward Mary and G.C., which he did not figure to do unless he were wounded, or to try for the next island of heavy cover, trees and thick brush, that was four hundred and fifty yards away to the north. To reach there he would have to cross open flat plain.

Now I figured that I was far enough to the left and began moving in toward the lion. He stood there thigh deep in brush and I saw his head turn once to look toward me; then it swung back to watch Mary and G.C. His head was huge and dark but when he moved it the head did not look too big for his body. His body was heavy, great and long. I did not know how close G.C. would try to work Mary toward the lion. I did not watch them. I watched the lion and waited to hear the shot. I was as close as I needed to be now and have room to take him if he came and I was sure that if he were wounded he would break toward me as his natural cover was behind me. Mary must take him soon, I thought. She can't get any closer. But maybe G.C. wants her closer. I looked at them from the corner of my eyes, my head down, not looking away from the lion. I could see Mary wanted to shoot and that G.C. was preventing her. They were not trying to work closer so I figured that from where they were, there were some limbs of brush between Mary and the lion. I watched the lion and felt the change in his coloring as the first peak of the hills took the sun. It was good light to shoot now but it would go fast. I watched the lion and he moved very slightly to his right and then looked at Mary and G.C. I could see his eyes. Still Mary did not shoot. Then the lion moved very slightly again and I heard Mary's rifle go and the dry whack of the bullet. She had hit him. The lion made a bound into the brush and then came out of the far side headed for the patch of heavy cover to the north. Mary was firing at him and I was sure she hit him. He was moving in long bounds his great head swinging. I shot and raised a puff of dirt behind him. I swung with him and squeezed off as I passed him and was behind him again. G.C.'s big double was firing and I saw the blossomings of dirt from it. I fired again picking the lion up in the sights and swung ahead of him and a bunch of dirt rose ahead of him. He was running now heavy and desperate but beginning to look small in the sights and almost certain to make the far cover when I had him in the sights again, small now and going away fast, and swung gently ahead and lifting over him and squeezed as I passed him and no dirt rose and I saw him slide forward, his front feet plowing, and his great head was down before we heard the thunk of the bullet. Ngui banged me on the back and put his arm around me. The lion was trying to get up now and G.C. hit him and he rolled onto his side.

I went over to Mary and kissed her. She was happy but something was wrong.

"You shot before I did," she said.

"Don't say that, honey. You shot and hit him. How could I shoot before you when we'd waited all that time?"

"Ndio. Memsahib piga," Charo said. He had been right behind Mary.

"Of course you hit him. You hit him the first time in the foot I think. You hit him again too."

"But you killed him."

"We all had to keep him from getting into the thick stuff after he was hit."

"But you shot first. You know you did."

"I did not. Ask G.C."

We were all walking up to where the lion lay. It was a long walk and the lion grew larger and deader as we walked. With the sun going it was getting dark fast. The shooting light was gone already. I felt wrung out inside and very tired. G.C. and I were both wet with sweat.

"Of course you hit him, Mary," G.C. told her. "Papa didn't shoot until he went into the open. You hit him twice."

"Why couldn't I have shot him when I wanted to when he was just standing there and looking at me?"

"There were branches that could have deflected the bullet or broken it up. That was why I made you wait."

"Then he moved."

"He had to move for you to shoot him."

"But did I really hit him first?"

"Of course you did. Nobody would have shot at him before you did."

"You're not just lying to make me happy?"

This was a scene that Charo had seen before.

"Piga!" he said violently. "Piga, Memsahib. PIGA!"

I slapped Ngui on the hip with the side of my hand and looked toward Charo and he went over.

"Piga," he said harshly. "Piga Memsahib. Piga bili."

G.C. came over to walk by me and I said, "What are you sweating for?"

"How far did you hold over him you son of a bitch?"

"A foot and a half. Two feet. It was bow and arrow shooting."

"We'll pace it when we walk back."

"Nobody would ever believe it."

"We will. That's all that matters."

"Go over and make her realize she hit him."

"She believes the boys. You broke his back."

"I know."

"Did you hear how long it took for the sound of the bullet hitting to come back?"

"I did. Go over and talk to her."

The Land Rover pulled up behind us.

Now we were there with the lion and he was Mary's and she knew it now and she saw how wonderful and long and dark and beautiful he was. The camel flies were crawling on him and his yellow eyes were not dull yet. I moved my hand through the heavy black of his mane. Mthuka had stopped the Land Rover and come over and shaken Mary's hand. She was kneeling by him.

Then we saw the lorry coming out across the plain from camp. They had heard the shooting and Keiti had come out with everyone except two guards that they had left in camp. They were singing the lion song and when they piled out of the lorry Mary had no more doubt about whose lion it was. I have seen many lions killed and many celebrations. But not one like this. I wanted Mary to have all of it. I was sure it was all right with Mary now and I walked on to the island of trees and thick brush the lion had been making for. He had nearly made it and I thought of what it would have been like if G.C. and I had to go in there to dig him out. I wanted a look at it before the light was gone. He would have made it there in sixty more yards and it would have been dark when we got up to it. I thought about what could have happened and went back to the celebration and the picture taking. The headlights of the lorry and the Land Rover were centered on Mary and the lion and G.C. was making the photographs. Ngui brought me the Jinny flask from the shell bag in the Land Rover and I took a small swallow and handed it to Ngui. He took a small drink and shook his head and handed it to me.

"Piga," he said and we both laughed. I took a long drink and felt it warm and felt the strain slip off me like a snake shedding his skin. Until that moment I had not realized that we had the lion finally. I knew it technically when the unbelievable long bow and arrow shot had hit and broken him down and Ngui had hit me across the back. But then there had been Mary's worry and being upset and walking up to him we had been as unemotional and as detached as though it were the end of an attack. Now with the drink and the celebrating going on and the photography, the hated and necessary photography, too late at night, no flash, no professionals to do it properly to make Miss Mary's lion immortal now on film, seeing her shining happy face in the glare of the headlights and the lion's great head that was too heavy for her to lift, proud of her and loving the lion, me feeling as empty inside as an empty room, seeing Keiti's gashed slant of a smile as he bent over Mary to touch the lion's unbelievable black mane, everyone cooing in Kikamba like birds and each man individually proud of this our lion, ours and belonging to all of us and Mary's because she had hunted him for months and had hit him in that barred phrase standing on her own two feet and when the chips were down, and now happy and shining in the headlights looking like a small, not quite deadly, bright angel and everyone loving her and this our lion, I began to relax and to have fun.

Charo and Ngui had told Keiti how it was and he came over to me and we shook hands and he said, "Mzuri sana Bwana. Uchawi tu."

"It was lucky," I said which God knows it had to be.

"Not lucky," Keiti said. "Mzuri. Mzuri. Uchawi kubwa sana."

Then I remembered that I had given this afternoon for the lion's death and that it was all over now and that Mary had won and I talked with Ngui and Mthuka and Pop's gun bearer and the others of our religion and we shook our heads and laughed and Ngui wanted me to take another drink from the Jinny flask. They wanted to wait until we would get to camp for beer but they wanted me to drink now with them. They only touched the bottle with their lips. Mary stood up now after the photography and saw us drinking and she asked for the flask and drank from it and passed it to G.C. They passed it back and I drank and then lay down by the lion and talked to him very softly in Spanish and begged his pardon for us having killed him and while I lay beside him I felt for the wounds. There were four. Mary had hit him in the foot and in one haunch. While I stroked his back I found where I had hit him in the spine and the larger hole G.C.'s bullet had made well forward in his flank behind the shoulder. All the time I was stroking him and talking to him in Spanish but many of the flat hard camel flies were shifting from him to me so I drew a fish in front of him with my forefinger in the dirt and then rubbed it out with the palm of my hand.

On the way into camp Ngui and Charo and I did not talk. I heard Mary once ask G.C. if I had not really shot before she did and heard him tell her that she had gotten her lion. That she had hit him first and that these things did not always go off ideally and that when an animal was wounded he had to be killed and that we were damned lucky and she should be happy. But I knew that her happiness came and went because it had not been as she had hoped and dreamed and feared and waited for all of six months. I felt terribly about how she felt and I knew it made no difference to anyone else and it made all the difference in the world to her. But if we had to do it over again there was no way we could have done it differently. G.C. had taken her up closer than anyone but a great shot had a right to take her. If the lion had charged when she hit him G.C. would have had time for only one shot before the lion would have been on them. His big gun was as deadly and efficient if the lion came as it was a handicap if he had to shoot it at two and three hundred yards. We both knew that and had not even joked about it. Taking the lion at the range she did Mary had been in great danger and both G.C. and I knew that at the distance he had brought her to she had, recently, a possible error of eighteen inches on live game. This was not the time to talk about that but Ngui and Charo knew it too and I had slept with it for a long time. The lion, by deciding to make his fight in the thick cover, where he was heavy odds on to get someone, had made his choice and had very nearly won. He was not a stupid lion and he was not cowardly. He wanted to make his fight where the odds were in his favor.

We came into camp and sat in chairs by the fire and stretched our legs out and drank tall drinks. Who we needed was Pop and Pop was not there. I had told Keiti to break out some beer for the lines and then I waited for it to come. It came as suddenly as a dry streambed filling with the high, foam-crested roar of water from a cloudburst. It had only taken time enough for them to decide who was to carry Miss Mary and then the wild, stooped dancing rush of Wakamba poured in from behind the tents all singing the lion song. The big mess boy and the truck driver had the chair and they put it down and Keiti dancing and clapping his hands led Miss Mary to it and they hoisted her up and started dancing around the fire with her and then out toward the lines and around the lion where he had been laid on the ground and then through the lines and around the cook fire and the men's fire and around the cars and the wood truck and in and out. The Game Scouts were all stripped to their shorts and so was everyone else except the old men. I watched Mary's bright head and the black strong fine bodies that were carrying her and crouching and stamping in the dance and then moving forward to reach up and touch her. It was a fine wild lion dance and at the end they put Mary down in the chair by her camp chair at the fire and everyone shook hands with her and it was over. She was happy and we had a fine happy meal and went to bed.

In the night I woke and could not get back to sleep. I woke very suddenly and it was absolutely quiet. Then I heard Mary's regular, smooth breathing and I had a feeling of relief that we would not have to pit her against the lion every morning. Then I began to feel sorrow that the lion's death had not been as she hoped it would be and as she planned it. With the celebration and the really wild dance and the love of all her friends and their allegiance to her the disappointment that she felt had been anesthetized. But I was sure that after the more than a hundred mornings that she had gone out after a great lion the disappointment would return. She did not know the danger she had been in. Maybe she did and I did not know. Neither G.C. nor I wanted to tell her because we had both cut it too fine and we had not soaked in sweat that way in the cool of the evening for nothing. I remembered how the lion's eyes had looked when he had looked toward me and turned them down and then looked toward Mary and G.C. and how his eyes had never left them. I lay in the bed and thought how a lion can come one hundred yards from a standing start in just over three seconds. He comes low down to the ground and faster than a greyhound and he does not spring until he is on his prey. Mary's lion would weigh well over four hundred pounds and he was strong enough to have leaped out over a high thorn Boma carrying a cow. He had been hunted for many years and he was very intelligent. But we had lulled him into making a mistake. I was happy that before he died he had lain on the high yellow rounded mound with his tail down and his great paws comfortable before him and looked off across his country to the blue forest and the high white snows of the big Mountain. Both G.C. and I wanted him to be killed by Mary's first shot or, wounded, charge. But he had played it his own way. The first shot could not have felt more than a sharp, slapping sting to him. The second that passed high through a leg muscle while he was bounding toward the heavy cover where he would make us fight would, at most, have felt like a hard slap. I did not like to think what my long-thrown running shot that was thrown at all of him, hoping to rake him and bring him down, must have felt like when it by chance took him in the spine. It was a two-hundred-and-twenty-grain solid bullet and I did not have to think how it would have felt. I had never yet broken my back and I did not know. I was glad G.C.'s wonderful distance shot had killed him instantly. He was dead now and we would miss hunting him too.

I tried to go to sleep but I started to think about the lion and what the moves would have been if he had reached the heavy cover, remembering other people's experiences under the same circumstances and then I thought the hell with all that. That's stuff for G.C. and I to talk over together and to talk with Pop. I wished Mary would wake and say, "I'm so glad I got my lion." But that was too much to expect and it was three o'clock in the morning. I remembered how Scott Fitzgerald had written that in the something something of the soul something something it is always three o'clock in the morning. For many months three o'clock in the morning had been two hours, or an hour and a half, before you would get up and get dressed and put your boots on to hunt Miss Mary's lion. I untucked the mosquito net and reached for and found the cider bottle. It was cool with the night and I built up the two pillows by doubling them over and then leaned back against them with the rough square balsam pillow under my neck and thought about the soul. First I must verify the Fitzgerald quotation in my mind. It had occurred in a series of articles in which he had abandoned this world and his former extremely shoddy ideals and had first referred to himself as a cracked plate. Turning my memory back I remembered the quotation. It went like this. "In a real dark night of the soul it is always three o'clock in the morning."

"Eagle Bait"

(from *True at First Light*)

After G.C. and his people were gone I was alone with Miss Mary's sorrow. I was not really alone because there was also Miss Mary and the camp and our own people and the big mountain of Kilimanjaro that everyone called Kibo and all the animals and the birds and the new fields of flowers and the worms that hatched out of the ground to eat the flowers. There were the brown eagles that came to feed on the worms so that eagles were as common as chickens and eagles wearing long brown trousers of feathers and other white-headed eagles walked together with the guinea fowl busily eating the worms. The worms made an armistice among all the birds and they all walked together. Then great flocks of European storks came to eat the worms and there would be acres of storks moving on a single stretch of plain grown high with the white flowers. Miss Mary's sorrow resisted the eagles because eagles did not mean as much to her as they did to me.

She had never laid under juniper bush up above timberline at the top of a pass in our own mountains with a *.22* rifle waiting for eagles to come to a dead horse that had been a bear bait until the bear was killed. Now he was an eagle bait and then afterwards he would be a bear bait again. The eagles were sailing very high when you first saw them. You had crawled under the bush when it was still dark and you had seen the eagles come out of the sun when it had cleared the opposite peak of the pass. This peak was just a rise of grassy hill with a rock outcropping at the top and scattered juniper bushes on the slope. The country was all high there and very easy traveling once you had come this high and the eagles had come from far away toward the snow mountains you could have seen if you had been standing instead of lying under the bush. There were three eagles and they wheeled and soared and rode the currents and you watched them until the sun spotted your eyes. Then you closed them and through the red the sun was still there. You opened them and looked to the side limit of the blind of the sun and you could see the spread pinions and the wide fanned tails and feel the eyes in the big heads watching. It had been cold in the early morning and you looked out at the horse and his too old and too exposed now teeth that you had always had to lift his lip to see. He had a kind and rubbery lip and when you had led him to this place to die and dropped the halter he had stood as he had always been taught to stand and when you had stroked him on the blaze on his black head where the gray hairs showed he had reached down to nip you on the neck with his lips. He had looked down to see the saddled horse you had left in the last edge of the timber as though he were wondering what he was doing here and what was the new game. You had remembered how wonderfully he had always seen in the dark and how you had hung on to his tail with a bear hide packed across the saddle to come down trails when you could not see at all and when the trail led along the rimrock in the dark down through the timber. He was always right and he understood all new games.

So you had brought him up here five days before because someone had to do it and you could do it if not gently without suffering and what difference did it make what happened afterwards. The trouble was, at the end, he thought it was a new game and he was learning it. He gave me a nice rubber-lipped kiss and then he checked the position of the other horse. He knew you could not ride him the way the hoof had split but this was new and he wanted to learn it.

"Good bye, Old Kite," I said and held his right ear and stroked its base with my fingers. "I know you'd do the same for me."

He did not understand, of course, and he wanted to give me another kiss to show that everything was all right when he saw the gun come up. I thought I could keep him from seeing it but he saw it and his eyes knew what it was and he stood very still trembling and I shot him at the intersection between the cross lines that run from opposite eye to opposite ear and his feet went straight down under him and all of him dropped together and he was a bear bait.

Now lying under the juniper I was not finished with my sorrow. I would always feel the same way about Old Kite all of my life, or so I told myself then, but I looked at his lips which were not there because the eagles had eaten them and at his eyes which were also gone and at where the bear had opened him so that he was sunken now and the patch the bear had eaten before I had interrupted him and I waited for the eagles to come down.

One came, finally, dropping like the sound of an incoming shell and breaking, with doubled-forward pinions and feathered legs and talons thrust forward to hit Old Kite as though he were killing him. He then walked pompously around and started working in the cavity. The others came in more gently and heavy winged but with the same long feathered wings and the same thick necks, big heads and dipped beaks and golden eyes.

I lay there watching them eat at the body of my friend and partner that I had killed and thought that they were lovelier in the air. Since they were condemned I let them eat a while and quarrel and go pacing and mincing with their selections from the interior. I wished that I had a shotgun but I hadn't. So I took the *.22* Winchester finally and shot one carefully in the head and another twice in the body. He started to fly but could not make it and came down wings spread and I had to chase him up the high slope. Nearly every other bird or beast goes downhill when it is wounded. But an eagle goes uphill and when I ran this one down and caught his legs above the killing and holding claws and, with my moccasined foot on his neck, folded his wings together and held him with his eyes full of hatred and defiance, I had never seen any animal or bird look at me as the eagle looked. He was a golden eagle and full grown and big enough to take bighorn sheep lambs and he was a big thing to hold and as I watched the eagles walking with the guinea fowl and remembered that these birds walk with no one I felt badly about Miss Mary's sorrow but I would not tell her what the eagles meant to me nor why I had killed these two, the last one by smacking his head against a tree down in the timber, nor what their skins had bought at Lame Deer on the Reservation.

"The Leopard"

(from *True at First Light*)

It was almost noon and very hot and we did not know it but all our luck lay ahead of us. We rode along through the park country and all of us watched every likely tree. The leopard we were hunting was a trouble leopard that I had been asked to kill by the people of the Shamba where he had killed sixteen goats and I was hunting him for the Game Department so it was permissible to use the car in his pursuit. The leopard, once officially vermin and now Royal Game, had never heard of his promotion and reclassification or he would never have killed the sixteen goats that made him a criminal and put him back in the category where he started. Sixteen goats were too many goats to kill in one night when one goat was all he could eat. Then, too, eight of the goats had belonged to Debba's family.

We came into a very beautiful glade and on our left there was a tall tree with one of its high branches extending on a straight parallel line to the left and another, more shaded branch extending on a straight line to the right. It was a green tree and its top was heavily foliaged.

"There's an ideal tree for leopard," I said to Ngui.

"Ndio," he said very quietly. "And there is a leopard in that tree."

Mthuka had seen us look and though he could not hear us and could not see the leopard from his side he stopped the car. I got out of the car with the old Springfield I had been carrying across my lap and when I was firmly planted on my feet I saw the leopard stretched long and heavy on the high right limb of the tree. His long spotted length was dappled by the shadows of the leaves that moved in the wind. He was sixty feet up in an ideal place to be on this lovely day and he had made a greater mistake than when he killed the sixteen unnecessary goats.

I raised the rifle breathing in once and letting it out and shot very carefully for the point where his neck bulged behind his ear. It was high and an absolute miss and he flattened, long and heavy along the branch, as I shucked the cartridge case out and shot for his shoulder. There was a heavy thunk and he fell in a half circle. His tail was up, his head was up, his back down. His body was curved like a new moon as he fell and he hit the ground with a heavy thump.

Ngui and Mthuka were whacking me on the back and Charo was shaking hands. Pop's gun bearer was shaking hands and crying because the fall of the leopard had been an emotional thing. He was also giving me the secret Kamba hand grip again and again. In a moment I was reloading with my free hand and Ngui, in excitement, had the .577 instead of the shotgun when we advanced carefully to view the body of the sixteen-goat-killing scourge of my father-in-law. The body of the leopard was not there.

There was a depression in the ground where he had hit and the blood spoor, bright and in chunks, led toward a thick island of bush to the left of the tree. It was as thick as the roots of a mangrove swamp and no one was giving me any secret Kamba hand grips now.

"Gentlemen," I said in Spanish. "The situation has radically changed." It had indeed. I knew the drill now having learned it from Pop but every wounded leopard in thick bush is a new wounded leopard. No two will ever act the same except that they will always come and they will come for keeps. That was why I had shot for the base of the head and neck first. But it was too late for postmortems on missed shots now.

The first problem was Charo. He had been mauled by leopards twice and was an old man, nobody knew how old, but certainly old enough to be my father. He was as excited as a hunting dog to go in.

"You keep the fucking hell out of this and get up on top of the car."

"Hapana, Bwana," he said.

"Ndio too bloody ndio," I said.

"Ndio," he said not saying, "Ndio Bwana," which with us was an insult. Ngui had been loading the Winchester 12-gauge pump with SSG, which is buckshot in English. We had never shot anything with SSG and I did not want any jams so I tripped the ejector and filled it with No. 8 birdshot cartridges fresh out of the box and filled my pockets with the rest of the cartridges. At close range a charge of fine shot from a full-choked shotgun is as solid as a ball and I remembered seeing the effect on a human body with the small hole blue black around the edge on the back of the leather jacket and all the load inside the chest.

"Kwenda," I said to Ngui and we started off on the blood spoor, me with the shotgun covering Ngui, who tracked, and Pop's gun bearer back in the car with the .577. Charo had not gotten onto the roof but sat in the rear seat of the car with the best one of the three spears. Ngui and I were on foot and following the blood spoor.

Out of a clot of blood he picked up a sharp bone fragment and passed it to me. It was a piece of shoulder blade and I put it in my mouth. There is no explanation of that. I did it without thinking.

But it linked us closer to the leopard and I bit on it and tasted the new blood which tasted about like my own, and knew that the leopard had not just lost his balance. Ngui and I followed the blood spoor until it went into the mangrove root patch of bush. The leaves of this bush were very green and shiny and the trail of the leopard, which had been made with bounds of irregular length, went into it and there was blood low on the leaves, shoulder high where he had crouched as he went in.

Ngui shrugged his shoulders and shook his head. We were both very serious now and there was no White Man to speak softly and knowingly from his great knowledge, nor any White Man to give violent orders astonished at the stupidity of his "boys" and cursing them on like reluctant hounds. There was only one wounded leopard with terrible odds against him who had been shot from the high branch of a tree, suffered a fall no human being could survive and taken his stand in a place where, if he retained his lovely and unbelievable cat vitality he could maim or grievously injure any human being who came in after him. I wished he had never killed the goats and that I had never signed any contracts to kill and be photographed for any national circulation magazines and I bit with satisfaction on the piece of shoulder bone and waved up the car. The sharp end of the splintered bone had cut the inside of my cheek and I could taste the familiarity of my own blood now mixed with the blood of the leopard and I said, "Twendi kwa chui," the stateman's plural imperative, "Let us go to the leopard."

It was not very easy for us to go to the leopard. Ngui had the Springfield 30-06 and he had also the good eyes. Pop's gun bearer had the .577 which would knock him on his ass if he shot it and he had as good eyes as Ngui. I had the old, well-loved, once burnt-up, three times restocked, worn-smooth old Winchester model 12-pump gun that was faster than a snake and was, from thirty-five years of us being together, almost as close a friend and companion with secrets shared and triumphs and disasters not revealed as the other friend a man has all his life. We covered the enlaced and crossed roots of the thicket from the blood spoor entry to the left, or west end where we could see the car around the corner but we could not see the leopard. Then we went back crawling along and looking into the darkness of the roots until we reached the other end. We had not seen the leopard and we crawled back to where the blood was still fresh on the dark green leaves.

Pop's gun bearer was standing up behind us with the big gun ready and I, sitting down now, started to shoot loads of No. 8 shot into the cross-tangled roots traversing from left to right. At the fifth shot the leopard roared hugely. The roar came from well into the thick bush and a little to the left of the blood on the leaves.

"Can you see him?" I asked Ngui.

"Hapana."

I reloaded the long magazine tube and shot twice fast toward where I had heard the roar. The leopard roared again and then coughed twice.

"Piga tu," I said to Ngui and he shot toward where the roar had come from.

The leopard roared again and Ngui said, "Piga tu."

I shot twice at the roar and Pop's gun bearer said, "I can see him."

We stood up and Ngui could see him but I could not. "Piga tu," I told him.

He said, "Hapana. Twendi kwa chui."

So we went in again but this time Ngui knew where we were going. We could only go in a yard or so but there was a rise in the ground the roots grew out of. Ngui was directing me by tapping my legs on one side or the other as we crawled. Then I saw the leopard's ear and the small spots on the top of the bulge of his neck and his shoulder. I shot where his neck joined his shoulder and shot again and there was no roar and we crawled back out and I reloaded and we three went around the west end of the island of rush to where the car was on the far side.

"Kufa," Charo said. "Mzuri kubwa sana."

"Kufa," Mthuka said. They could both see the leopard but I could not.

They got out of the car and we all moved in and I told Charo to keep back with his spear. But he said, "No. He's dead, Bwana. I saw him die."

I covered Ngui with the shotgun while he cut his way in with a panga slamming at the roots and brush as though they were our enemy or all our enemies and then he and Pop's gun bearer hauled the leopard out and we swung him up into the back of the car. He was a good leopard and we had hunted him well and cheerfully and like brothers with no White Hunters nor Game Rangers and no Game Scouts and he was a Kamba leopard condemned for useless killing on an illegal Kamba Shamba and we were all Wakamba and all thirsty.

Charo was the only one who examined the leopard closely because he had been mauled twice by leopards and he had shown me where the charge of shot at close range had entered almost alongside the first bullet wound in the shoulder. I knew it must have as I knew the roots and the bank had deflected the other shots, but I was only happy and proud of us all and how we had been all day and happy that we would get to camp and to the shade and to cold beer.

Selected Bibliography

Works by Ernest Hemingway

There is a wealth of unpublished writing by Ernest Hemingway at the Hemingway Archives of the John F. Kennedy Library in Boston, including letters, pages from journals, and a number of stories and articles in various stages of completion, as well as family scrapbooks, old hunting licenses and other ephemera. The following is a selected list of sources relating to Hemingway and hunting.

Across the River and Into the Trees. New York: Charles Scribner's Sons, 1950.

By-Line: Ernest Hemingway. Selected Articles and Dispatches of Four Decades. Edited by William White. New York: Charles Scribner's Sons, 1961.

The Complete Short Stories of Ernest Hemingway. The Finca Vigía Edition. New York: Charles Scribner's Sons, 1987.

Dateline: Toronto, the Complete Toronto Star Dispatches, 1920–1924. Edited by William White. New York: Charles Scribner's Sons, 1985.

Selected Bibliography

Death in the Afternoon. New York: Charles Scribner's Sons, 1932.
Ernest Hemingway: Selected Letters, 1917–1961. Edited by Carlos Baker,
New York, Charles Scribner's Sons, 1981.

Numerous references to hunting may be found in the published letters, in which Hemingway sometimes writes of his works, such as *Green Hills of Africa*, or of the thrill of the hunt and his love of the great outdoors, as well as of his much greater commitment to writing. The following letters are those which I found particularly interesting, illuminating and, at times, generally amusing.

To: Clarence E. Hemingway (5/2/22); Clarence E. Hemingway (11/7/23); Clarence E. Hemingway (3/20/25); Waldo Pierce (8/23/28); F. Scott Fitzgerald (9/13/29); Henry Strater (c. 6/20/30); Henry Strater (c. 9/10/30); Archibald MacLeish (11/22/30); Henry Strater (12/10/31); Henry Strater (10/14/32); Guy Hickok (10/14/32); Patrick Hemingway (12/2/33); Arnold Gingrich (7/15/34); Sara Murphy (7/10/35); Marjorie Kinnan Rawlings (8/16/36); Arnold Gingrich (9/16/36); Eugene Jolas (c. late March 1938); Arnold Gingrich (10/22/38); Charles Scribner (c. 8/15/40); Maxwell Perkins (c. 10/12/40); Charles Scribner (c. 11/20/41); Hadley Mawrer (7/23/42); Patrick Hemingway (11/19/44); General Charles T. Lanham (11/2/46); Charles Scribner (8/19/49); Harvey Breit (6/29/52); Bernard Berenson (10/14/52); Bernard Berenson (9/15/53); Harvey Breit (1/3/54); General Charles T. Lanham (11/10/54); Charles Scribner (8/14/56); Gianfranco Ivancich (1/7/59); Patrick Hemingway (8/5/59).

A Farewell to Arms. New York: Charles Scribner's Sons, 1929.
For Whom the Bell Tolls. New York: Charles Scribner's Sons, 1940.
Green Hills of Africa. New York: Charles Scribner's Sons, 1935.
Men at War. Edited with an Introduction by Ernest Hemingway. New York: Crown Publishers, 1942.
"My Pal the Gorilla Gargantua." *Ken*, July 28, 1938.
"Safari." *Look* Magazine, January 26, 1954.
True at First Light. With an introduction by Patrick Hemingway. New York: Charles Scribner's Sons, 1999.

A Very Brief List of Works About Ernest Hemingway
(especially his life as a hunter)

From the wealth of essays, articles and books written about my grandfather, I have found the following works particularly helpful and relevant to his hunting and his writing as it relates to the sport he so loved.

Arnold, Lloyd R. *High on the Wild with Hemingway.* Caldwell, Ida.: Caxton Printers, 1968. The best source for hunting during the Idaho years, with many excellent photographs by the author.

Baker, Carlos. *Ernest Hemingway: A Life Story.* New York: Charles Scribner's Sons, 1969. Still a fundamental resource, with much information on Hemingway's hunting life.

Bredahl, A. Carl, and Susan Lynn Drake. *Hemingway's Green Hills of Africa as Evolutionary Narrative.* New York: Edwin Mellen Press, 1990. A scholarly revisionist assessment of *Green Hills of Africa* that finds it an impressive work in its own right and a central piece in the development of Hemingway's writing.

Buckley, Peter. *Ernest.* New York: Dial Press, 1978. An excellent collection of photographs from every period in Hemingway's life, combined with a thoughtful biographical essay by a personal friend.

Bull, Bartle, *Safari: A Chronicle of Adventure.* London: Viking Press, 1988. An entertaining book that places Hemingway and his work in the context of the history of the African safari.

Cappel, Constance. *Hemingway in Michigan.* Petoskey, Mich.: Little Traverse Historical Society, 1999. This book contains a reprint of the story "Judgement of Manitou" and other early Hemingway fiction.

Hemingway, Gregory H. *Papa: A Personal Memoir.* Boston: Houghton Mifflin, 1976. My father's honest memoir filled with personal insights.

Hemingway, Hilary and Jeffrey P. Lindsay. *Hunting with Hemingway.* New York: Riverhead Books, 2000. Tall tales of hunting adventures with EH.

Hemingway, Leicester. *My Brother, Ernest Hemingway.* New York: Fawcett World Library, 1963. Particularly good for recollections of hunting expeditions in the early years.

Hemingway, Mary Welsh, *How It Was.* New York: Alfred A. Knopf, 1976.

Hemingway, Patrick, "The Elephants of Tsavo: The Failure of Stewardship," *Sacred Trusts: Essays on Stewardship and Responsibility.* ed. Michael Katakis. San Francisco: Mercury House, 1993. Pp. 98–111. A fascinating case study of an area of East Africa in the years after Hemingway's safaris.

Howell, John M. *Hemingway's African Stories: The Stories, Their Sources, Their Critics.* New York: Charles Scribner's Sons, 1969.

Meyers, Jeffrey. *Hemingway: A Biography.* New York: Harper & Row, 1985. An excellent one-volume biography.

Percival, Philip H. *Hunting, Settling and Remembering.* Agoura, Calif.: Trophy Room Books, 1997. A personal glimpse into the days of pre-automobile hunting safaris as well as remembrances of his times with EH.

Reynolds, Michael. *The Young Hemingway.* New York and London: W. W. Norton, 1986.

———. *Hemingway: The Homecoming.* New York and London: W. W. Norton, 1992.

———. *Hemingway: The 1930's.* New York and London: W.W. Norton, 1997.

———. *Hemingway: The Final Years.* New York and London: W. W. Norton, 1999.

Ross, Lillian. *Portrait of Hemingway.* New York: Random House, 1997. An interview with Papa in 1950, written for *The New Yorker,* that captures some of his complex character vividly.

Turgenev, Ivan. *A Sportsman's Sketches.* First published in 1852. One of Hemingway's favorite collections of stories about hunting.

Voss, Frederick, with an essay by Michael Reynolds. *Picturing Hemingway: A Writer in His Time.* New Haven and London: Yale University Press, 1999. A beautifully illustrated catalogue that accompanied a centennial exhibition on Hemingway held at the National Portrait Gallery in Washington, D.C.